THE CHANCE THAT MADE ME

Anglo-Saxon Riddle

I am puff-breasted, proud-crested,
a head I have, and a high tail,
eyes and ears and one foot,
both my sides, a back that's hollow,
a very stout beak, a steeple neck
and a home above men.
*   Harsh are my sufferings*
when that which makes the forest tremble takes and
*   shakes me.*

Here I stand under streaming rain
and blinding sleet, stoned by hail;
freezes the frost and falls the snow
on me stuck-bellied. And I stick it all out
for I cannot change the chance that made me.

                                      (The solution is a weathercock.)

For Chris and Helen (another 56 vintage!),
with all good wishes,
Christopher

Dec '06

THE CHANCE
THAT MADE ME

CHRISTOPHER JARY

Privately published
in a single, limited edition

First published October 2006

© Text copyright Christopher Jary

© Illustrations copyright various

All rights reserved. No part of this publication may be reproduced, stored in a retrieval system, or transmitted in any form, or by any means, electronic, mechanical, photocopying, recording or otherwise, without the prior permission of the publishers.

Printed by Ospec Printing Limited

Bound by Masters Book Binding

DEDICATION

*In memory of Little Nanny,
the bravest of the brave,
and of Bill and Winnie,
who deserved better.*

CONTENTS

	An explanation	i
1.	Meet my family	1
2.	Sources	9
3.	Victorian respectability	17
4.	Illiterate peasants	23
5.	Either you *are* County or you are *not* County	29
6.	Banishment and reconciliation	35
7.	Sid's Boy's Boy on Sid	40
8.	The long shadow of tragedy	46
9.	Brothers on the Somme	54
10.	Spring at Arras	61
11.	The end of spring	67
12.	Summer at Ypres	73
13.	Christen her what you like. I shall call her Peggy.	81
14.	A bit of a disappointment	87
15.	Tennis, skating, flying, love and war	93
16.	Air Force wife	99
17.	Return to ops	106
18.	Fair stood the wind	113
19.	To Arnhem on foot	118
20.	Bulge, Bedburg, Bremen and a Nazi	124
21.	Victory in Europe and Bognor Regis	130
22.	Nobby and me	136
23.	The shadow of war	141
24.	At The Gallop	150
25.	A Sunday at Ilford	158
26.	No relations of ours	165
27.	A remembered landscape	171
28.	School	177
29.	Lois	183

30.	A pair of Lightfeet	189
31.	Dogs and Derbyshire	196
32.	Some family snaps	202
33	Dorset, daughters and dogs	209
34.	In Government	216
35.	My friends pictured within	224
36.	Fitting in	231
37.	More than a disappointment	237
38.	Waiting for women	244
39.	Valletta revisited	253
40.	The view from here	259
	Who's Who? Faux, Fletcher etc family tree	271
	Who's Who? Jary, Rogers etc family tree	273

An explanation

Walking up our village street carrying an envelope, I may be dropping a cheque into Winston's shop to pay our monthly butcher's bill, or posting a birthday card to my friend Steve on the Orkneys or a letter to Charlie, a friend of a friend, in Western Australia. Whatever it is, however far it's going, its journey will be through space. These letters will also travel through space, but they're designed mainly to travel through time. Their destination is about a hundred years from now.

Written during the first part of this year, with my 50th birthday coming in October, they're addressed to someone I'll never really know. I may meet one or two of my great-grandchildren just as they're appearing and when I'm ready for the off, but I won't know them as adults and they won't remember me. These letters are for them when they're old enough to wonder what life was like for us, a century or so earlier, and how it was, earlier still, for the forebears we share. The playwright Alan Bennett claimed that all families have a secret, which is that they're not like other families. This is true of mine but, although all the people described in these pages had their *own spark of divine fire*, their experiences are typical of their time. So I hope these letters may also bring their reader closer to the generations and times they portray.

Because I'm not a poet, perhaps some explanation is required about the origin of the two poems about my great-uncles, Wally and Len. Early this year I discovered a bit more about their tragically brief service in the Army in the First World War. One new fact, apparently of little significance, was that Wally had enlisted at Clapham Junction. The first line of the poem came unbidden to my mind, followed by the second. The lines had the rhythm of a train, and a picture formed of a nervous, excited young man in his Sunday best sitting staring out of the carriage window at the sunshine of August 1914. The rest followed with little conscious thought, since when I've barely revised it. A day or two later the idea came about Len, spring and Bullecourt and its devastating effect on his sister Winnie, my grandmother. Although I tinkered a bit more with one or two words in this poem, again the lines and verses came unconsciously, fully formed. I make no claims for either poem except this: they're true. But both were a curious experience.

Like most ideas, the one for this book has several origins. One was a conversation over dinner in Belfast with my friend Paul Grant. Born less than two years apart and brought up within three or four miles of each other, we were trying to fathom why our childhoods and many of our adult attitudes were so different. It set me thinking…

Clare Shaw, Susan Jones, Joy Taylor, David and Robin Betts, Don, Dene and Carole Pickard, Sean Lusk, Graham Davies, Amanda Bausor, Pat Baxendale, Alan and Kathleen Stagg, Jean Proctor, Alison Bennett, Graham Davey, Sue Calthorpe, and Nuala Swords-Isherwood and her friends in her Manchester women's reading group all read these letters in draft and encouraged me to persist. They have only themselves to blame, but they also have my gratitude.

My thanks also to Tiina End, Julie Sharpe, Jim Johnstone, Colin Belcher, Nigel Holman and Ed Watt for their invaluable help throughout the writing process, to Elizabeth Gibson of Wield for the Westbrook family photographs, to the Commonwealth War Graves Commission for the photographs of the Le Touret and Arras Memorials, to Mike Jameson for his enthusiastic technical help and advice, to Marie Webb for her marvellous design for the dust jacket and to Phil Lawrence and Chris Jarvis for their enthusiasm and professionalism. And, finally, to Lois, Alex and Vicky, without whom these letters would make much less happy reading.

Since the New Year this book has possessed me. The draft's never left my side as, wherever I've been, I've sat trying to reconstruct the times and characters I'm describing. Some of the people have appeared so vividly to me that it's felt less like writing than conducting a séance. Sometimes I could even hear their voices. I felt I was conjuring ghosts.

Christopher Jary
Odiham – London – Dunblane – Stormont –
Pilsley – Delhi – West Bay – Lyzzick – Ypres
January - August 2006

1: Meet my family

Odiham
Hampshire

Thursday, 12th January 2006

Dear G,

There comes a point when the past becomes history. No one's quite sure when or how it happens, but suddenly we realise that a yesterday that seemed quite recent and not very different from today is no longer either of these things. We've drifted imperceptibly away from it, leaving it stranded over there, apart from us, distinct, preserved unchanging in our memory. The people there, even if their older selves are still alive today, look different from us. They'll stay there for as long as we're here to remember them, but they're set in their time and, even if we can hear their conversation in our heads, their voices seem somehow to come from further away, across the water.

I'm fifty in October and it's already happened to my own childhood. I was born and grew up in what was widely called *post-war Britain*. As its name suggests, it began at a fixed point on the day the Second World War ended, but at some time in the last thirty years – and we could spend some very entertaining hours debating when exactly it happened – post-war Britain finally ended. That time, including my own childhood, is still within sight but it's separated from the present me by an uncrossable expanse of years. It's populated by some familiar faces, siblings, parents and grandparents: people I knew personally and remember directly. So, before I explain exactly how these letters will work and introduce you properly, let me take you to the house I lived in as a boy and show you some of the main characters and how they seemed to me when I first came to consciousness. I don't know about you, but I usually find starting with me by far the most interesting way to begin anything…

The landscape of my childhood was dominated by two colossal mountain ranges that seemed to tower over most aspects of our lives. The more distant of the two was the First World War; much closer was the Second War, from which both my parents had descended alone into the tranquil valley where my sisters and I were raised. What had happened in those mountains to the middle-aged and elderly people I knew? What had they seen and done? What had they been like before? And what of the people I never knew, who had been denied a gentle descent into peace and maturity and whose bones were left somewhere on the rock-strewn ledges and slopes above us?

You'd have had your own glimpse of most of the survivors if you'd called at my home in the mid-1960s. If you'd come from London, you'd have caught a train from Victoria which wove its sluggish way through Clapham, Streatham, Norbury, Croydon, Waddon and Wallington before, fourteen miles from the capital, finally stopping at a small, suburban station rustically announcing itself as Carshalton Beeches. The beeches were there, but were invisible from the platform; they lined the road above the station. Crossing the road bridge over the railway, you'd pass Quattrucci's off-licence and Mac's sweet shop, run by Mr Quattrucci's brother, before you turned right, down a steep hill towards the shops.

That road down the hill was vintage 1930s suburbia, whose net-curtained, semi-detached security now surrounded you for several sedate miles in every direction. To those of us who were brought up there it seemed a fixture. We'd have been startled to hear that practically every house and almost every road, avenue, close and crescent had only been here for thirty years. Until then, this had been farmland and parkland on the Derby estate. Lord Derby, famous for his horse races and infamous for the enthusiasm with which he propelled other men to the trenches during the First World War, had lived a mile and a half away at what was now The Oaks' Park. Arthur, our gardener, who also worked for my grandfather, had been one of Derby's stable boys, but happily was too young to be packed off under his master's enlistment scheme to the

Somme or Ypres. He was one of the lucky generation, just too young for the Great War and just too old for the Second.

At the bottom of the hill is a crossroads. To right and left run parades of small shops on both sides of the road: two newsagents called Coates' and Taylor's, two butchers, an iron-monger's, a couple of grocers' shops, two bakers, a fishmonger's and, of more interest to the ten-year-old me than all the rest put together, Church's toy shop, where I have my eye on a Winchester rifle. But, if you're coming to my house, you need to keep straight across the crossroads and start to climb the hill opposite. The houses near the bottom of the hill are semi-detached and mostly have three bedrooms. Half way up the hill they start to get a bit bigger. Ours is on the right. It's covered in grey-brown pebbledash: squirrels can run right up the side, the tiny pebbles providing a sure footing up to the red roof.

Open the gate, walk down the path flanked by two lilacs, one purple, one white, and you're at the front door. But, before you have a chance to knock, a ten-year-old boy appears at your right side. Since he's heavily armed and wearing a steel helmet, you decide to take him seriously.

"I've come to tell you that we're in the garden. If you come this way, I'll show you round. Close the back gate behind you. Our dog has no road sense."

An elderly fox terrier approaches and stops to be patted. On the left the backdoor stands open into the kitchen, and a brown and white rabbit lies stretched out, fast asleep, on the sunlit step.

"No need to worry about him with the dog. They ignore each other most of the time – although the rabbit did once bite him."

Navigating your way cautiously round a huge holly bush, you see the lawn in front of you. Three people are sitting in deckchairs, a couple of girls are sitting on a groundsheet and two elderly ladies are further down the garden, inspecting a rose bush. The man coming to meet you is my father. A short man, with receding black hair, he's wearing a crumpled, cream summer jacket and striped regimental tie. He takes off his sunglasses, revealing conjoined, bushy eyebrows, and blinks slightly in the bright sunshine as you shake hands.

"Come and meet my wife. This is Peggy."

My mother, blonde once but now grey-haired, appears from behind you where she's been making tea in the kitchen. She's wearing a cotton dress with an RAF brooch on the collar. On the third finger of her right hand is a diamond and sapphire ring. She enquires politely about your journey and asks if you'd like a cup of tea. She'll be calling us in in a few minutes. While she and my sister Anne disappear indoors and my father goes off to lay the table, I am detailed to show you the garden and introduce you to the rest of the family.

"Here in the deckchair's my grandfather Faux: my mother's father. He calls me Horace Horsecollar. I don't know why – he always has. He's very funny and takes me to the zoo sometimes. He loves dogs and lets me steer his Rover 95 down the drive and was a soldier in the Great War. He can be very sarcastic sometimes but today he's in a good mood, so you're all right."

The white-haired man in the deckchair wears a grey-green sports coat, a maroon tie, grey flannel trousers and brown leather shoes. He's fast asleep, the newspaper with its half-completed crossword balanced on his lap. It seems a shame to wake him.

"And over there's Nanny Jary, my father's mother. She says I have her hair and remind her of her brother, Len, who was killed in the Great War."

By the rose bed a small, sad looking woman with thick white hair cut short is listening to a much taller one with a prominent chin.

"The tall lady who's talking a lot is my Nanny Faux. She rode my bike the other day. It's a full-size man's bicycle and she rode it all round the garden. Here she comes."

"Good afternoon. Wake up, Billy! There's a guest here. You'd better get out of that deckchair and make some room to sit down."

"Come down the garden with me and I'll show you the railway line where the foxes live. I was letting off some bangers last winter and one came into the garden and watched me. You'd think they'd be scared of the bangs, but he wasn't. That's the shed where I keep my bike. There's an old wheelbarrow in there and, if you turn it upside down, the handles point up into the sky like that. If you light a banger and drop it down the handle and then quickly light another one and drop that in on top of it, the first one shoots the second one up in the air. Then it explodes over Mr Novissimo's garden over there. My dad says it's called airburst. But you can only get them in November so I can't show you now."

Looking back up the lawn towards the house, you see a balding man with two walking sticks standing by the birdbath, talking to a teenaged girl with blonde hair. He's talking and she's smiling at him as she listens.

"The old chap with the walking sticks is Grandpa Jary and that's my sister Elizabeth with him. He likes her but I don't think he likes me much. I don't like him either. He gambles money on horses and takes his false teeth out to eat and talks with his mouth full. He's just had a big operation on his hips and is learning to walk again. He lied about his age and was in the artillery in the Great War. He used to play cricket but now he plays bowls instead."

Here they all were, the two previous generations of my family, and, as neither of my parents had any brothers or sisters, these six were all there were. As with any family, I liked some of them and had certain reservations about others, but one thing stood out proud even to my ten-year-old eyes: the lives of both my parents and at least two of my grandparents had been transformed by the two world wars. Their speech, attitudes and behaviour were shaped by two cataclysmic events that would dominate their lives till their last breath. And their values and attitudes helped to form mine.

Beyond this particular island in my memory, peopled by these few characters I remember vividly, lie more remote stretches of the past populated by people I never met but who were clear in the memories of people I knew. Great-grandparents usually inhabit this region. My wife, Lois, and our younger daughter, Vicky, met none of theirs. I'm told I met one of my great-grandmothers, but I'm not sure which. Alex, our older daughter, met her great-grandmother and made her rock with laughter but, although it's a happy memory for me, Alex doesn't remember anything about it. Great-grandparents usually stay just out of reach, slightly beyond the point where the past starts to become hazier, less personal, part of history. So it's unlikely you and I will meet and, even if we do, you won't remember me.

When Alex was born, Lois got a letter from Great Aunt Mamie, who was born in the last but one year of the nineteenth century – when the young Churchill charged with the 21st Lancers at Omdurman. She had crocheted a jacket for our new baby. Her letter began: "You don't know me, but you married our Christopher so you must be nice." A big assumption, but I was touched by the principle behind it: that, although Auntie Mamie had never met Lois, she would assume she was a good thing until she proved otherwise. I'm extending this same principle to you.

As for the people I'm describing, I'll try to be as objective about them as possible. Inevitably, though, what follows will reflect my perspective, my own subjective opinion. As you read it, if you think I'm being a bit unfair to someone, allow for it. If they were writing about me, it would not be the same story. Happily, though, I'm holding the pen.

What to call you? How about *G* (for Great Grandson or Great-Granddaughter)? I hope that's OK. I'm hopeless at maths but I'm told population increases geometrically, rather than arithmetically. All being well, Lois and I – who currently have two children (and a dog called Harris, but he doesn't count in this respect) – should have four or five grandchildren and perhaps ten or more great-grandchildren, of whom you may be one. If you're not actually a great-grandchild, perhaps you're a great-great-niece or -nephew instead. I can call you G too, and I hope this book will still be of some interest. You and I – Lois thinks this sounds pompous, but I can't think of a better metaphor – are both tributaries of the source I'm describing. Whoever you are, if you're not gripped by what these letters offer, please pass them on to someone who is, pausing only to accept my best wishes, which come to you all the way from Odiham in Hampshire in January 2006. If, though, this sort of thing appeals to you (and I hope it does), please read on.

Adopting Auntie Mamie's admirable principle,

With love,

Christopher

PS In case you don't know, our Jary rhymes with Mary, and Faux sounds like forks.

2: Sources

Odiham

Friday, 13th January 2006

Dear G,

In my desk drawer here I have a letter – you may have read it because, by the time you read this, it will belong to you, or perhaps to your parents or an aunt, uncle or cousin. It's on faded blue paper with a Victorian penny red stamp and it's from 1854 – actually, it's dated 1853, but the aged writer got the date wrong. It's from my thrice-great-grandfather, William Faux. He's writing rather formally, by my standards and probably by yours too, to his son, also called William, who has just left home to work for a bookseller in Clapham. Despite the emotional, social and language constraints of his time, his feelings for his son sound no different from those of most loving parents of any century. It's rather touching.

However much I feel your absence I sincerely rejoice to hear you are very comfortably situated, a consideration with me that soars above all others. I trust your services will always be alike appreciated which will in some measure reconcile you to the recluse and quiet way of life, on which you are now entered. Nevertheless, any separation from those so dear to you, by very natural tyes of affection, must at times give you pain, and I need not assure you the separation tugs heavily on my heart, and altho' 'tis said "time wears away human affections like chaff before the wind", my love for my children can only escape but with the last sigh! I am pleased to say we are all tolerably well and your brothers & sisters desire their love to you and will be happy to see you as soon as you can make it convenient.

The letter is enclosed in another sheet of paper, which has been annotated twice. The first note is from the son himself, William, who died in 1906.

This letter I recd from my dear father a few days after leaving home for the first time – I was then 21. I hope my son Christopher will retain it as a souvenir of his Grandfather and also as a specimen of good writing for a man 70 years old.

The second annotation refers to the first. It's from the second William's son, Christopher, and it reads:

This letter from my dear father came into my possession Mch 11 1907 the 42nd anniversary of his wedding day. F. C. Faux

From this you may conclude that the Faux family had a slightly self-important sense of posterity. You may be right, but so were they: the letter's already survived 150 years. F.C. Faux was Christopher or Kit. (He's your 4 x great-grandfather, while the writer of the letter is your 6 x great-grandfather.)

As I write this, a century on from Kit's note on his father's note on his grandfather's letter, to me they all sound distinctly ponderous – and the younger William frankly rather pompous. I hope it's not inevitable that the voices of previous generations sound like this. I'll try to avoid it. But, as you read on, I hope you'll make the same allowances for me that I try to make for poor old William. Like him, I may sound a bit odd, but I mean well.

The same drawer that holds that letter contains a lock of Kit's hair, taken when he was eighteen months old in 1867. And it's exactly the same colour as my daughters' hair was when they were young. I never met Kit, who died just before the Second World War. To my daughters, Alex and Vicky, he seems a very remote figure. They bear no physical resemblance to the face that stares at us from various photographs: small and bird-like like all the Fauxes and with the inevitable moustache. (You'll be relieved to hear that neither Alex nor Vicky has one of those – at least up to the time I'm writing this.) Nonetheless, Kit's hair in the late 1860s is identical to how theirs was in the 1980s. So he's passed something on that we know about, and there may be much more of him in us than we will ever know.

I can't help feeling it would be nice to know a bit more about him and other ancestors – partly because it brings us closer to the times they lived in, partly because each of them has added his own ingredients to the cocktail that is me and to the similar cocktail that's you.

Kit's son, Bill, whom I knew and who died when I was twelve, passed things on a bit more directly. I sneeze just like him – loudly and with impressive dramatic effect. Quite often I find myself using expressions he used when I was a boy. "Here they come in their teeming millions: all the world and his wife." "It hurts like billio." Don't ask me what "billio" is, or how to spell it. I haven't a clue. It's an expression I inherited with as little conscious choice as Alex and Vicky inherited the colour of Kit's hair. And Bill's daughter Peggy, my mother, has left us even more. Alex is like her in looks, speech and manner. Influential stuff, that DNA. So what are you like? What have all these people left you? I bet something I'm about to mention will strike you as a characteristic you share or recognise in a relative. I wonder what it will be.

Humanity has a short collective memory for detail. If you're like most people, you'll know a lot about your parents, a lot less about your grandparents, less still about your great-grandparents and very little indeed beyond them. My perspective is similarly telescopic. From where I stand now I can see my own life full scale, my parents' lives half-scale, my grandparents' quarter-size and so on. But, reading this will enable you to stand on my shoulders, see further than most of your contemporaries and perhaps have a better understanding of how people lived and loved long before you arrived on the planet. This in itself I think is interesting. Where have we come from? Were our ancestors like us? But there's a wider purpose as well. If this idea works, it will give you an unusually full picture of the late twentieth century where I have come from and the early twenty-first where I am now which, to you, may otherwise seem a distant age.

I took a reasonable interest in my grandparents' and parents' lives but, now they've gone, there are lots of things I wish I'd asked while I had a chance. These letters are to answer those sorts of questions by telling you a bit about these people who were our fore-runners, yours and mine. As it seems unlikely you'll have met either of us, I'll tell you a bit about Lois and me, your great-grandparents, too. And I may throw in a bit about your grandmother and great-aunt (who are – respectively – either Alex and Vicky or Vicky and Alex). I expect you'll remember them well. I hope you liked them. I only wish you could tell me a bit about you and your family as well. But, whatever scientific advances there may have been by the time you read this, I doubt you'll be able to manage that.

My predecessors have gone now, taking most of their memories with them, their lives, long or short, reduced to a few glimpses prompted by some haphazard memories, by the stories some shared while we were together, and by their few remaining possessions which surround me. There's furniture. Great-grandfather Fletcher's upright writing desk, which has seen so many of our comings and goings. It began its life in an Edwardian study, spent the 1930s and 1940s in my grandfather's home, stood in my bedroom throughout my childhood and now occupies a corner of my sitting room. Opposite stands the same great-grandfather's mahogany chest, holding a tea service made by a French factory that was destroyed by German shelling in 1915. On the wall is a watercolour of Abbeville, bought by my grandfather in 1917 to show his mother where he had been.

There are a few pieces of jewellery. An engagement ring, bought in 1912, made of Kimberley diamonds. My great-grandfather Fletcher's gold watch chain with a Victorian halfpenny, illegally engraved "LUCK 1912". Another watch chain – my great-grandfather Jary's – heavy and thick with enormous gold links. Another ring, of sapphire and diamonds set at an angle, bought at great cost for my mother in the year of the Munich Agreement by a young man called Jack then earning thirty bob (£1.50) a week.

There are books. My grandfather Faux's *History of the 89th Brigade*, inscribed by some friend now forgotten, "To Old Bill of the 90th". There's his pocket prayer book, bound in faded khaki cloth, inscribed by his mother-in-law in 1915 and pressed flat during the twelve months it was carried in a tunic pocket from the Somme to Passchendaele. There's Jack's blue pilot's logbook, begun in immature writing to record the weekend flying of 1936 and closed by an unknown hand seven years later with the single word "Missing".

There are oddments. A pair of steel spurs used by my grandfather Jary to encourage recalcitrant horses and mules to pull the guns. The mother-of-pearl-handled knife with which great-uncle Wally Rogers cut his 21st birthday cake in 1913. The gilt box, originally containing chocolate and cigarettes, sent by "The Princess Mary and friends at home" to wish Wally and his fellow soldiers a happy Christmas 1914. Today it contains Wally's medals, with his brother Len's. Too large to fit in the box are two bronze plaques sent by the King to my great-grandparents Rogers, but which could never be used because Wally and Len have no graves.

There are letters. Bill's letters, scribbled in filthy trenches with blunt pencil on scraps of now fading paper, preserved first by a father who died in 1939 and then, for another thirty years, by Bill himself. An affectionate note from Jack, scratched in cheap, war-rationed ink to my mother on a stormy March afternoon from a bomber station in Yorkshire. And, dated the next day, an official letter of condolence, inexpertly typed with two fingers by an aircraftsman clerk, and signed by the squadron's commanding officer.

Finally, there are photographs. Among them, a sepia-tinted picture of my grandfather wearing his captain's uniform and the pepper and salt moustache his colonel ordered him to grow to make him look older. A black and white one of him at his retirement lunch, hosted by his Fleet Street colleagues, wearing a city suit and an insincere, faintly cynical smile. A colour postcard of a church window commissioned by my great-grandfather Rogers to memorialise his dead soldier sons. A cracked school photograph of a short, introverted boy, my father, his face half-hidden by the shadow of an outsized cap. Behind it, an army photograph, ten years later, of the twenty-one-year-old veteran he became, with three pips on each shoulder and the white and purple ribbon of the Military Cross on his chest. A snapshot taken one day in March 1943 outside a Lincolnshire farmhouse of a Flight Lieutenant, his young, blonde wife and their baby, at the end of his last leave before catching the train back to his airfield near York.

Redolent with memories, each object evokes a clear but tantalisingly incomplete glimpse of its owners at a particular moment. My grandfather, shivering in his greatcoat in the snow-covered drainpipe that served as his company headquarters near Arras, trying to write a cheerful note to his anxious father in Southport. A month later and two miles away at Bullecourt, twenty-year-old great-uncle Len in his first and only battle, crouching low in a newly captured trench trying vainly to shelter under his steel helmet from the pitiless German barrage that lasted all day. A quarter of a century later, Jack sitting in the mess at Linton-on-Ouse, the rain lashing at the windows as he scribbles a quick note to his young wife. Next morning, my mother hanging out my half-sister's nappies to dry in the orchard near Grantham, not knowing that, ninety miles north, a letter is being typed that will change everything forever.

You'll own or will have seen some of these objects I'm describing but, unless someone tells you whose they were, they'll just be things. Like facts, they may or may not be attractive in themselves, but they become really interesting only when someone explains not just what they are, but what they mean. These letters, from someone you'll never meet, are to help you to put characters to faces in faded photographs and to connect people and stories to possessions. Let's take these photographs and possessions as our starting point as we try to conjure back to life just a few of the forerunners you and I share.

Most of these letters run to between six and eight pages so you can read the whole thing in small digestible chunks, and, where I could, I've included a photograph or two to help you picture the people I'm describing. Events are mostly covered chronologically, so we start by looking back at the four families (Faux, Fletcher, Jary and Rogers) which gave me my grandparents. But, as with any human enterprise, there are complications. I actually had five or six grandparents – you'll find out why later on – and, although one grandmother is no blood relation, you'll see why I think she more than earned her place here. A generation further back, the circumstances of my grandfather's birth are so melodramatic that I simply had to tell you a bit more about his mother's family, the Westbrooks, who lived not far from where I am now. So, like the human story it tells, it's not a straightforward journey from A to B.

I've not tried to improve or simplify the story by tinkering with what I think is the truth. My sources have been mainly family oral tradition and partly my own research. I found out about the Westbrooks and the deaths of Uncles Wally and Len, and this is the first time any of it has been written down. My grandfather Faux probably knew little about his Westbrook ancestry, while my grandmother Jary didn't know what befell both her brothers in the trenches – and perhaps it's as well.

These letters are about people; they're not about war. There are other things here too – poverty, intolerance, generosity, love, bereavement – the stuff of all human life, and particular to you and to me because each bit contributed to what we both are. But there's a lot of war in them. Although, happily, I've very successfully managed to avoid any form of violence – and so did most of my more distant ancestors – my parents and grandparents were demographically unlucky. My grandparents and their siblings came to adulthood just in time for the First World War, my parents punctually for the Second. My father's world view was formed by his war, his mother and my mother were both casualties of war as surely as if they had lost arms, legs or eyes, and my mother's father was embittered and made cynical by his experience from the Somme to

Passchendaele. It's impossible to describe the last two generations before mine without mentioning, as first and greatest among all the influences upon them, the two wars that dominated their century. Their experiences at once developed, damaged and defined their characters for the rest of their lives.

Memory seems to work like a muscle. In exercising mine to describe the events and people here, I seem to have strengthened it and found I could recall much more than I'd thought possible. Occasionally it conjured for me not only the scene, but also the me who witnessed it. In that first letter the ten-year-old me who showed you round the garden wasn't a convenient literary device; he came to my mind, complete with his khaki shorts and short-sleeved shirt with its pictures from the Bayeux tapestry, unbidden from 1966 to show me what – and who – he can see in his present tense. So, especially in the later letters which describe things I remember, you'll meet several contemporary mes from those times.

You'll also meet me, the fifty-year-old from 2006 who's writing the letters and who, although they're not really about him, will tell you a bit about himself when the story concerns him personally. Finally, there's the me we need to be most careful about: the one who's remembered, chosen, ordered and described everything in these pages. In doing so, like it or not, he's plastered his fingerprints and DNA all over them. Even when he thinks he's being objective, he'll be giving you only his view, and inadvertently he'll be revealing things about himself he didn't intend to share or didn't even know himself. We'll both have to keep an eye out for him as we go through the pages that follow.

With love,

Christopher

3: Victorian respectability

Odiham

Saturday, 14th January 2006

Dear G,

Let's start with the Faux family, three generations of whom figure in that 1854 letter and its two annotations. Sadly, I can tell you very little about the William Faux who wrote the original letter. Born in London in 1784, he died seventy-five years later in Brighton, where he'd lived for many years. He seems to have been a clerk, sometimes an accountant or accounts clerk, in a number of different sorts of business. His handwriting's good – clerks needed that – but his spelling isn't all it might be. He's said to have been a prisoner of the French during the Napoleonic Wars which may explain his marriage rather late in life. His wife had the unusual name of Andalusia, which suggests its own Peninsular War connection, and they had several children. One was William, born in 1833, another the first recorded Christopher in the family.

Family tradition holds that the family came from a village near King's Lynn, and that one of our forebears was baptised by Admiral Nelson's father, the Rector of Burnham Thorpe. Often these stories have a basis in fact but, if this one has, I've found no evidence except that Norfolk is one of the three or four areas where people called Faux lived at around that time. Intriguingly, the Norfolk Chronicle of 10th March 1781 carries a report of a William Faux from those parts.

Escaped from Justice, out of the Gaol of the Borough of King's Lynn, Norfolk, in the Night of the 6th Inst., William FAUX, charged upon Oath with having obtained Money of one Richard HOMES, under divers Pretences. The said William FAUX is by Trade a Carpenter, about 46 Years of Age, five Feet seven Inches and a half High, Sandy Eye brows and beard, Pitted with the Small Pox, and hath lost a front Tooth in his Upper Jaw. Had on when he went away, a Brown strait Coat, with Buttons of the Colour, Black Waistcoat, Black Corderoy Breeches, Black and White Silk and Worstead ribbed Stockings, and a Light Brown curled Wig, with two Rows of Curls.

Whoever will Apprehend the said William FAUX, so that he may be conveyed back to the said Gaol and brought to Justice, shall on his being delivered there receive a Reward of Ten Pounds, and all Reasonable Charges from James CRAWFORD, Gaoler.

Was this William Faux that first William's father? Did he disappear to London and there, three years later and presumably with the help of a wife or partner, produce a son? That sandy hair is familiar – like Kit's – although the rest of the description paints a less than attractive picture. I have to admit finding it a seductive thought that the respectable, faintly pompous Fauxes descended from this disreputable-sounding character. If self-important old William knew about this, he most certainly would have kept it to himself.

That William (the one born in 1833) took great pains to preserve his respectability. His first job at the Clapham bookseller led to a life in publishing, first with Chatto and Windus but mainly with W H Smith, where his career prospered. As head of Smith's library service, he was widely respected as a man of substance and judgement. He knew Thomas Hardy, offended George Moore by refusing to stock one of his books on moral grounds and is even described in *First with the News*, the history of Smith's, as *an eminent Victorian*. George Moore himself left a much less flattering portrait of his moral censor, describing his "tangle of dyed hair... bald skull... false teeth... and withered face". But I suppose he would, wouldn't he? It's always unwise to offend a writer.

In his early thirties, William took a wife fourteen years younger, Mary Ellen Alabone, who came from a family of clock-makers from Newport on the Isle of Wight. Francis Christopher – Kit – was their first child, born in

1866 at Basingstoke, a few miles from where I live now. Several other children followed after the family settled at New Malden in Surrey, where William built and steadily enlarged a family house called Fairmead. Although William himself and one or two of his less critical offspring spoke of it as a sort of southern Chatsworth, it was a not quite house. It was not quite large enough – which is why he steadily extended it. It was not quite attractive enough. In fact, some thought it a dark, ugly, Victorian monstrosity. And it was not quite in the right place. The spot he chose was near the railway and exactly where, fifty years later, there would be enormous inexpensive development as the London suburbs grew. It was finally sold in the 1940s on the death of one of William's sons, who lived there all his life. Fairmead's only memorial today is a close of small houses named after it, while Mary Ellen Faux has her own memorial in the pulpit of Old Malden Church.

Mary Ellen knew exactly how to deal with her domineering husband. Forbidden to go to London, she'd simply wait till he'd left for the city and catch the next train. After a pleasant day's shopping she'd get back to Waterloo to catch the train before the one he always caught home. Sometimes she climbed into another carriage of the same train. He never found her out.

Born four years before the Victorian age began and dying five years after its end, William Faux was a man of his time. In fact, he seems to personify his era: self-educated, self-made, industrious, unimaginative, rigid, pompous and sometimes cruel. His was an aspidistra world of dark wainscoting, graduated social hierarchies and heavy moral certainties. His hard-won status in society and his family's – perhaps newfound – respectability are important factors in the story that followed, when the behaviour of his oldest son, Kit, undermined all his father's social ambitions. And the product of that scandal, which included deception, disinheritance, a twelve-year banishment, a false marriage and birth certificate, and a secret that was maintained for eighty years, was my grandfather – your thrice-great-grandfather – Bill.

The scandal began some time in 1888, when 22-year-old Kit, who was still living with his parents at Fairmead, fell in love with 19-year-old Alice, one of their housemaids. Events took the turn then that they often take now, and that I imagine, however well such things may be organised, they still will in your time. In the first couple of months of 1889, realising she was pregnant, Alice quietly left Fairmead and settled in Croydon, where her oldest brother Robert and his family lived. Here she took another job as a maid and awaited the birth of her baby.

Bill was born in August 1889 in a tiny terraced house in Union Road. You may well ask at this point what Kit was doing. We can't, of course, know in detail but it seems he tried to keep a foot in both camps, seeing Alice but continuing to live at home. To my late twentieth century ears, a man in his early twenties behaving like this sounds pretty feeble. I wonder how it strikes you? But before we condemn Kit too harshly it's worth remembering that he was probably entirely dependent on his father financially. To jump ship and try to be independent would have carried the risk of failing and having no money to support Alice and the child. It was a tough position to be in and he made his own choice.

Kit and Alice married at Croydon registry office in March 1889, making, on their marriage certificate, several false claims. Kit exaggerated his age, gave his name as *Christopher Francis* – rather than Francis Christopher Faux – and described his father as *William Francis deceased*. As we know, William was neither of those things. Meanwhile, Kit continued to live at Fairmead long after the birth of his son, whom they called – with loyalty or a touch of insurance? – William (after his paternal grandfather) James (after his maternal grandfather) Christopher (after his father) Francis (their adopted alias).

Census night in January 1891 found Kit Faux still living comfortably with his prosperous family at Fairmead, Alice Francis working as a live-in maid for a family in Croydon and their sixteen-month-old son farmed out to Alice's brother, Robert and his wife, at another address in Croydon. And that was the welcome that the well-heeled Faux family and the affluent last decade of the Victorian age offered my grandfather, Bill. It seems to me a bleak start in life. God knows how it must seem to you.

With love,

Christopher

4: Illiterate peasants

Odiham

Sunday, 15th January 2006

Dear G,

Do you look like your parents? My grandfather, Bill, and his two brothers didn't look a bit like Kit and the other Fauxes. They were larger, stockier and more powerful. Bill in particular, unlike his father, was an impressive and handsome man. Physically he resembled his mother's family, the Westbrooks. Mostly farm workers, they lived twelve miles from where I live now. Because they didn't move about much, we've been able to trace them as far back as the parish registers allow. It's worth mentioning that a number of houses and streets in the nearby market town of Alton are called Westbrook because the name describes half of Alton (west of the brook) delineated by the Normans when they arrived 940 years ago. Don't be misled into thinking this makes the Westbrooks in any way rich or important: all it means is that, when one of them moved away from Westbrook in Alton, he was identified in his new village as *John of Westbrook* and, over the years, the *of* was dropped. I'm told this is how some surnames developed.

Six centuries after the Norman Conquest, our Westbrooks lived at a village called Bentworth a few miles on the Alresford side of Alton. By the end of the 18th century they'd moved a couple of miles further down the road to Upper Wield. Along the way, their fortunes had waxed briefly and then waned. The first Westbrook to settle in Upper Wield was 21-year-old Thomas, who arrived from Brown Candover to marry Jane Finden there in 1780. He had thirteen children: five by Jane and then another eight by his second wife, Jemima. One of Thomas's sons, James Westbrook, left the village and enlisted in the 14th Light Dragoons, serving in the Peninsular Campaign as Wellington pushed Napoleon's army out of Portugal, across Spain and back across the French borders. A distant relative of Alice's mother, meanwhile, one of the Woodmans from Upton Grey, was killed in the final victory at Waterloo.

For the less adventurous members of the family the woods around Wield provided a living. Jemima's son, Thomas, was a wood dealer and her grandson, James, was a woodman's labourer, while his younger brother, Colin, made hurdles, which he sold on the green.

It gave me a bit of a jolt when I was sent a print of an old photograph of Colin, who was born in 1842. He's wearing a hat and Victorian outdoor working-man's rig, and has a long white beard, behind which hide the familiar features of my grandfather, Bill, his great-nephew.

Today Upper Wield is an idyllic English village with thatched cottages, a pond and long views across gently undulating Hampshire countryside. I go clay-pigeon shooting near there once a fortnight and always take a detour through the village simply because it's so pretty. But in the mid-nineteenth century it wasn't so pretty for Jemima, who ended her long life in poverty, in a lean-to wooden shack beside the chalkpit.

James, born in 1839, was Alice's father. Her mother was Charlotte Knight, whose father was a local builder. There's a stone inscribed with his initials on one of the houses. These Knights were a poor, distant branch of the same family to which Jane Austen, who lived nearby, was related. And here for me is the most startling fact about them all. Despite these remote but impressive literary connections, neither James nor Charlotte ever learned to read and write. Does it shock you that relatives of ours who died as recently as 1908 couldn't read a book or a newspaper headline or write a letter or even their names? Or does 1908 seem to you so long ago that it doesn't surprise you as much as it does me? For me it's less remote – less than fifty years before I was born. But now perhaps we're getting closer to why Kit was frightened to tell his father that he wanted to marry Alice. The self-educated William Faux, who had made himself eminent in the world of books and literature, would have been horrified at the prospect of his eldest son regressing by marrying the daughter of an illiterate peasant.

Alice was born into an era that to you and me seems entirely alien. No schools, no readily available medical care, no plumbing. In winter she'd have been cold a lot of the time – or occasionally too hot when she sat too near the open fire in Caiger's farmhouse, where the family lived. Sometimes, in otherwise unheated houses, you could manage both at once and be too hot down the side near the fire and too cold the side away from it. Compared with Jemima's life, though, theirs was comfortable.

**Charlotte Westbrook in the doorway of Caiger's Farm
with some of Alice's sisters and sisters-in-law**

And, at just the right time for Alice, who was born in 1869, a school appeared in Upper Wield. She was one of the first village children to benefit from the 1870 Education Act, and hers was the first generation of this branch of our family, since the decline of their fortunes in the early 18th century, to read and write. Such was the power of education that, within a few years, her younger sister was the village schoolmistress. Alice's own writing was firm, clear and correct; not, perhaps, as refined as Kit's copperplate hand, but – educated.

Walking to Upper Wield from nearby Bentworth today, you approach along a long straight lane flanked by trees. Beyond the trees on all sides are green fields and, on your left, the small chalkpit near where Jemima lived. Turn right here, past the school and glance in at the playground where Alice and her younger brothers and sisters played between lessons. Just up here on the green over on the left Colin Westbrook had a stall selling hurdles. He did well, even exporting some as far as Jersey. Around the green and beyond it along the lane stand several thatched cottages of various sizes, and down there on the left is the tiny Methodist chapel, which stands almost beside the tree-encircled parish church. And there, close to the church, under an ancient yew, is the grave of Alice's parents, your 5 x great-grandparents, James and Charlotte. They died, James very soon after Charlotte, in 1908, having spent their entire lives in the village.

Their children moved further afield. Their oldest son, Robert, moved to Croydon in the early 1880s. He was born in 1861 before James and Charlotte married – something else that would have horrified William Faux. Although James acknowledged paternity, Robert maintained the name Knight for the rest of his life. His brother, Arthur, followed Robert to Croydon, where in the 1890s a colony of four Westbrook siblings settled within a few roads of each other. Six feet tall and a member of the Salvation Army, Arthur was a coalman's labourer. A year apart, Alice and Arthur seem to have been close. She called her second son Arthur Vernon after him and he named his daughter Alice. Arthur's own son, Arthur James, was destined to travel furthest of them all. As a private soldier in the Queen's, he would land at Suvla Bay, Gallipoli, in the summer of 1915, fight in Egypt at the first Battle of Gaza and die at Beersheba, aged 23.

Inevitably, the secret Kit had taken such pains to hide came out, and banishment and disinheritance predictably followed. Kit finally moved in with his wife and baby son in Croydon, where Vernon was born in 1897. As his career, also in publishing, advanced, the young family moved to Ipswich, to Birmingham and finally to Southport in Lancashire. Then, as Kit's sentimental note on his grandfather's letter suggests, there was A Great Reconciliation. Bill, who up to his early teens had been William Francis, became William Faux. An honour indeed. I think I'd have told them where to put the Faux name, wouldn't you?

Except for a slight Hampshire burr in her voice, Alice's origins were deeply buried in the past. Far from holding Kit back, as William had feared, as Kit's career prospered Alice blossomed into a loving mother, a loyal wife and a socially confident mistress of her house. How many of the members of the affluent Southport and Ainsdale Golf Club guessed that their formidable lady captain was the daughter of an illiterate woodman's labourer? She learned to hold her own – even in the future with Bill's ruthlessly argumentative wife.

In the middle of one of many rows, her daughter-in-law exclaimed: "This is what comes of marrying beneath you."

"You?" Alice replied. "You couldn't marry beneath you."

Bill remembered her fondly and, because she died three years before I was born, I've always felt rather sorry to have missed her.

With love,

Christopher

5: Either you *are* County or you are *not* County

Odiham

Monday, 16th January 2006

Dear G,

Because, thirty years ago when Lois and I got engaged, I wasn't earning any money and couldn't afford an expensive ring, my mother suggested we use Bill's and Dora's engagement ring. Dora had worn it from 1912 until her death in 1969, since when it had spent seven years in my mother's jewel case. I don't know which of you has it now. You may have seen it: a gold ring with five Kimberley diamonds set in a straight row. This is one of quite a lot of things we have from Dora and the Fletchers, who were probably the most socially secure (if not the wealthiest) branch of the family. In the corner of my sitting room, for example, stands Dora's father's upright writing desk. On it is a blue and white plate recording the birth, on 3rd December 1738, of Elizabeth Fletcher, Dora's 4 x great aunt and your 9 x great aunt. I expect you've seen them in someone's house.

By the time my great-grandfather bought the writing desk in my sitting room, the Fletcher family fortunes were already on the wane. When records began they were yeomen farmers and chapmen in the village of Walton-le-dale, near Preston. It's an odd thought that our first recorded ancestor, Barten Fletcher who was born in 1579, may have glimpsed from his cradle the young schoolmaster who's said to have spent the next two years under the protection of their local landlords, the Catholic Hoghtons. He'd come all the way from Stratford and his name was William Shakeshafte, or Shakespeare.

Succeeding generations made steady economic and social progress until, by the mid-eighteenth century, Elizabeth's brother was describing himself as a gentleman. And gentlemen – in the sense, at least, that they did no paid work – they remained until the 1880s, when my great-grandfather and his brother appalled their father, John, with the news that they intended to train for the law.

Marriage three generations earlier with the Walmsley family had brought them Ashton House at Ashton-upon-Ribble, where both Fletcher sons were born in the early 1860s. The House remains – at the moment it's a smart nursery school. Dora's father's name memorialised this zenith of their fortunes. He was christened Richard Ashton Fletcher. In many ways he was the antithesis of his father, John. John was extravagant, Richard simply generous. John travelled extensively abroad by coach; Richard travelled little and was essentially a local worthy. John left his wife and family and took a mistress in Brighton. Richard remained devoted to his wife at the centre of a large family. John never worked; Richard established a successful solicitor's practice in Southport. John had three legitimate children and one illegitimate one; Richard had six daughters and two sons, all conceived in highly respectable wedlock.

Ada Fletcher and six of her children. Dora is second from left, Gladys on right. Mamie sits on Dora's lap while Alwyn peers over Walter's hat.

Three of these contrasts explain the decline in the Fletcher fortunes. John's infidelity resulted in his wife's family ensuring that her substantial estate reverted to them. Richard's large family and his generosity – he'd never send a bill for his services to a friend or a widow or anyone in need – severely depleted whatever wealth he may have inherited. Throughout his life, however, he remained a man of substance, although reduced from the estate into which he was born, to a large, redbrick Victorian villa in a leafy avenue in Southport. Here, in solid, upper-middle-class comfort, he and his wife, Ada, raised the eight children born to them between 1887 and 1901.

Dora was their second child, born in March 1889, eighteen months after the birth of Lily, with whom she would fight cat-and-dog for the rest of her life. Seventy-five years later, I remember Lily visiting briefly from her home in Cape Town. The two old ladies had barely been reunited for ten minutes before there was a loud shout of "Liar!" followed by slamming doors and the inevitable argument that ended the reunion. Dora and Lily relished a fight. Their next sister, Gladys, must have been a great disappointment to them: she was my favourite great aunt: quiet, determined, unexcitable and sensible. But their first brother, Alwyn, remained true to their pattern, joining in their battles with gusto. On one occasion, memorable for its noisy violence even by Fletcher standards, he was pursued up the stairs by Lily brandishing a carving knife. The endless offensives and counter-offensives of his childhood seem to have given Alwyn a taste for warfare that never left him. Not content with serving in both world wars, he even volunteered to fight in the Spanish Civil War when time hung heavy in between.

With so many adventures available within the family home, Dora was unreceptive to education and at her private day school acquired the nickname "Monday Morning Dora". Her teacher would start each week with the same greeting. "Good morning, girls. Good morning, Dora." Her parents generally allowed her to stay home for the rest of the week. When, during the Second Boer War at the turn of the century, Mafeking was relieved, all the schools in Southport were granted a holiday except Dora's. Her father kept her home for the day, which cannot have come as any great surprise to anyone. Despite this lack of formal teaching and an apparent lack of intellectual curiosity, she remained throughout her life a voracious reader of fairly heavyweight literature such as *The Herries Chronicles* and the works of Charles Dickens, with whom the Fletchers claimed a tenuous connection. (Dora's mother was distantly related to Dickens's friend, the now-forgotten author William Harrison Ainsworth.)

Dora's was a stereo-typical upbringing for an Edwardian upper-middle-class girl. Her parents were well respected, well heeled and over-indulgent. Her mother, born to an Army family – the Denhams – with several brothers in the Guards, was a home-maker and an excellent cook, a skill she passed on to all her daughters. Whenever as a boy I visited my grandmother or any of her sisters, they had the same air of excitable, quick-fire conversation and they all cooked the same meals in the same way. Their father, a gentleman solicitor and a leading light in the freemasons, was a pillar of Southport society. He gave generously to his children and expected little of them.

Secure in their social position, the Fletchers looked back to previous generations who had not had to work. I remember my grandmother reminiscing about how all the land around Ashton House – "as far as the eye could see" – belonged to her family. When a neighbour once referred to a socially ambitious local family having "gone county", Lily replied in terms worthy of Lady Bracknell: "*Gone* county? *Gone* county? You can't *go* county. Either you *are* county or you are *not* county." In this life the Fletcher family expected to occupy the front row of the stalls, and in the next they cheerfully anticipated similar advantages.

Richard himself was a man of his time and class. Self-effacing and gentle to the point of weakness inside the family home and with those he thought vulnerable, he could be ruthless in defence of his home and position. To the family's horror, during the First World War he discovered that one of his younger daughters was pregnant as the result of a liaison with a local boy recently posted to France. Somehow, in the middle of the war to end wars, he successfully manipulated the military machine to return the boy at once to England to marry his daughter. Because, however, he regarded him as socially unacceptable as a son-in-law, he first insisted he sign a humiliating document to the effect that he understood that he was unworthy to marry into the Fletcher family and would make no claims upon the privilege.

His two older daughters, however, married appropriately, and their weddings were celebrated in 1912 and 1913 with suitable display as well as warmth and good will. Alice's parents lay buried under the yew tree in Wield churchyard and her brother, Arthur the coalman, was bringing up his family two hundred miles away. It seems unlikely that anyone ever enlightened Bill's father-in-law about Alice's background. Even had they done so, I doubt he would have opposed the marriage. By the time the Fletchers and Fauxes joined in marriage, Kit and Alice had firmly established their middle-class credentials. Richard welcomed the marriage, giving his second daughter a huge wedding and an impressive mahogany canteen of cutlery engraved with the letter 'F' for Faux. The Fletcher's own cutlery, of course, carried the family crest. Lois and I still use Bill's and Dora's cutlery but, after the Second World War, Lily took the Fletcher stuff with her when she emigrated to Cape Town, where it was stolen. I wonder who's using it now, crest and all?

The status, security and spoiling of her childhood seem to have allowed Dora to become snobbish, selfish and aggressive. In any gathering she would expect to be centre-stage and, when this didn't happen naturally, she took whatever steps were necessary to contrive it. She would expect her husband, as her father had done, to provide a home in which she could bestow her smiles only when she felt inclined. Sixty years later, at her lunch-table in front of guests, she glared at her defeated-looking husband and announced in characteristically strident tones: "My father was the best man who ever lived – bar none."

With love,

Christopher

6: Banishment and reconciliation

Odiham

Tuesday, 17th January 2006

Dear G,

A faded photograph taken in the summer of 1901 provides us with what I've long thought is the theme for Bill's story. A tea table has been laid in an Ipswich garden and the young Faux family are having fun. Bill's father sits centre-stage, wearing a moustache and a large hat, and obviously in the throes of telling the sort of funny story that requires a lot of arm-waving and face-pulling. Bill's mother and an aunt look on; they are both smiling. So are four-year-old Vernon and even Reg, the curly-haired infant who sits on Bill's lap, peering over the tea pots. That Edwardian photographer captured a happy moment. For everyone, that is, except twelve-year-old Bill who, in his stiff white collar and dark suit, simply looks sad.

This tea-time photograph in that Ipswich garden was taken just after the magnanimous family reconciliation that enabled them to revert to their real name. Is it fanciful to think that, at twelve, Bill had already sensed that his very arrival had to some been unwelcome or that he was unimpressed by some unknown relatives expecting him to be grateful for this sudden change of name?

The Fauxes had a curious attitude to names, seldom calling their children by any of the names with which they were christened, and often inflicting on each other and those around them faintly disparaging nicknames. Bill was uniquely fortunate in two respects: his three Christian names were all perfectly sensible and he was called by the first of them. Although Vernon used his second name, for some unfathomable reason he was known in the family as "Tooks". The third brother, Reg, fared worse still, Bill saddling him with the insulting nickname "Whelp".

Two years later, the family had moved to Birmingham, where Bill attended King Edward VI's School for Boys. At fourteen, however, he was removed and sent to work as a clerk. The Faux family subscribed to the philosophy that their sons should start at the bottom. Despite their new literary tradition, they did not believe in education and shared with many of their class a deep suspicion of cleverness. Reg, born in the first year of the twentieth century, would be the first to receive any form of higher education when, in the early twenties, he trained to be a doctor. To justify his investment, his father expected him over the dinner table each evening to recite the main points of every lecture he had attended that day. When he protested that his father would not understand some of the more scientific information, he was told: "Never mind. If I'm paying for this, I want to know I'm getting my money's worth."

There was a touching, slightly Pooterish simplicity to Kit, who would sit in his drawing room pedalling enthusiastically at the pianola and waving his arms about to the strains of Sibelius's *Finlandia*. *Finlandia* was "the finest tune ever written", just as *The Last of the Mohicans* was "the finest book ever written". In 1936, shortly after his 70th birthday, my mother remembered Kit walking into Southport, proudly telling passers-by: "I'm seventy, you know."

Alice was more down-to-earth. One of her favourite tales was of being invited to dinner at a house in Southport where the family still maintained a butler. At the table, the butler approached her first as the senior lady guest. He was bearing an impressive silver dish, from which he grandly removed the gleaming cloche cover, revealing six sausages. There were eight guests at table. My great-grandmother did some hasty mental arithmetic as the butler enquired: "Will madam have half a sausage or a whole one?"

Meanwhile, Bill's early career followed the pattern of his father's, grandfather's and great-grandfather's. The only attempt at a break with tradition ended in failure. In 1910, when he was twenty-one, he was sent to embark on a new career in India. His ship docked at Calcutta, he was taken seriously ill in the searing summer heat and he returned to England in a matter of months with a dose of recurrent malaria as the only souvenir of his visit to the sub-continent.

Three characteristic pictures emerge for me from Bill's early manhood. The first is of him, in straw boater and plus fours, bicycling to Fairmead to see not his grandfather, William, but his cousin Jon on summer days in the first decade of the new century. (Kit's sister's son, Jon had, of course, been christened Fabian, after Kit's brother, who was known as Tim!) Jon had been born in Calcutta in 1895 but his mother returned to England six years later with three children but minus her husband. She kept the two younger children with her but left Jon in the care of his septuagenarian grandfather at Fairmead, where discipline was maintained with the aid of a whip. William may have left psychological scars on Kit and Bill, but the scars he left on Jon were physical as well. Six decades later, when they both shared our Christmas dinner table, Uncle Jon's gratitude for the respite represented by my grandfather's visits was still readily apparent.

The second picture is another Edwardian vignette. It is of Kit and Bill, now in his late teens, standing by a piano in a dark, Edwardian drawing room, singing *Friend o' mine*. Appropriate, somehow, because, despite Kit's blinkered view of education, his heavy-handed humour and his superficial tightly-buttoned pomposity, Bill had an excellent relationship with both his parents which lasted all their lives, broken only by the frequent family arguments mostly instigated by Dora. Years later, when both his parents were dead, an elderly Bill would draw an unspoken but bitter contrast between his wife and Alice. "My mother was a good sport," he said.

The final picture is a wedding photograph from around 1912. It's in Southport, where Kit and his family have now lived for several years. It's a Fletcher wedding and therefore a pretty grand affair. Dora's older sister, Lily, is marrying a man called Simpson.

Big hats and grand adornments are on display. On the right, little great-grandfather Fletcher, in his pince-nez and gold watch chain with the shiny new halfpenny on the end, freshly engraved "LUCK 1912" to mark Bill's and Dora's engagement, is dwarfed by the bridegroom's mother's enormous hat on display beside him. On the left, Dora's mother, standing beside the bridegroom's father, has yet managed to upstage the bridegroom's mother's hat by the simple expedient of adding half an ostrich to her own, which was already an impressive creation. Dora and her sister Gladys, as white-clad bridesmaids, also wear massive headwear adorned with long scarves, falling low over their shoulders.

Invisible in the photograph, on Dora's left hand sparkles a new engagement ring of Kimberley diamonds.

Edwardian high summer and the upper middle class in their brightest colours.

Ada Fletcher stands second from left and Richard second from right. Gladys is seated left and Dora second from right. Alwyn stands at right beside Richard.

And there, at the back, cigarette in hand, stands the purchaser of that engagement ring, Dora's fiancé, Bill. Somehow he manages to look detached, faintly sardonic. Is it marriage he's facing next year or a take-over bid by the Fletcher family?

With love,

Christopher

7: Sid's Boy's Boy on Sid

Odiham

Wednesday, 18th January 2006

Dear G,

Most years in my childhood we went as a family to the Royal Tournament at Earls Court. Despite the huge crowds, I loved it. Does it still run? This evening before the show there had been a Spitfire parked among the many exhibits in the huge display hall outside and, after hours of queuing, I'd been allowed to climb into its cramped cockpit, surrounded by dials, to breathe its atmosphere of metal, oil and leather. Then we'd been shown to our seats by the smartest soldier I'd ever seen. He wore a large hat with its brim pinned at a jaunty angle by a tiny black badge in the shape of a bugle. Not much taller than me, he gave an impression of irrepressible alertness and professionalism. I'd never met a Gurkha before. And now we were listening to Suppé's *Light Cavalry* and watching eight gun teams of the King's Troop of the Royal Horse Artillery as they cantered below us, criss-crossing and avoiding collision only by split-second timing and each driver's skill in controlling his team of gleaming horses. Even in the 1960s their thirteen-pounder field guns looked archaic.

When they unlimbered and fired them, it was like a re-enactment of a scene from the Napoleonic Wars. I remember being startled when my father leant over and whispered: "Those are like the guns my father used in the Great War."

It was hard to make any connection between this spectacle and the old man in the thick cardigan we used to visit on Sundays in his flat in Ilford. It was as hard to associate my grandfather with those field guns at the Royal Tournament as it was to associate their ancient design with anything that had happened in the twentieth century. But it was true. For three years Sid had served on the Western Front as a gunner in the Royal Field Artillery. One day he proved it by giving me the steel spurs he had worn.

Born in the Mile End Road in 1898, my grandfather was the second son of Frederick and Harriet Jary. Both came from Great Yarmouth, where Frederick owned the two trawlers in this photograph.

In the last decade of Queen Victoria's reign he had moved to London and opened a business in Billingsgate Market, where the fish he caught could be sold wholesale. His four children, Het, Fred, Sid and Stan, were therefore all born within the sound of the Bow bells. As his business prospered, they were also born into relative affluence: despite their father's addiction to horse racing, they lived very comfortably. Soon after the birth of their youngest son in 1901, the family moved to a large Victorian house in suburban Ilford where, except for three years away at the war, my grandfather remained for the rest of his life.

Like the Fauxes, the Jarys had difficulty with names which they resolved by the curious stratagem of seldom using them. Where the Fauxes simply christened their offspring by one name and then called them something quite different, the Jarys addressed members of all subsequent generations either as "Boy" or "Girl". When referring indirectly to them, to avoid the inevitable confusion this would create, they became more specific, identifying them according to their relationship to themselves or their siblings. My father was therefore "Sid's boy" and I became "Sid's boy's boy", while my sisters were "Sid's boy's girls". Confusion was not, however, entirely avoided because they employed the same nomenclature for the people we married; so my mother was also "Sid's boy's girl" and, in this way, my sister's new husband became "Sid's boy's girl's boy". It really was a very cumbersome system, but at least it enabled them to side-step the requirement to get to know any of the younger members of their family.

When as a small boy I was taken to visit my grandfather's brother Fred and ushered into the seated presence of a small, frail prototype of my grandfather, neither he nor his wife, Ethel, was even mildly disconcerted by the fact that neither knew their great-nephew's name. I, on the other hand, was deeply disturbed by my first sight of my great-aunt who, peering suspiciously round her half-closed front door, said in quietly sinister tone: "Come in, boy."

The three Jary brothers all seemed to look alike and they seemed to get smaller as they got older. I remember Fred as small, my grandfather as medium-sized and Stan as fairly substantial. All I knew about Uncle Fred was that he had served in the London Scottish as an infantry soldier throughout the Great War, and that he and my grandfather seldom spoke because there had been some disagreement between them about the distribution of money from the family business, where they had both worked all their lives.

During my great-grandfather's life, the business thrived and made them a lot of money. Despite their affluence, however, they were and would remain peasants, with many of the virtues and vices that went with it. They were prejudiced and ignorant but independent-minded and had what might charitably be regarded as a healthy scepticism about the value of knowledge and education. My father remembered a Christmas quiz, set by his uncle, in which many of the answers were simply wrong. When presented with the evidence of encyclopaedia or dictionary, the Jarys spoke with one voice: "You don't want to believe all you read in books…" Their opinions were generally ill-informed and often wrong, but they were at least their own. My grandfather's peculiar motives for volunteering for the Army in early 1915 are a case in point.

Having attended a private day school in Ilford, Sid joined his father and elder brother in the business at Billingsgate Market. After a year or two he decided he should have a rise and, knowing how irascible his father could be, he waited until Sunday lunch to ask him. This strategy proved unsuccessful and his request was refused. When he asked why, his father replied with characteristic bluntness: "Because you're not worth it." Perhaps unsurprisingly, Sid took umbrage, left the house and enlisted in the Army, lying about his age as at that time he was just seventeen.

He was posted to a battery of field artillery with whom he served as a driver in France and Flanders from the end of 1915 until the Armistice.

I once saw a snapshot of him taken during those years, wearing his gunner's uniform with a leather bandolier around his chest. He's wearing his soft cap at a distinctly unmilitary angle and the slightly vacant grin traditionally adopted by wily private soldiers reluctant to reveal any intelligence in case they're given a job to do. He looks humorous and slightly feckless.

At various times he found himself on the Somme, at Arras and in the Ypres salient but, as an artilleryman, his was quite different from the war the infantry knew. He never found himself forward of the transport lines, never spent a night in a trench or faced the enemy riflemen and machine-gunners. His trips up to the line were at night, when the gunners took their limbers up to the reserve positions to deliver fused Mills bombs to the infantry, and the main danger was shelling either when his battery were on the move or when the German artillery engaged the British guns with counter-battery fire. As a driver, he seldom personally fired his troop's guns. Knowing the Jary family's renowned incompetence (which I've inherited) with things mechanical, I imagine his officers and NCOs soon recognised the danger of letting him loose with an 18-pounder field gun. His job was to look after the horses and mules which pulled the guns and limbers. But, as the long lists of gunner casualties attest, his was still a dangerous job and, given his life-long love of horses, it must have been a heart-breaking experience watching so many animals being worked to death, wounded and killed. So, for the three formative years from seventeen until the age of twenty, he endured the dirt and discomfort that were the dismal lot of every soldier on the Western Front.

The three Jary sons were unusually lucky. Although Fred was wounded in the arm at Passchendaele, he and Sid survived, while Stan, born in 1901, was too young for the War. All three sons joined their father's business and, in 1921, Sid married Winifred Rogers, whose parents also lived in Ilford. They were both twenty-three years old and both their young lives had been dominated by the recent war.

With love,

Christopher

8: The long shadow of tragedy

Odiham

Thursday, 19th January 2006

Dear G,

While my grandfather Sid talked often about the war, although with an inconsequential vagueness that omitted concrete facts and conveyed little understanding, his wife seldom spoke about the events that effectively destroyed her life. Winifred's way of managing unpleasant truth was not to speak of it. It was impossible, however, to be in her presence for longer than an hour without sensing an all-pervading sadness. Born the last of five children, by the time she was eighteen she was the only survivor. Her older sister, Edith, died of septicaemia in her early teens, another sister died in infancy and both her brothers, Wally and Len, were killed in the Great War. They were a presence with her always, but she kept them to herself. It was as if she had enveloped herself in an impenetrable cloud of bereavement which, however much one sympathised, one could never hope to relieve because she so seldom spoke about her siblings other than in the most superficial and fleeting terms.

She was born in Ilford in 1898 to Walter and Edith Rogers, who were both Londoners. Walter was born in Stepney, and Edith in the Mile End Road, although her family, the Ayrtons, were originally Scots. As their family and Walter's small engineering company in East London grew, they moved out to Ilford to a quieter life. Their first child, Wally, was born in Stepney in 1892. Winifred was their last, arriving close on the heels of Len, who was a year older. Theirs was a quiet upbringing of gentle middle-class values constrained within narrow, suburban, Edwardian horizons.

Her brothers, especially Len who I suspect was closest to her emotionally as well as in age, remained with her to the end. And yet, on her death aged eighty-nine, I found I knew virtually nothing about them. I have no idea what they looked like, although at one time she remarked that I had a look of Len, which suggests that he, like my grandmother and me, may have had fair hair. I knew that one of them – was it Len again? – was very short-sighted. I knew that they had both been infantry soldiers, and that Wally had been killed in 1915 at Givenchy, while Len had died two years later. But, apart from this handful of very insubstantial facts, I knew only that their deaths cast a seventy-year cloak of sadness over her life, effectively obscuring all human detail of them as people. They were our family's unknown soldiers: tragic, individual but somehow faceless and impersonal.

I remember her showing me their medals, which she kept in her bedroom in the gilt box that Princess Mary had sent to Wally and all the other soldiers at Christmas 1914. I remember being struck by the watered silk ribbons of their Victory Medals in their rainbow colours, and the red, white and blue ribbon of Wally's 1914-15 Star. She explained that Wally had gone to France two years before Len. He therefore had three medals, Len two. I remember too my astonishment when suddenly she asked if I would like to keep them.

It was not until twelve years after my grandmother's death that I uncovered what little information survives about what happened to Len and Wally. The few facts about their deaths more than vindicated her instinctive sadness. Two years apart, both had enlisted as private soldiers in the London Regiment, both had gone to France with a fresh battalion and both had been killed within a few weeks, on their first day in action.

The Le Touret Memorial, on which Wally is remembered

Soon after the outbreak of war, Wally had crossed London to Clapham Junction to enlist in the 1st/23rd London Regiment. Shut your eyes and you can see him: a young man like those in the newsreels, quietly dressed in a dark suit and a boater, queuing among many others at the drill hall in St John's Hill. Here, on a warm day in late summer, he was examined by a doctor and took the oath.

The autumn and winter were spent in England learning the skills required of infantrymen and practising techniques of open warfare which no one would be able to apply until the summer of 1918.

Until then, the field gun and the machine gun would dominate every battlefield, spawning the stagnant trench existence, stirred only by occasional episodes of unimaginable carnage, that characterised the First World War experience. On that first Christmas of the war – the one by when they'd all said the whole war would be over – every soldier received the gilt box containing chocolate, cigarettes and a card 'from Princess Mary and friends at home'. Do you still have Wally's box somewhere?

When they landed at Le Havre on 15th March 1915 the 1st/23rd were part of the first Territorial Army division to arrive in France. Spring came for them here as they settled comfortably into camp on the hills overlooking the port. The unbroken ranks of khaki tents were their home for the next six weeks while they breathed the healthy sea air and trained in the new trench warfare, which had yet to become infamous in our culture.

May found them in reserve in the flatlands around Béthune. A long wet day in a rattling train that stopped and started had taken twenty hours to transport them the last twenty-five miles to the line. Here, between Festubert and Givenchy, the British had just launched a new offensive against armour-plated, concreted positions, strongly defended by machine guns and artillery. The ground was littered with the rotting corpses of the British and Indian troops who had failed to cut their way through the thick German wire that had withstood the British bombardment. Thousands of them had been cut down by machine gun fire or obliterated by pounding shelling. By 23rd May, a fortnight into the offensive, the British had advanced three-quarters of a mile.

Meanwhile, the incessant rain and the relentless shelling of both sides had turned the battlefield into a quagmire. In the flat, bare fields the rain-fed grass had grown tall and coarse. Among it were strewn tangles of barbed wire, the brick remains of a few cottages and the splintered stumps of what once were fruit trees in what once were orchards. Hidden from view, until you stumbled into one of them, was a mass of ditches full of mud and slimy water.

Two miles behind the line, the Londons could hear the thunder of artillery and the rattle of machine guns as, on that Sunday morning, standing bare-headed in the waterlogged open fields at Beuvry, they attended their last religious service before joining the battle. Next day they marched in column, company by company, through driving rain, across the La Bassée canal, to relieve another battalion in trenches at Givenchy. Their damp, serge uniforms clung to them uncomfortably, chafing and chapping their skin. Filing finally into their new positions, the unlucky companies in the forward trench would spend their first night in the line soaked, cold and sore.

Next morning, barely settled into their new trenches and dug-outs, the battalion were ordered to attack a German trench system two hundred yards to their south. They would lead the attack with their sister battalion, the 1st/24th, and they were promised artillery support to protect them once they'd captured the German forward trench. Because this was the first battle of a territorial unit, their performance would be closely watched. Great things were expected of them.

When their officers' whistles blew, fifteen hundred men from both battalions leapt from their trenches and ran forward in groups, employing the newly learned tactic of 'alternate rushes'. As they crossed No Man's Land, each group threw themselves down three or four times, pressing their bodies and faces hard into the waterlogged, broken ground to avoid the defenders' machine gun fire. Each rush was timed differently from the next group's so that the Germans never had a single, complete target.

At each rush, fewer soldiers arose from the ground, but their final dash took them into the German front line. The defenders vacated rapidly, running back to their support trenches two hundred yards to the rear. Elated by their success, the Londons pursued them and bombed them out of the last of their support trenches as well. The unblooded territorials had exceeded their objective and won the day. Now they flooded into the German trenches and prepared to defend them against any counter-attack, hacking rough and ready firesteps into the wet, chalky soil.

Once the remnants of the German infantry had retreated, their artillery took a terrible revenge. Shells began to whistle down on the Londons as they tried to adapt the German trenches to face the other way. All they could do was keep their heads down and wait for their own artillery to provide the promised support. But the British gunners had run out of ammunition. For hours, untroubled by any form of retaliation, the German guns hammered the narrow, tightly packed trenches.

While Wally and his friends crouched low and covered their heads, wondering what had happened to their artillery support, the air above shrieked death, the ground below them shook and stretches of trench beside them subsided under the onslaught. Because the British Army had been slow to adopt the steel helmet, they had no protection from the blast and flying splinters. Four hundred men of the 1st/23rd Battalion were killed or wounded in the next few hours. Wally was one of those killed. His may have been one of the hundred and twenty bodies recovered and buried a couple of days later but, if it was, his grave has since been lost. Given the intensity of the shelling, there may have been no body to bury.

Wally: August 1914

Chugging down to Clapham Junction,
Smiling at a cloudless sky,
Boater on the seat beside you,
Sunday-suited, sober tie,
Keen to join and patriotic,
Twenty-two, prepared to die.

Join the queues at Clapham Junction,
Swell the ranks of other men,
Leave the office and the suburbs,
Sister Winnie, brother Len.
Will whatever waits in Flanders
Bring you back to them again?

Chugging home from Clapham Junction
On this tranquil August day,
German gunners near Givenchy
Seem a million miles away.
But their barrage, which will kill you,
Falls nine months from now – in May.

Sixty years later, as my coming-of-age party approached, my grandmother gave me the pearl-handled knife Wally had used in 1913 to cut his 21st birthday cake. It was the one time I recall my father being superstitious. He wouldn't let me use it. On the night, for my grandmother's sake, Wally's knife lay prominently beside the cake-stand but, surreptitiously, I used another knife to cut my cake. I have it still, but it has never been used.

With love,

Christopher

9: Brothers on the Somme

Odiham

Friday, 20th January 2006

Dear G,

The very names of the villages on the Somme have a memorial resonance for me, sometimes poetic, often horrific: Bapaume and Carnoy – each with its echo of Sassoon's poetry – Montauban, Delville Wood, Mametz Wood, High Wood or Beaumont Hamel, each name tremulous with the horrors of trench warfare. Do they have the same impact on you as you read them? After the four-month Battle of the Somme, war, society, the continent of Europe and even the English language would never be the same again.

Today, near Albert, a rickety museum displays a haphazard collection of relics of the battle: shell cases, rusted weapons, badges and bits of uniform and photographs. Outside it they've preserved some original stretches of trench. But they've preserved them not as a sanitised, concrete memorial but *as they were in 1916*, in all their dank, muddy dereliction. It was there, standing alone in those trenches on a sunny July afternoon in 1998, that I caught a glimpse of my grandfather as a young man. Here, in late July 1916, had been Bill's first exposure to modern warfare in all its filthy horror. To arrive here from what was still at heart provincial Edwardian England, to leave a young wife and a new home, to find oneself living like an animal in holes scraped in the ground, to be shot at and shelled… Bill must have felt he'd been thrown down in a desolate landscape that belonged in hell.

A mile down the road, the Commonwealth War Graves Cemetery held ranks of graves from his regiment, the Manchesters. While the rest of my party from the Somerset Light Infantry sought out Somerset graves, I put poppy crosses on a few of the Manchester ones and tried to remember my grandfather and his young brother.

After their marriage in 1913 Bill and Dora had bought a house in Harrogate, where he'd followed his father and grandfather into W H Smith. Then, in 1915, long before conscription, he suddenly enlisted. Like Wally Rogers and many young men in 1914 and 1915, his eighteen-year-old brother Vernon had decided to join up. To reassure their anxious mother, Alice, Bill decided to go with him to look after him. Significantly, he omitted to tell Dora until he had taken the oath and the King's shilling. Dora's mother, Ada, gave him a khaki prayerbook, inscribed: "With best love to Billie and wishing him the best of luck. AEF. 1915." Alex still uses it. Dora's contribution was to give up the house at Harrogate and move back to her parents' home for the duration of the war.

We have a photograph of Bill in his new second-lieutenant's uniform, a black armband marking the death of Lord Kitchener when *HMS Hampshire* was sunk in June 1916.

With it is the typed order posting a draft of five officers to the 17th Battalion in France, including Second-Lieutenants W J C Faux and A V Faux. The 17th were a pals battalion, drawn from the City of Manchester. Pals battalions encouraged friends to enlist, train and fight together. Sadly, they also enabled them to die together, and one consequence was the devastation of particular streets, areas, villages and towns across Britain. They were brigaded with their sister battalions, the 16th and 18th, and a regular army battalion, the 2nd Royal Scots Fusiliers. As that inscription in Bill's *History of the 89th Brigade* suggests, this was the 90th Brigade.

Bill and Vernon joined their new battalion near Montauban. Here, on 1st July 1916, the first day of the battle, the 16th and 17th Manchesters, advancing into a whirlwind of machine-gunfire, had swept through the German lines, capturing hundreds of prisoners and three German field guns, before taking Montauban itself. But the German machine guns had culled both battalions to a little over a third of their fighting strength. Eight days later, the survivors led the dawn attack on Trones Wood, which they captured easily. Then the shelling began. When it stopped, the 17th Manchesters, seven hundred and fifty strong ten days earlier, had a hundred men left. Over the next fortnight the battalion was rebuilt, with a new colonel and many new officers and soldiers, fresh from England or drafted in from other regiments.

Finally captured a week later, Trones Wood now became the patched-up battalion's start line for their next part in the offensive: to take the village of Guillemont. This would be Bill's and Vernon's first battle. After an interminable night spent digging assembly trenches, they trudged wearily up through the wood to support the attack in the misty hours before dawn on 30th July. Barely a tree remained among its shattered acres, tangled with brambles, pock-marked with shell-holes and littered with the stinking, fly-covered corpses of the Manchester Pals.

The news from the leading battalions was good. They had already taken Guillemont. But German shelling and machine guns made it almost impossible for anyone else to reach them. The few score survivors who braved the shelling and crossed the machine-gun-swept approach to Guillemont, found their way blocked by uncut barbed wire. Finally they found a gap in the wire near the Montauban road, but German riflemen and machine-gunners in the surrounding orchards turned the narrow gap into a killing ground crammed with corpses. No one could reach the soldiers in Guillemont, if any of them remained uncaptured and alive. Having lost another thousand men, the 90th Brigade was withdrawn to receive more reinforcements, to train and to recover from the carnage of the previous month. Bill's first battle was over. July, which had begun for the Manchesters with startling, though costly, success, had ended with equally costly failure.

Bill and Vernon didn't return to the Somme until early October. August found their battalion in the area of Béthune, licking their wounds and training more drafts of reinforcements. The month began with an inspection by the army commander, General Rawlinson, after which their brigade major cheered everyone up with a vitriolic report on their turn out. The divisional general, he said, had expressed himself "extremely dissatisfied".

September took them further north for their first experience of Flanders' trenches. Here, at Festubert, a couple of miles from where Wally had died sixteen months before, the ground was so waterlogged that trenches were mere scrapings in the ground, protected by piles of sodden sandbags. This sector, though uncomfortable, was a quiet place for Bill and Vernon to adapt to the routines and procedures of trench life. To reverting to a troglodyte existence in an alien landscape, living in holes gouged in the damp ground. To monotonous days which began with stand-to in the chill silence of daybreak and ended in a sunset framed by mud. To the lonely hours of the night watch, smoking and stamping one's feet to keep warm, staring up at a starry sky. To managing one's bodily functions without privacy here, where the enemy rendered the latrines inaccessible. To sharing a tin of cold pork and beans or Maconochie, or larding an army biscuit with plum and apple jam with a dirty knife and filthy hands. To feeling frightened, ill or homesick some of the time. To being cold, dirty and damp all the time. Southport, a hot bath and clean sheets all began to seem to belong to another life.

By the time they returned to the Somme, it was autumn. Guillemont had been captured and the front had moved north, to just below Bapaume. Despite droves of reinforcements, none of the Manchester battalions could muster more than five hundred of their full complement of seven hundred and fifty. Their objective was a ridge overlooking Bapaume itself, and the

17th Battalion would lead the attack, which would be preceded by a brief but very intense artillery barrage.

Throughout a pouring wet morning, Bill and Vernon squatted with the rest of C Company in their assembly trenches at Factory Corner beside the road to Ligny-Thilloy, waiting for the barrage to start. Early in the afternoon it finally broke upon the German trenches opposite, and the German gunners retaliated, bringing down thunder-clap concentrations on the Manchesters' trenches. Meanwhile, had anyone among the Manchesters been able to lift his head above the parapet, he would have seen the German marines opposite lying some way back from their trenches to escape the British shelling. After five ground-shuddering minutes, the British barrage lifted, the Manchester officers blew their whistles and the men started to clamber from their trenches. The German marines raced forward to reoccupy their lines and to take up their weapons, and a hurricane of machine gun fire burst upon No Man's Land. No one in C Company got beyond thirty yards. They lay in the mud, dead, bleeding or pinned immobile by bursts of fire scything a few inches above their heads. Somehow Bill survived the whirlwind but thirty yards out there, where no one could move to help him, lay nineteen-year-old Vernon, wounded and terrified. The attack foundered in the face of the merciless machine guns. Of the officers, only Bill and two others survived unwounded.

All that day, Vernon lay wounded, pinned down out in No Man's Land, and Bill, the older brother who had enlisted to protect him, could do nothing to help. That evening the 16th Battalion reinforced them and in the darkness some of the morning's wounded, including Vernon, were at last rescued and carried back. One of Bill's letters, written the following spring to his father, provides a tantalising hint of what happened.

Tell Tooks that blighter Edwards came back two days ago with his usual grin. He has had three months in hospital with what he calls 'scabies'. The medical report said something different. Tell Tooks I have taken him on again as servant. I felt very wild with the beggar, but remembered what he had done for Tooks last October, so am giving him another chance.

This was the end of Vernon's war. The teenager who had volunteered so patriotically was now safely out of it while his older brother, who had loyally gone along to support him, was left to soldier on alone. Meanwhile, the Battalion had taken another pasting, the autumn rain was turning the country into a quagmire and the Somme offensive of 1916, for which so many had hoped so much, was grinding to a murderous, muddy halt.

Out with his men next day digging some new trenches beside the Longueval road, Bill heard an unexpected clanking and the sound of a large engine working hard. A huge steel machine was grinding its solitary way forward, where it would provide welcome support to the infantry who faced the next grim attack. Bill hadn't the remotest idea what it was. Fifty years later, standing in our dressing gowns at the kitchen sink doing the breakfast washing up, my grandfather told me about this, his first glimpse of a tank.

With love,

Christopher

PS   Maconochie was a tinned stew which, like pork and beans which always contained considerably more beans than pork, was much more stew than meat – and the provenance of what meat there was was always doubtful.

10: Spring at Arras

Odiham

Saturday, 21st January 2006

Dear G,

After the Somme, Bill's battalion and its exhausted survivors withdrew from the line. At the end of the month they moved north again, a few miles south of Arras. Here they received reinforcements and, on 6th November, relieved the Scots Fusiliers in the line at Bellecourt. The Arras sector was a quiet place and few of them can have had any inkling of what would happen to them there in the spring.

In the 18th Battalion there remained some unfinished business from the Somme. On 14th November they shot one of their soldiers for desertion in the face of the enemy. On 1st December they shot two more. Privates Longshaw and Ingham had joined up together from the Salford goods yard of the Lancashire and Yorkshire Railway Company, had served together on the Somme and finally had run away together. Now they were shot by the same firing squad and buried together in the cemetery at Ballieulmont. It seems unlikely that the acute brain that originally conceived the Pals battalion foresaw its ideals of comradeship taking this particular twist. Happily, there were no executions in Bill's battalion.

In a quiet sector like Arras leave came round more regularly, the roster artificially accelerated by their casualties in October. Bill was lucky. Although he had just taken over A Company, his first home leave materialised at just the right moment, enabling him to spend Christmas in Southport. A rush to Boulogne, across to Dover, the leave train to Charing Cross, a taxi to Euston and a long journey north delivered him to his in-laws' house in Cumberland Road, where he enjoyed a brief return to family life and home comforts. Here were Dora and his parents, whom he had not seen for six months, and Vernon, whom he had last seen being carried away from Flers on a stretcher.

Leave, as always, passed too quickly and, by early January 1917, Bill found himself back in the trenches at Bellecourt. On the 11th, after the Manchesters had moved back into corps reserve, Bill found time to write a letter to his father, Kit.

It suddenly flashed across my mind this morning, when I was shaving, that tomorrow will be your birthday. I am sorry this letter will not reach you in time, but I wish you many happy returns of the day and hope that you will celebrate many more to come in the future and under happier and more peaceful circumstances.

I wrote Mother two days ago and told her we were out of the line resting and are likely to be for a month. Tres bon, n'est-ce pas? It is a relief to get back from the sound of the guns.

Am having a very busy time just now. We are rearranging all coys to get new formations, as the Army have just brought out a new scheme, copied from the French, which I think will be all to our advantage. I can't tell you about it, but it entails a fearful lot of work for coy commanders and I hardly get time to breathe.

My captaincy hasn't come through yet, but I have my second pip, which is a nice little lift. It was in the Gazette of Dec 24th, if you want to have a look at it. No news to tell you, except that I am fed up with the War and wish to goodness we could finish this show off and come home to peace and comfort again.

Many of 'em once again.

Best love to you all,

Your loving son,

Bill

The wintry weeks that followed were spent out of the line, building a railway line to supply the Arras offensive when it began in the spring.

Then came good news. In early March, Bill wrote enthusiastically:

Good biz this retirement of the Bosche in front of Bapaume. Tooks will have told you how we were connected last October with some of those little villages in front of Bapaume we have just taken. We can hear the guns going hell for leather from where we are and thank goodness we are out of it.

Sorry you still suffer from your cold a bit. Mine has gone and I feel as fit as a fiddle.

Three weeks later, he wrote again.

I am writing this sitting in my Coy HQ which consist of an old wide drain pipe dug in the side of a rly embankment. We have been up in the line since the advance last Sunday up to Saturday morning, and were then relieved and came back into reserve (ie drainpipe). I haven't had an hour's consecutive sleep for six days until we arrived at the drainpipe, but I had a good night last night. The only trouble is that it is so infernally cold at nights. Our water bottles freeze every night. Still the men are in fine spirits and it is great to advance over Bosche country and to see the old devil on the retreat. We had absolute hell of an artillery strafe when we got to our new line, but we didn't have many casualties, although it is dashed trying to the nerves. Have had my usual strokes of luck and managed to get through without a scratch, although I had some devilish close squeaks. We are being relieved in two days and shall go out for a short rest. What joy to think about it. Fancy blankets again and my dear old valise.

I do envy you blighters this Sunday afternoon, sitting in your cosy armchairs and with a nice fire and poor old me with a mackintosh and tin hat on and shivering like hades with feet like lumps of ice and can't even sit up straight. Who the devil invented wars! Still, the swines are on the retreat now so nothing else matters.

Opposite them the Germans were indeed retreating. They were withdrawing to strengthen the massive defences of the Hindenburg Line, part of which would be the Manchesters' next objective.

On the last day of March Bill wrote again.

What a lot of misery there is about. A French countrywoman has just come into the cottage where I am billeted and I can hear her talking to the people in the next room. Her son has been badly wounded down at Verdun and is not expected to live. Poor woman. She is crying like anything. Curse the war and to hell with the Bosche.

Ask Tooks if he remembers young Nixon, one of C Coy's runners. He was very badly hit the last day we were in the line. Had one arm taken off at the elbow and a bad leg wound. It is doubtful if he will live. Only 22 and married with one kiddie. Poor fellow. I bandaged him up temporarily until the stretcher-bearers arrived and wrote to his wife for him. I'm sick of war – wish I could get a blighty and have a rest for a time. Cheer-ho!

Happily, Nixon survived. Bill's concern about the young father and his own desire to get home may have been heightened by recent news that Dora was expecting their first child in September.

On 12th April, Bill's battalion were relieved by the 2nd Royal Welch Fusiliers, who took over the old German third-line trench they occupied. The second-in-command of one of their companies was Siegfried Sassoon, whose name would have meant nothing to Bill at that time – or, quite probably, later – but whose poetry always captures for me the language of the trenches which my grandfather would speak for the rest of his life

Haig's spring offensive had pre-empted the arrival of spring, which came late that year. On the 21st, Bill wrote home:

Yes, by gosh, we have cursed the weather this month good and plenty. Just our infernal luck in an advance, when men have to live in little narrow trenches and no dug-outs, to have snow and sleet and mud everywhere. The lines of communication are awful too. You see artillery horses lying by the roadside in hundreds everywhere you go in the forward area. All dead through overwork and exposure. The ration and ammunition limbers have instructions that they must work horses at all costs even if they drop dead, as the stuff has to be got up somehow and the roads are ghastly.

Can't see any signs of leave for a bit. Too busy out here. I have been left out of the line this time for a rest. Our fellows are now right up in the thick of the advance. Feel a bit of a worm not being with them but very glad of my first rest since coming out.

In any major attack some troops and officers were left out of battle to provide a cadre on which any unit could be rebuilt. Bill therefore handed over A Company to Alan Holt, his young second-in-command. From the comfortless safety of the Battalion's transport lines he wrote to Kit.

You will be sorry to hear our Battalion has been in action again and over the lid this morning. The only news we have yet received at the transport lines is that we gained our objective, took nearly 300 prisoners and have had a fair number of casualties. All the officers in my company were either killed or wounded. The one killed would have been all right as he was wounded first and, instead of lying still, tried to run back to our trenches and was again hit and killed. One of the wounded, tell Tooks, was Holt, who was at Béthune with us and he was acting second-in-command to me. I believe nearly all our casualties have been light wounds, which is some consolation. Report says Cartman is wounded again but I'm not sure of this. We shall get all the news tonight as I expect the Bn will be relieved. I suppose I should have got my blighty by now had I been in the show. Feel an awful worm sitting here at ease when they have been through it so up there.

Before dawn A Company had advanced into heavy artillery fire. German machine guns, set in concrete emplacements, traversed No Man's Land with their fire. Of its three officers, Holt was captured, Cartman wounded and nineteen-year-old Second-Lieutenant Walter Palmer was killed. For all practical purposes, Bill's company had ceased to exist. The 17th Manchesters' two hundred and sixty survivors were withdrawn from the line and went into reserve for training. But the Arras offensive wasn't quite over. Its final act, the Battle of Bullecourt, was about to claim the life of Winnie Rogers's brother, Len.

With love,

Christopher

11: The end of spring

Odiham

Sunday, 22nd January 2006

Dear G,

One expects to lose one's parents. In the natural course they should die before us. But to lose a child – happily something that has never happened to Lois and me – must, I imagine, be something one never really recovers from. Before the war Walter and Edith Rogers had already lost two daughters. In 1915 the war, still only nine months old, had taken their elder son. Of their five children, only eighteen-year-old Len and seventeen-year-old Winifred remained, and Len now followed Wally's example, enlisting in the 2nd/4th Battalion of Wally's regiment, the Londons.

Wally's loss, reinforced in the minds of Winnie's parents by the news of the hundreds of thousands of casualties at Loos, Ypres and the Somme, must have made France synonymous with death. One can imagine their sense of dread when, in January 1917, Len's battalion were posted to France. During the much-delayed spring, while the Germans retreated a few miles behind the prepared defences of the Hindenburg Line around Arras, they were held in reserve. While the guns flashed and roared continuously on the eastern horizon they trained to prepare themselves for the much-anticipated Spring Offensive. All around them massive preparations were under way. Not far away Bill Faux's battalion of Manchesters laboured to extend a railway line to supply the offensive when it came, while Sid's artillery mules struggled through the snow and ice that epitomised the spring of 1917. And now, suddenly, the weather changed. The snow melted and the sun shone, bringing heat more reminiscent of mid-summer than April.

The village of Bullecourt straddled the Hindenburg Line south east of Arras. In early April the village had been virtually untouched by the war; by early May not one of its cottages remained standing, its streets reduced to corpse-strewn rubble, plagued in the early summer heatwave by an army of swarming flies. Here, Australian troops had punched a small hole in the German defences, creating a tiny bulge – or salient – east of Bullecourt. It was these troops in their virtually surrounded, heavily battered section of the old German positions whom Len's battalion relieved just after midnight on 14th May.

The Hindenburg Line at Bullecourt May 1917

The Londons crept forward in darkness, the ground shaking with sudden explosions as the Germans shelled their communication trenches, the night air sickly with the chemical smell of burst shells mingling with the nauseating stench of the hundreds of rotting bodies lying unburied around them. The falling shells killed several of their soldiers, including the battalion's doctor, before they'd even reached the front line.

Ejected from their elaborate trench system, the Germans were determined to restore the tiny bulge in their long defensive line. On the slope below the Londons' new position, their infantry clung onto a random, unconnected series of shell holes. Soon after the Australians had left, an alert sentry heard a German patrol just below their positions. One of the company commanders, a primary school headmaster called George Leake, leapt over the parapet into the darkness beyond to attack them single-handed. He shot four German soldiers with his revolver, returning with three prisoners and the machine gun they'd been trying to establish to turn on the Londons' trenches.

Shortly after midday, the German shelling stopped. Down the slope, near the remains of some sort of factory, the Londons thought they could see enemy infantry collecting for an attack. The British gunners brought down a lightning, accurate barrage on the assembled Germans, who scattered or were killed. But the British shelling evoked a thunderous response from the German artillery that roared unbroken for nineteen hours. Exposed in their deadly salient, throughout that interminable day and all through the long night, the Londons were shot at and shelled from three sides. Shells ripped through their positions, blowing up most of their ammunition and bomb supplies, collapsing their trenches and killing, wounding and burying alive many of their soldiers. Unlike his older brother, Len had a steel helmet, but it offered little protection against a sustained barrage of this kind. Like Wally, Len crouched low and pressed his face to the trench wall, waiting for an end.

Just before their second dawn in these positions the deafening shelling stopped again. In the silence the elite troops of the 3rd Prussian Guard rushed forward to recapture their old trenches. While the British artillery opened up, some platoons from the reserve trenches dashed to what remained of the forward trench and reinforce the two depleted companies there. With their rifles and Lewis machine guns the novice London troops were able to repulse the attack before it reached their line. The surviving Prussians fled back down the hill to their shell holes, leaving the slope littered with the grey figures of their dead and wounded. Then the shelling began again.

The Londons' first battle cost them two hundred and seventy casualties, among them the gallant Captain George Leake and twenty-year-old Private Len Rogers, who both fell victim to the remorseless German bombardment. Leake died in a Rouen hospital three weeks later. Len died where he fell. Like Wally, he has no known grave.

Somehow my two great-uncles seem to stand for the two faces – and phases – of the First World War: Wally, the patriotic early volunteer going keenly, perhaps naively, to an unknown war; Len, still a boy, joining the massive machine that despatched a million young men to the industrialised slaughter of the Somme, Arras and Ypres. Like his older brother's brief experience of trench warfare two years and a dozen miles distant, Len's lasted little more than twenty-four hours and was ended by German shelling. The American soldier-poet Louis Simpson suggested that *being shelled is the main work of an infantry soldier*. In their single day of front-line soldiering neither of my uncles seems to have had a chance to learn much about their work as infantrymen, but they certainly learned that.

The memory of both her brothers remained for another seventy years in my grandmother's heart, but locked privately away and never spoken of. My only recollection of her revealing anything personal about them was her once describing how, some time in the early summer of 1917, she and her mother had been washing the dishes at the kitchen sink when suddenly her mother shuddered and quietly said: "Oh. Len." The long-dreaded telegram had come a couple of days later. Winnie, not yet nineteen, was now the only survivor.

Len: May 1917

Spring never came to Bullecourt.
Fierce summer came instead
To melt the dregs of April's snow,
And putrefy the dead.

The flies came up to Bullecourt
To feast upon the dead.
By day they flew and buzzed and swarmed
And gorged and bit and fed.

The Londons came to Bullecourt
By night and, under fire,
Relieved the tired Australians
Beyond the German wire.

The Prussians came to Bullecourt.
At dawn their Guards were sent
To drive the novice London troops
Out of their salient.

The Prussians left at Bullecourt
Their silent, sprawling dead,
But then their gunners strafed the line
To blast them out instead.

The trenches up at Bullecourt
Collapsed as they were shelled,
And splintered, buried, choked and crushed,
But still the salient held.

Deep in the clay at Bullecourt
Lies twenty-year-old Len.
For his young sister, Winnie,
Spring never came again.

The Arras Memorial, on which Len is remembered

Thus ended the Rogers family's active part in the war to end wars. When, eighteen months later, the church bells rang to celebrate Europe's deliverance from German aggression, what comfort can they have sounded for Walter, Edith and Winifred and for so many other families, whose sons, brothers and husbands had bought that deliverance with their blood? The four bloody years had cost a million young men's lives, devastated an entire generation, changed a confident nation's view of itself and cast a perpetual shadow over the families whose lives they had darkened. My grandmother's family was just one of many for whom the light never returned.

With love,

Christopher

12: Summer at Ypres

Odiham

Monday, 23rd January 2006

Dear G,

In early May 1917, just as Len's Londons were moving up to Bullecourt, the remnants of Bill's Manchesters began a long march back to the coast.

Well, we've moved again but still further back from the scrapping. We aren't far from the sea coast now. By gosh it was some march yesterday. Fourteen and a half miles and it took us from 9am to 4.30pm to do. We looked like millers we were so white with dust when we arrived here. You would never think there was a war on here. No sound of guns, glorious scenery and perfect weather. I am as brown as a berry already with the sun.

Six new officers coming tonight so I am hoping for a bit of relief from all the fiddly little things I have had to do lately.

And, five days later on 11th May:

Just had a long letter from Tooks. He seems pretty fed up with Eaton Hall. I don't wonder. I think if I came back wounded, and they shoved me into one of those places to get convalescent, that I should tell them to go to Hades and clear off home. It must be jolly hard on married men.

Weather is terrifically hot here. Nearly killing me. Feeling as limp as a rag.

The Battalion were marching north for their first tour of duty in the Ypres salient. Like a large-scale Bullecourt, Ypres was exposed simultaneously on three sides to enemy shelling. Also like Bullecourt, the town itself had been shelled out of existence. The British generals planned another huge offensive here in late July.

On 25th May Bill described the rigours of life on the march.

Sorry I have been so long answering… We have been on the move for the last eight days – as it is by march (as the Army calls it) we don't get much time for letter writing. We march all day, halt for the night and then on again in the morning. They gave us one day's rest after three days, which gave us a chance to recuperate. I hear tonight that we are staying here for four or five days and then are pushing on again. I feel so sorry for the men with full pack and rifle. It gives them hell this hot weather.

Just heard from Tooks who tells me has touched for £140 wound gratuity. He has done jolly well out of the Army, the lucky young beggar.

I should like to see the garden now. I should say it is top-hole. Hope I shall see it soon.

By mid-June, the Battalion were back in the line at Hooge, near the Menin road, from where Bill wrote to his youngest brother, Reg.

My dear Whelp

If you will persist in addressing your revered brother by his full cognomen every time you write to him, the aforesaid revered brother will be under the painful necessity of screwing your nose and toeing your rear when he returns to his ancestral abode. Lord only knows when that will be as leave seems to be at a standstill for officers at the moment. I am getting fed up as it is six months since I had leave. You're a lucky little beast to be so young and to be out of this war. Wish I was.

Visions of the bathing pool float before me now as I sit sweltering in the heat. Do you know I haven't had a bath for a fortnight and no chance of getting one. Water is so scarce here that it all has to be used for drinking purposes. The only washing water is a little slimy, muddy, chemical-laden water out of adjacent shell holes. And it's not pleasant to wash in, I can tell you.

However, enough grousing, shall hope to see you all soon.

Above all, it was the filth that depressed Bill. He could not bear feeling dirty. At one point during the campaign he acquired half a barrel, which his servant contrived to keep with them for some time, in which when out of the line he could bathe.

Five days later, they were pulled out of the trenches again and Bill was writing to his mother.

I note you have a rumour that I am coming home on leave. I hope it will come true but I am beginning to wonder. The men are still getting leave, but the officers haven't had one for over a fortnight now.

We have been travelling again and we have got back to a village miles back from the line. We are only ten miles from the coast and only 35 miles from England. It might as well be 3000 miles for all the good it is. We are going to have ten days training to get our new reinforcements into shape. Then into the thick of it again.

I wish you could persuade Dora to come and stay with you. I'm sure it is too rowdy for her at Cumberland Road at present and she ought to have a quiet time of it, instead of taking part in all that housework and bustle.

No other news to tell you except that I am very brown and very fit and well.

The beginning of July found them back in the line near Zillebeke, where their working parties built and fortified the network of trenches. With the offensive looming, officers' leave was severely disrupted and Bill was becoming more and more anxious about Dora and their baby, due in September.

Can't get this wretched leave through. There has been a hang-up and the fellow in front of me hasn't gone yet. It is so sickening because I know Dora must be worrying herself ill. I shall have to ask for special leave. I think I am entitled to one under the circumstances, don't you?

In the end, the officer ahead of Bill in the leave roster generously stood aside and allowed Bill to take his place. In early July Bill was therefore able to enjoy a second leave at home before returning for the forthcoming battle.

On 19th July he wrote:

I have felt very fed up since coming back till yesterday. I began to feel a little more resigned to it then and am feeling much brighter today. You have no idea how mopey you feel coming back to this pig's life after feeding and living decently for ten days. I had a great time at home with you all and wish to goodness it was just starting instead of finished. Never mind, I have pleasant memories to look back on, thank goodness.

We are at present under canvas. It is quite pleasant although it poured with rain last night and my bally tent leaked all over my blankets. They are now out drying in the most gorgeous sunshine.

I suppose the house seems very quiet with Tooks gone to Cleethorpes. Never mind, we have been very lucky to get home twice running at the same time as each other.

Two days later he wrote his last letter from the front, trying to send his father some photographs.

At last a few of those photographs we had taken about six weeks ago have arrived and I am sending you along a group of our officers. The ones I had taken of myself and a cheval have not arrived yet, but I will send one as soon as they do.

I am feeling horribly fed up and sick, but it is wearing off by degrees. I felt like nothing on earth when I first arrived back. We are still behind, but expect our turn for the line will come along soon. Well, we've had a good rest so mustn't grumble.

The officers sitting down in the photo are from left to right: the Adjutant, Captain Orr, the Colonel, Captain Sadler and me. The fellow who gave up his leave for me is the tall chap on the extreme left standing up with an eye-glass. He has had his own leave since and came back two days ago. Clayton, my second-in-command and nephew of old Alderman Clayton, is the fourth from the left standing. The chap on the extreme right is our Interpreter. He is a great lad and has been in the French cavalry. He started in August 1914. He is married to an English girl and lives at Teddington, but has not the honour of GRF's acquaintance.

Dora seems to be enjoying herself with you at Balfour Road from her letters. It is much nicer for her to have a quiet, restful time with you than the bustle of Cumberland Road.

Well, I must dry up now.

With best love to you all,

Your affectionate son,

Bill

I can't find an envelope big enough to take that photograph, so I am sending it with a lot more different ones in a parcel to Dora. She will give it to you and you can of course have any of the others you care for. None of them are very good, I'm afraid. These Frenchies can't take good photos.

I didn't see the picture of Bill and his 'cheval' until 1994, when Michael Stedman's *Manchester Pals* was published. And there he was, astride the beast, leading his company out of the line, east of Ypres.

What historians call the Third Battle of Ypres opened before dawn on Tuesday, 31st July 1917. The Manchesters' part in Haig's Summer Offensive began at four in the morning, when the 16th and 18th Battalions emerged from their sodden trenches to fight their muddy way through Sanctuary Wood up to the Menin road. An hour and a half later, Bill's battalion was unleashed to pass through them and to cross the road. Each step was a struggle as the long preliminary bombardment had churned up ground already waterlogged by days of heavy rain. In the grey light of dawn German aircraft roared low below the slate-coloured clouds, firing their machine guns at the advancing troops.

Soon after dawn, Bill was leading his company into the attack across the road when he was hit in the thigh by a machine gun bullet. Bowled over by the impact, he fell into deep mud and was only saved from drowning by six men who stopped to pull him out. He was soon on a stretcher and on his way back, out of battle, to the regimental aid post and a casualty clearing station, where his wound was dressed.

The following Sunday found him in a sunlit hospital ward in Yorkshire, writing to his father, who had visited him the day before.

I had a gorgeous night's sleep last night and felt very refreshed today. I wheeled myself in a chair to the bathroom this morning and spent an hour scrubbing the superfluous muck off me. It made me very weak and tired doing it, but I thank goodness I made the effort as it is delightful to feel clean again. The sister wanted to wash me in bed but I didn't cotton to the idea at all.

Bill had finally got his blighty wound. After exactly a year in the filth of France and Flanders, he had thankfully been removed from it. He would now be at home for the birth of Dora's baby due in late September. His first cousin, Arthur Westbrook, was less lucky. On Friday 10th August 1917, he died at the railhead in Egypt where General Allenby was preparing his attack on the Turkish line at Beersheba. He was buried in the little cemetery at Deir el Belah, south of Gaza. Since there was no fighting at this time, his death must have been the result of accident or disease, but no one remembers any more. He was twenty-three and his parents' only son.

Bill never returned to the trenches. By early 1918, his wound healed, he was due to go back, but a recurrence of the malaria he had contracted in his ill-fated foray to India eight years earlier prevented it. Malaria probably saved his life. He would otherwise have returned in good time to face the German onslaught of March 1918, when the 17th Manchesters were overwhelmed and virtually destroyed. As it was, Bill had already been extraordinarily lucky to have survived twelve months as an infantry platoon and company commander. He was lucky, too, in the nature of his wound, which healed and gave him no further trouble. Dora's brother Alwyn, wounded and a prisoner of the Germans, would walk with a limp for the rest of his life.

Meanwhile, Bill's pre-war employers, W H Smith, seemed unenthusiastic about his return and a grateful government offered him a disused railway carriage to live in with his wife and baby daughter. It must have made the danger, horror and sacrifice of the last four years seem so worthwhile.

With love,

Christopher

13: Christen her what you like. I shall call her Peggy.

Odiham

Tuesday, 24th January 2006

Dear G,

On the wall of the small sitting room my grandparents used when they were alone hung a sequence of sepia-tinted photographs, framed together, of a ten-year-old girl in Dutch costume. Despite their generally grey-brown effect, you could see that she had blonde hair above a roundish face with a short nose. But, while the pictures caught a lively glint in her eyes, they couldn't show you that they were bluish-green. Today, I see that look frequently in the face of Alex, my older daughter. As a boy, I simply looked at those pictures and wondered vaguely what my mother must have been like when she was my age. The photographs were taken when Peggy was at school in Southport. She'd been born there on 25th September 1917: a fact which caused her children huge amusement when, as teenagers, we learned that her father had been granted leave from the trenches to spend Christmas 1916 at home. My mother's response was that she personally found it reassuring to know that her father *had* been granted Christmas leave.

Characteristically, there was a dispute between her parents about what she should be called. Predictably, her mother had her way and she was christened Marjorie Alwyn, after Dora's brother Alwyn and his current but ultimately transient girlfriend. Equally characteristically, Bill said: "Christen her what you like. I shall call her Peggy." It was in the Faux tradition to call her by neither of her names, and Peggy she remained.

On Bill's demobilisation from the army, he joined the *Daily Mail* in London, and the young family moved south, briefly to Catford and then to Carshalton Beeches in Surrey. Most of my mother's early memories were therefore of the same area in which I later grew up.

Bill and Dora would have no more children. Nor did Dora seem especially keen to keep her only child with her. A fortnight before her eighth birthday Peggy was sent to boarding school in Southport, two hundred miles from her parents. At the start of each term – apart from her first, when he travelled with her to Southport – Bill would take Peggy to Euston Station, where he would install her in a compartment and ask the guard to ensure she changed at Manchester. For an eight- or nine-year-old girl, this must have seemed a long, lonely and worrying journey. Having had two daughters of that age, I find it almost impossible to imagine how any parent could take such a risk.

Both Faux and Fletcher grandparents lived nearby but, since Dora had instigated a perpetual state of warfare with her in-laws, this meant that Peggy's only family contact for most of her school career was with her Fletcher grandparents. She therefore got to know Dora's parents, Richard and Ada, much better than Bill's, and came to love them for their kindness. They offered what any child at boarding school dreams of: a comfortable family home, plentiful meals and, above all, love. Now that their argumentative offspring had left home, they gave what Peggy needed most of all: stability, tranquillity and consistent affection. Surprisingly, Peggy's school also provided these things. Run by Miss Crabbe and Miss West, two spinster daughters of clergymen, Metfield provided an unacademic education for young ladies. It also provided a strict but stable environment for Peggy to grow up in. Peggy's descriptions of her days at boarding school and weekend visits to the Fletchers' house in Cumberland Road suggest to me that all four adults – Richard and Ada Fletcher, Miss Crabbe and Miss West – recognised the defects of her parents' relationship and silently determined to compensate for them.

All four proved a lasting influence on Peggy's life. Ada, a marvellous cook and indulgent mother, provided a model of what a secure family home should feel like, while Richard's generosity, gentleness and kindness to the vulnerable – their maids, some of his poorer clients and Peggy herself – helped form Peggy's model of a gentleman. Throughout her life, she'd expect the men around her – Jack, Sydney and me – to live up to this model. It wasn't a bad one by any means, but, because none of us ever had as much money as Richard, it could sometimes be costly.

While her developing mind silently codified the admirable aspects of her grandparents into standards of behaviour, Miss Crabbe and Miss West were dealing more explicitly with such standards. Integrity was a *sine qua non*. Because all good manners were founded on putting others first, they lay at the root of Christian morality. At table Metfield girls were forbidden to ask anyone to pass anything. If no one thought to pass you a vegetable dish or the salt, you went without. Standards of dress and appearance, though simple and certainly not ostentatious, were unbending. In her old age, my mother would still run back into the house to collect her gloves, muttering, only half-humorously: "Coat without gloves! Coat without gloves! What would Crabbe and West say?"

And she'd still quote her grandfather often.

"I know you have to eat a peck of dirt before you die, but I'd rather not have mine all at once."

"All folk are willing. Some are willing to work and the rest are willing to let 'em."

"Blessed are they that itch. They shall know what a pleasure it am to scratch."

Metfield was not an expensive school. Perhaps as an echo of his early upbringing, perhaps simply because the Faux family had a tendency to be tight with money, Bill always tried to live on half his income. Because Dora wouldn't allow his meanness to impinge on her personally, Peggy bore the brunt and therefore spent most of her childhood and adolescence feeling less well dressed and less well equipped than most of her friends and cousins. A generation on, my sisters and I benefited from the legacy of Bill's parsimony. My mother was determined, whatever the cost, that we should always be well equipped and well dressed, and never feel at a disadvantage among our peers as she had done among hers. At the same time my father did his generous best to compensate for Peggy's penny-pinching upbringing. Curiously, though, whenever Peggy acquired anything of value, whether a watch, a new coat or a sofa, Bill would be despatched forthwith to buy Dora one exactly the same, or perhaps a touch more expensive.

Many of her school friends were the daughters of Empire whose parents were serving in India. They saw their parents for one long holiday every three years. The parents of one of her closest friends were missionaries in China who would see their daughter only every five years. At first glance, Peggy may have seemed luckier: she went home every holiday, but hers was – by my standards and probably by yours – a deprived childhood. She remembered trying to eat her dinner at her grandparents' while her parents, who were visiting, bickered with each other. Grandpa Fletcher silenced them both with a sentence: "This is my table and, while you're sitting at it, you won't behave like that in front of Peggy."

Their rows, and Dora's ceaseless offensive against the Faux family, created a volatile, often unhappy home. Dora's grip on Bill prevented his showing Peggy the paternal affection she felt instinctively was there, and Bill's own obstinacy caused further heartbreak. His refusal to put dogs on leads resulted in Peggy returning from school several times to find that another of her beloved terriers had been run over.

When, in the early 1930s, Bill was posted to Manchester and he and Dora moved back to Southport, they took Peggy away from Metfield and installed her in a school in North Wales. Presumably Dora had concluded that she did not want her daughter round the corner. Removed from Miss Crabbe and Miss West and the affection and comfort of Granny and Grandpa Fletcher, Peggy was deeply unhappy. Although some families at that time had a tradition of sending their children away to school, it's perhaps worth mentioning that neither Bill nor Dora was sent to boarding school and that Dora, as a child, had enjoyed the certainty of the care, love and attention of a secure and indulgent home. Seen in this light, her treatment of her own daughter seems savage.

Being sent away so young left its scar: throughout her life Peggy clung like a limpet to her home. Moving house (which we did only once in my childhood) was an enormously emotional experience with my mother insisting, the night before the move, that she didn't want to leave her home. Even going on holiday upset her until we reached the hotel, while putting her beloved dogs in kennels was to her an emotional betrayal.

Peggy left school at fourteen and, apart from a secretarial course and a brief period working in London as a typist, was never allowed the sorts of opportunities that most middle class boys would have had. Hers was perhaps the last generation where this would have been regarded as the norm. Many – perhaps most – women of my generation have been treated much more fairly. But my mother never had the chance to realise her ambition of training as a physical education teacher. It's ironic, however, to attempt to apply modern standards of women's equality to Dora. Like a few middle class women of her time, Dora didn't seem to do very much. Unlike some of her female contemporaries, she did at least cook the family's meals and, like her mother, she cooked well. But that was about the limit of her contribution to family life. For Dora, equality with Bill would have been a backward step.

With love,

Christopher

14: A bit of a disappointment

Odiham

Wednesday, 25th January 2006

Dear G,

What's your earliest memory? Mine is of building a snowman in our back-garden with my sister Elizabeth and her friend Diana Wilson. I think it dates from the winter of 1959-60, when I was three. Alex's is more precisely dateable: she can remember sitting on a wall eating Smarties and watching some monkeys. Lois and I remember the incident too. The monkeys were Barbary apes, the wall was part of some fortifications and the date must have been some time in the week of 6th September 1984, while we were in Gibraltar on holiday. Alex was exactly two and a half on 5th September 1984. This seems a very early memory. My father, on the other hand, claimed to be able to remember nothing until he was about ten! Life at home, he explained, was so uneventful when he was a child that his brain had recorded nothing at all. I wonder.

Once, when we were visiting his parents, my father showed me a school photograph. It's not unusual, when someone presents you with a large group photograph from long ago, not to be able to find the person who's smiling and looking at you expectantly. What was unusual this time was that, even when he had pointed out the boy who was him, I still couldn't see the smallest similarity between that boy and my father. The schoolboy, small, sitting cross-legged and head-bowed, looked insignificant, introverted and cowed. The sort of boy any professional teacher would worry about and keep a close, protective eye on.

The picture didn't lie. Sydney's interests were solitary: sketching and, from an unusually early age, music – especially the works of Frederick Delius. This, plus his extraordinary lack of prowess on the games field, led inevitably to bullying at school where, perhaps because they sensed his apartness from them and perhaps because of his black hair and his father's hooked nose, the larger boys called him "Syd the Yid". At home he was of little interest or consequence in his father's eyes. Sid, the talented cricketer and affable team-player, had no patience with this alien child, who was a bit of a disappointment to him.

His understanding and advice never got beyond exhorting his son "to take it on the chin". Only once was he persuaded by Winnie to intervene to protect Sydney, who was being persistently assaulted not just by other pupils but by a form-master who delighted in inflicting physical pain and moral humiliation on his young charges. Sid returned smiling and with a tale to tell. He'd had to do nothing. As he'd walked in the gate, he'd encountered the towering figure of Captain – , a Merchant Navy captain.

"Have you come to see ----?" the Captain enquired, naming Sydney's form-master. "No need. I've just kicked his arse all round the football field."

A heart-warming and convenient discharge for Sid from his parental responsibilities. Is it unduly cynical to wonder, after all these years, if it was true?

One reason my father's memories didn't stretch back into his early childhood may have been choice, born of simple unhappiness. One thing was clear for all to see: his parents were ill-assorted. Sid was gregarious, lazy, publicly affable, sporting, loud and confident. Winnie was reserved, dutiful, inhibited, introverted, quiet and humble. Years later, during the Second World War, travelling home on leave with another officer, Sydney was met from the train by Sid and one of his friends. Throughout his life, Sid's friends were always rowdy, sporting types with loud voices, often from the betting world. They barged into the carriage, making a lot of clatter and shouting at one another while Sydney's fellow soldier looked on in amazement. Finally, recovering the power of speech, he enquired: "Do you know these people?"

In London on another leave my father met by chance another young officer in his regiment who happened to be a hereditary member of the House of Lords. He suggested they met for lunch at his club a few days later, and my father accepted. This was too much for his mother, who knew her place. Inhibited and conformist, Winnie spent the next day or two subtly undermining his confidence, suggesting that the invitation hadn't really been meant and that he wasn't really the sort of person to lunch with a lord. This was how Winnie customarily controlled Sydney. First she chipped quietly away at his self-confidence by making him feel he'd said or done something foolish, and then she simply fell back on a son's natural pity for a mother who'd lost all her brothers and sisters and had married unhappily. My father made an excuse and declined the invitation.

**Winnie on left, Sid on right. Beside Sid sits his mother, Harriet.
Peggy is between Winnie and Harriet and, in front, is Anne.
The picture dates from 1947.**

What did Winnie and Sid see in each other? Opposites are said to attract and one can see why Sid might have wanted to marry blonde, attractive, respectable, malleable Winnie. But heaven only knows why she married him. For a young woman brought up in a strict, inhibited Edwardian family to marry a Jary seems inexplicable. Her parents were quiet, gentle people, comfortably and respectably situated in a sedate, middle-class suburb. The family she joined were quite different. Richer, louder, more confident, less intelligent, they had emerged from the First World War largely unscathed and considerably enriched: fish had become a profitable business during wartime rationing and food shortages. While Winnie's father was a gentleman of quiet pleasures and reticent manners, saddened by the loss of his children, Sid's was a rowdy peasant with a black moustache, a harsh voice, an unquenchable thirst for gambling and a spittoon beside his chair. Many years later, my grandmother gave us our only clue about why she had married Sid. "He was a nice boy," she remembered. "He changed in his late twenties." Sydney, their only child, was born when his father was twenty-six.

Where did the music come from? The wireless, which my father listened to a great deal. Why Delius? Two reasons, perhaps: one practical, one emotional. The mid-thirties was the era when Sir Thomas Beecham was first championing the highly individual music of Frederick Delius, who died in 1934. Emotionally, this intangible, often very beautiful, always highly characteristic music is the stuff of dreams and as far removed from 1930s Ilford and his father's life, bordered by Billingsgate Market, the cricket field, the race course and the bookmakers, as it is possible to imagine. Twelve-year-old Sydney probably wouldn't have known the word 'escapism', but he'd found it.

At school he was selectively idle and lop-sided, excelling at history, geography, creative writing and art, but achieving nothing in arithmetic, geometry, algebra or any of the sciences. However abysmal, his work was always neatly presented in his regular, tiny writing. He failed School Certificate because, although he'd won distinctions in the arts papers, he'd scored no marks at all in any of the maths exams. He loathed his school, regarding its institutionalised intolerance and bullying as crueller than anything he later saw on the battlefield. It was a minor public school called Chigwell and he attended as a day-boy. His last two years there involved cycling through the Blitz, wearing a steel helmet and sometimes carrying his bicycle around new, smoking, stinking bombsites to continue his hazardous journey.

The school cadets (then known as the Officer Training Corps) were affiliated to the local Home Guard. Always an enthusiast for firearms, Sydney found he excelled and before he left was promoted to the OTC's most senior rank. What he didn't know was that his service, which included all the duties of adult members of the Home Guard, would qualify him for his first campaign medal before he'd even left school. From somewhere he acquired a .455 service revolver and for a shilling (five pence) illegally bought a single round of ammunition, which he fired down the garden into a home-made butt. To reduce the noise, he fired from just inside the kitchen door with a colossal bang. His mother's long-suffering maid, who was washing up at the sink at the time, later complained that she "was not partial to the dischargation of firearms", which formed no part of her duties.

His school fees were probably paid by his grandfather Rogers. Education would not have been a priority for Sid. Like his own father, Sid was a gambler, and the small family's fortunes fluctuated according to the extent of his losses. Winnie would find that the house had been remortgaged; her father would pay it off. Without her knowledge, it would then be mortgaged again to settle fresh debts. Sydney remembered the gas or electricity being cut off because his father hadn't paid the bills. Although they lived in apparent middle class comfort and conformity, just below the surface of his parents' marriage lay a turmoil of uncertainty and resentment. Nonetheless, their marriage lasted more than sixty years.

Given her brothers' experience a generation before, one can imagine Winnie's feelings when her only son enlisted in the Army in the middle of the Second World War. He was just eighteen. It was 1942. If that school photograph is a true picture of him, Winnie's son had "another tragic victim of war" written all over him.

With love,

Christopher

15: Tennis, skating, flying, love and war

Odiham

Thursday, 26th January 2006

Dear G,

Remember that my mother grew up in exactly the same area I did? Remember how you came to my house in the first of these letters and I showed you round my garden? First of all I directed you from the station over the bridge, along Beeches Avenue past Mr Quattrucci's off-licence – can you picture it? Well, if, instead of turning right down the hill towards the shops, you'd continued about half a mile along Beeches Avenue, you'd have come to a sign "Carshalton Beeches Tennis Club". You arrived at the station in the summer of 1966 but, as you walk along in the shade of the beech trees, you realise the years are regressing. The suburban houses either side of the road remain the same, but the traffic's thinning. There's a lot less of it and that bus – the 213 – looks a bit of a museum piece. There, behind it, is that an Austin Seven?

By the time you reach the Tennis Club sign, you've travelled thirty years. Turning up the narrow lane towards the tiny wooden club house, you realise it's about eight o'clock on a June evening in 1936. You can hear laughing and voices and the noise of balls hitting racquets. In the car park is a black Morris Ten and a brick-red three-wheeler, open-top Morgan. Your eyes haven't quite acclimatised yet. You inspect the Morgan closely. It looks considerably less sophisticated than a motor bike and you quietly wonder to yourself what sort of idiot would take to the road in a death-trap like that. But you're interrupted by a tall, middle-aged woman in tennis whites who is advancing towards you, hand outstretched.

"Good evening. I'm Dora Faux. Did you have trouble finding us? My husband's over there. Billy!"

Without waiting for a reply, she takes you to a middle-aged man who has been sitting at a table chatting with some other members. Bill stands up gingerly and massages his leg as he introduces himself and the people round the table.

"My daughter's on court now, playing a mixed doubles with her young man." He winks at you ironically. "I'll show you round the courts and you can meet them – they'll be finished in a moment. I'm afraid I'll have to take it a bit steadily. I pulled a muscle in my match earlier on and it still hurts like billio."

All the courts are occupied and most have a few spectators, sitting on rugs or deck-chairs, watching the match, chatting and enjoying the gentle warmth of the amber evening sun. A young blonde girl and a young blond man are playing mixed doubles against a taller couple. It's energetic, not especially skilful stuff and there's a lot of laughter going on, much of which seems to centre on the blond, round-faced young man who, now you come to look at him, seems unusually short. He and his eighteen-year-old partner look very similar. Are they brother and sister?

"That's my daughter, Peggy. And that's Jack, her young man."

The match is over and Jack makes a big play of pretending not to be able to reach over the net to shake hands with his opponents. No one seems to have bothered much who won. They pick up their sweaters, tie them round their necks and leave the court. Here they are. Let's introduce them.

Jack and Peggy had met a year before at Purley ice rink, when a friend of Peggy's had suggested she join a group of other friends who were going skating. Jack, whose parents lived in West Wickham, was one of the group. On 7th December 1935, at Jack's twenty-first birthday party in London, Peggy had not only been invited; she was seated at his right at dinner. Now, six months on, they were an established couple, but with no money and therefore no prospect of being able to marry. Jack earned thirty bob (£1.50) a week working for his father's paper business while Peggy was given ten bob a week to stay at home to help Dora. But, providing you didn't want to marry and buy a house, living was cheap. Jack's pipe tobacco cost less than a shilling (5 pence) an ounce (25 grammes), a cinema ticket was also a shilling and that Morgan parked by the tennis club had cost thirty bob. Whether he'd got a bargain was debatable: the car broke down often, its handbrake didn't hold it on a hill and its engine protruded from the front. Jack's mother, Gertrude Wetherly, viewed it with intense suspicion.

Like many young men of his time, Jack wanted to fly. After an entirely undistinguished school career at Whitgift, a minor public day school in Croydon, he'd applied to Cranwell but failed the medical on high blood pressure. When he met Peggy, he'd been trying to reduce his blood pressure before re-applying but meeting Peggy had decided him not to re-apply for the Regular RAF. Instead, he would apply for their Volunteer Reserve and learn to fly with them at weekends. There'd been great excitement that evening you visited the tennis club because he'd recently heard that he'd been accepted and his flying training would begin later in the summer.

One morning a couple of months later, Bill and Peggy dropped Jack at Hanworth, near what's now Heathrow airport, for his initial flying training. The course would last seven weeks. As they drove into the RAF station, a tiny bi-plane misjudged its landing on the grass strip in front of them. It completely overturned and came to rest upside down. Peggy thought this an unpropitious start to Jack's flying career. Jack's pilot's logbook – on the shelf in front of me as I write this – opens on 24th August 1936 when he spent fifteen minutes aloft with Flight-Lieutenant Jennings in a Blackburn B2. He learned taxiing and handling of engine (including action in case of fire) and effect of controls (including aileron drag). A fortnight or so later, after 11 hours' instruction, he recorded his first solo flight, which he underlined in red to show its significance. At the end of the course, he'd earned his wings and was promoted Sergeant-Pilot.

From the autumn of 1936 on, Jack spent a great many weekends flying from Redhill, progressing from training aircraft like the Blackburn B2 and De Havilland Moth to the fighters and bombers of the time, Hawker Harts and Audaxes. All of these were bi-planes. Only a few of the RAF's front-line squadrons had the new Wellingtons and Whitleys, Spitfires and Hurricanes. Five out of six RAF squadrons were still equipped with obsolete aircraft. Meanwhile, Hitler's Germany was re-arming. They had reoccupied the Rhineland unopposed, were breaching the terms of the post-1918 Peace by building a substantial air force unchallenged and were casting threatening glances at their smaller neighbour, Czechoslovakia.

Munich weekend 1938
Jack centre, Bill beside him, Vernon on right. Peggy sits behind Bill.

In late September 1938 Bill, Dora, Peggy and Jack went to Southport to celebrate Peggy's twenty-first birthday. While they were there the Prime Minister, Neville Chamberlain, flew to Munich to negotiate with Hitler about the fate of Czechoslovakia, and Peggy and Jack announced their engagement. During the birthday cum engagement party, people kept slipping from the room to listen to the latest news on the wireless. In between, however, we can be sure her cousins and aunts did all the usual things, including admiring the unusual engagement ring Jack had chosen. A deep-blue, square-cut sapphire, flanked by diamonds, mounted at an angle to its gold ring, it had cost him all his flying pay for two years.

For the moment, the immediate threat of another world war receded as Chamberlain agreed to sell half of Czechoslovakia to Hitler in return for a few months more peace. Six months later Hitler snatched the other half, still unopposed by the British and French governments. One year on, despite all sorts of cautions and threats, Hitler invaded Poland and Chamberlain finally, reluctantly declared war.

Jack and the generation who enlisted in September 1939 had fewer illusions than Wally and his contemporaries had had. There was little enthusiasm and little doubt about what lay ahead. Their fathers and uncles had told them about the Somme, Arras and Ypres. They quietly went away to an unpleasant task that couldn't be shirked. The tennis club packed away its nets for six years, its younger members scattered across the world. The pre-war flying weekends ended too as Jack and his VR colleagues were embodied into the Royal Air Force for the duration – however long that might be. Meanwhile, Jack's RAF pay enabled them to marry.

On 30th September, a few days after Peggy's twenty-second birthday, they married in Southport from Uncle Vernon's house. Some snaps taken at the wedding show Jack in uniform and Peggy wearing a hat with a large brim. It's a striking hat, reminiscent of Ingrid Bergman's in the final scene of *Casablanca*. Auntie Gladys had bought it for her with the rest of her outfit when Dora decided that a white wedding was inappropriate because Jack wasn't an officer. Jack's standing between Peggy and her bridesmaid, Gladys's daughter Pat, doing a Charlie Chaplin impression and making everyone laugh.

A happy moment at a terrifying time in history.

With love,

Christopher

16: Air Force wife

Odiham

Friday, 27th January 2006

Dear G,

If Jack had been a soldier, he'd either have been sent overseas or have stayed safely in England until posted to some theatre of operations. For his young wife, his war would have been a distant, though worrying, phenomenon; she'd have seen none of it, hearing about it only long afterwards at second hand. The lot of the RAF wife was quite different. She was never far away and lived a tour of operations almost as vividly as her husband did. If Jack's night terrors were flak, fighters and foul weather, which he faced with his crew, Peggy's were the same, but she faced them at home, in the small hours, alone.

They led a gypsy life. During the three and a half years of their marriage Peggy followed Jack to Tern Hill in Shropshire, Harwell on the Thames, Stradishall in Suffolk, Moreton-in-Marsh in the Cotswolds, Montrose in North East Scotland and Grantham in Lincolnshire. She lived his short career alongside him and, despite its many anxieties and ultimate tragedy, my mother was unrepentant about it, arguing that, had she not done so, they would have had no married life at all.

After learning to fly Barnes Wallis's sturdy Wellington bomber, Jack arrived at Stradishall on 3rd September 1940, which coincidentally was the first anniversary of Chamberlain's declaring war. Here he joined 214 Squadron and a crew captained by Pilot Officer Hartford. A tall young regular officer with a missing front tooth, Hartford was known as "Lechy" while Squadron-Leader Balsdon, the flight commander, was called "God". One can only guess the origins of these nicknames…

After the collapse of France, invasion seemed imminent. The Germans were assembling barges in the French and Belgian ports. Once Goering's pilots had won air supremacy over southern England, the barges would ferry invading German troops across the Channel. While Fighter Command's Hurricanes and Spitfires tangled with Messerschmitts, Heinkels and Dorniers over Surrey, Kent and Sussex, Bomber Command bombed the collections of barges, which is why Jack's first operations were to Calais and Ostend.

In his first month he also attacked the railway yards at Hamme, an aluminium plant at Merseburg and Osnabruck, whose anti-aircraft guns scored three hits on their Wellington, G-George. In front of me now I have one of the patches with which one of the holes in her canvas skin was repaired. Sergeant Stevens, the rear-gunner, decorated it with a reverse swastika to commemorate this piece of bad luck, which happened in the very early hours of Friday the 13th. Until his death a couple of years ago Steve used to phone me from Seattle, where he settled after the war. I was sad when the phone calls ceased and I heard he had died, but he didn't do badly. He was the only one of three brothers even to reach thirty: one was killed on Bomber Command, the other with the army in the Po Valley.

They flew all their operations at night because, by day, their bombers would have been shot out of the sky by German fighters and anti-aircraft guns. Later in the war bomber operations became much more sophisticated with airborne radar devices, radio navigational aids, flares for marking targets on the ground or through cloud, and bomber streams that concentrated a lot of aircraft over the target in a very short time. In 1940 there were none of these things. Jack and his crew simply took off in the dark and tried to map-read their own way to the target and home again. On clear nights this was difficult; on cloudy nights it was impossible. If they couldn't see the ground, they relied on the stars and a sextant. Inevitably, their bombing was often inaccurate and seldom effective but, at a time when only Britain remained unoccupied and in the war, they were the only force capable of attacking Nazi Germany on the European mainland.

The crew of G-George
Jack on right, Steve Stevens third from right. Fourth from right is Lechy Hartford.

And so the operations continued: Berlin, Hanover, Kiel (when Steve told me they got lost and nearly bombed Malmo in neutral Sweden by mistake), Hamburg, Emden... All the time the weather deteriorated, winter approached and the danger grew. As they discovered over Osnabruck, there was always the threat of anti-aircraft fire. There was also a growing threat from the expanding German night-fighter force. But perhaps the biggest danger came from their aircraft's complete lack of navigational equipment. They faced a real risk of getting completely lost returning from the target, missing England altogether and flying out over the Atlantic until there wasn't enough fuel to turn back. This nearly happened to Jack returning from trying to bomb the pocket battleships *Scharnhorst* and *Gneisenau* in Brest harbour. He and his navigator just managed to get into Manston airfield with a drop of fuel left in the tanks. If you go to the Runnymede memorial by the Thames, you'll see how many aircrew were less lucky and disappeared into the sea. Even if they did find their base, the dangers weren't over. Returns from operations in the early hours of the morning were especially perilous in winter, with the ground obscured by low cloud or fog. Many crews who'd found their way home from distant targets crashed on their final approach back at base and were killed.

Through all this Peggy and Jack lived in a flat over the fish and chip shop in nearby Haverhill. Jack lived out so, on a day when he was briefed for an operation that night, he'd come home for dinner before returning to the airfield. Knowing Jack was flying over Occupied Europe, Peggy would then endure a long, lonely, worrying night which ended only when, in the early hours of the morning, she'd hear his key in the lock and realise with a flood of relief that he was safe home. But during the days and when Jack had leave, it was a different story. Newly, happily married and independent for the first time, they created a home wherever they went. Despite their night terrors, their six months at Stradishall was a happy time.

In late November Jack was appointed captain of his own crew and arrived home with a tall young officer who shyly introduced himself as Ian Lawson. Ian had just arrived on the squadron and had been allocated to Jack's crew as second pilot. My mother remembered him as almost silent but an enthusiastic eater: an ideal guest.

With Ian and his new crew Jack flew another fourteen operations, finally completing his own tour of operations with an attack on the Focke Wulf aircraft factory at Bremen on 12th March 1941.

The crew of A-Apple
Jack on right, beside him Ian Lawson. Nigel Walker second from left.

Of Jack's crew of six, only two survived the war. One was the navigator, Nigel Walker, whom I met as an old man living in an elegant flat in Oxford. The other was Ian Lawson, who remained my friend until his death in 2000. His vivacious wife Bunty, whom we often visit in Wiltshire, has become an honorary great-aunt to my children. Jack's short flying career cast a very long shadow indeed.

Joining an Operational Training Unit as a staff pilot, flying fledgling navigators around the country as they learned their trade, provided both a rest from operations and a happy eleven-month interlude in a yellow-stone Cotswold village. Except for frequent crashes when clapped out training aircraft mishandled by inexperienced trainee aircrew fell from the sky, and occasional sad news of friends still on operational squadrons being killed or posted missing, it was an idyllic life in beautiful surroundings.

They made new friends, made a home and made the most of it and, because Jack's career as a bomber pilot was now behind him, they decided to start a family.

When they arrived at Montrose in late January 1942, they found the place frozen up. Although Jack had been sent here to learn to be a flying instructor, the weather decreed there should be no flying on which to instruct. Instead, they took leave, staying with Auntie Gladys in Southport, where Jack drew a sketch of A-Apple, his 214 Squadron Wellington, in Cousin Wendy's autograph book. Fifty years later the sketch was reproduced in *Portrait of a Bomber Pilot*.

A posting to instruct at the RAF College Cranwell found Jack and Peggy living with Nellie and Lewis Hilliam at Rauceby in Lincolnshire. Here, in the hot summer of 1942, my sister Anne was born. Peggy felt very much at home with the Hilliams, who adopted the young couple and their new baby, so she was very sorry when Jack was sent back to Montrose to instruct instructors. But this was a return to friends too: Ray Holmes, who had rammed the Dornier that bombed Buckingham Palace on 15th

September 1940, the decisive day of the Battle of Britain; John Fletcher with the huge moustache – "a moustache isn't a moustache unless it can be seen from behind," he claimed – who like Jack had done an early tour on bombers; and Joe Urbanski, who'd escaped from Poland to fly with the RAF. A good pilot and a natural instructor, Jack was in his element and, sharing a house with Ray and Betty Holmes, they settled happily again.

The twenty-two month idyll ended abruptly when Jack arrived home to tell Peggy he'd been posted back to a bomber squadron in Yorkshire. They made their sad farewells to Ray, Betty and their friends at Montrose, and caught the train south, where Peggy and Anne returned to the Hilliams' farm in Lincolnshire. Fifty years later Ray wrote to me: "He was sad – we all were – when he was posted. He seemed to have a premonition."

With love,

Christopher

17: Return to ops

Odiham

Saturday, 28th January 2006

Dear G,

Sometimes events one didn't see are so vivid that one thinks one was there. If they happened during our childhoods, we may never know if we saw them first-hand or if our brains have simply reconstructed the pictures from photographs and other people's stories which have become engraved on our memories. One that's clear to me can only be the latter because it dates from thirteen years before I was born.

A chill March day. My mother in the black winter coat that cost so many clothes coupons of her government ration last year. Jack, his six days' leave over, is back in uniform, cap and brown leather gloves. They pause outside the farmhouse for him to say goodbye to eight-month-old Anne who sits, muffled against the cold, propped up in her pram in the weak winter sunshine. Mrs Hilliam, who has come out to say goodbye, produces a camera and records the moment for us to look at now. Time stands still for an instant.

Then a brisk goodbye to Mrs Hilliam, who promises to keep an eye on baby Anne while Peggy walks Jack to the bus stop. Staccato, slightly stilted conversation: trivialities interspersed with pressing demands to take care of yourself. The silence presses heavily on them as the remaining moments together tick away.

At the deserted bus stop nervous humour. Nostalgic mentions of what fun the last few days have been. Peggy nervously twists the sapphire engagement ring, beside her wedding ring on her finger. Jack stamps his feet to keep warm, peering round every few seconds to see if the bus is coming.

Then the rumble of its engine as it approaches down the winding road, appearing between the bare trees. It's here. A kiss and a gentle pressure on her shoulders.

"I'll be back."

Forced smiles and a wave as he finds a seat and stares out at his wife through the glass that now separates them. The growl of the engine as the bus pulls away. He's gone and suddenly, melodramatically, she realises she'll never see him again.

Alone, back up the muddy lane towards the farm. Above, the brave March wind is sweeping huge white clouds across a blue sky, forming a pattern that will remain imprinted on Peggy's memory for the rest of her life. Inside, emptiness.

Jack had arrived at RAF Linton-on-Ouse, near York, in early February, having spent the last few weeks learning how to fly the Handley-Page Halifax. With its four Rolls Royce Merlin engines, the Halifax was a much larger and more complex proposition than the Wellington. In fact, such was the brute strength needed to control the aircraft, had Jack been one inch shorter he would not have been allowed to fly it. In the next month he'd flown twelve operations. He'd twice bombed the German U-Boat bases at Lorient, the port of Wilhelmshaven and the city of Nuremberg, returning the first time through a colossal electric storm. He'd attacked Cologne and Essen, the centre of the German arms industry, in the Ruhr. The attack on Essen had been especially successful. It was the opening of Air Chief Marshal Harris's main offensive and the beginning of Bomber Command's most effective, and most costly, phase. He'd bombed the port of Hamburg, the Siemens factory at Munich, Stuttgart and the big one, Berlin.

Over the blazing city the roar of the Halifax's four engines muffles most external noise. Explosions on the ground bubble and burst silently red and yellow in the fiery cauldron below. White tracer hosepipes across the black sky, approaching lazily in a gentle parabola before suddenly accelerating and cracking past like a whip. Through all this the bomber sails steadily on, its crew silent except for the bomb-aimer, lying on his stomach in the nose of the aircraft, directing the pilot.

"Right. Right. Steady. Right. Steady."

Flak bursts black around them and the bomber rocks as it's buffeted by the force of a nearby explosion or as it hits the slipstream of an aircraft just ahead.

"Steady. Left a bit. Steady. That's good."

The bomb-aimer continues his running commentary as the ground below moves slowly through his glass bombsight.

"Bombs gone!"

The Halifax leaps in the air as it releases its heavy load into the inferno below. For a few moments Jack keeps the aircraft straight and level while a photograph is taken to record the fall of their bombs. Then he puts K-King's nose down to accelerate out of the deadly target area into the welcome darkness beyond. All being well, if they can avoid prowling fighters and the flak batteries scattered across Occupied Europe, they'll be home in bed in just a few hours. But with each operation they know the odds against their survival lengthen. The frequent disappearance of friends is a constant reminder of their own frail mortality.

On 1st March the Squadron lost two crews on Berlin, one of them captained by Squadron-Leader John Fletcher, Jack's friend from Montrose. Hamburg cost another friend, Bill Golding, with whom Jack had converted to Halifaxes at Riccall. The two Essen operations cost two more crews. As Jack had gone on leave, losses had been mounting.

Back at Linton by mid-March, operations were interrupted by clear skies and the full moon. Jack played tennis on the hard courts and wrote to thank Bill, his father-in-law, for sending him some snaps of Peggy and Anne. Behind lay forty operations. Ahead lay another ten ops before his second tour was over, after which he wouldn't need to fly operationally again. The next six weeks before leave fell due again would probably see it all over, one way or another, and there was the new job of flight commander to think about, with its promotion to squadron-leader. Meanwhile, his duties as deputy commander of A Flight kept him busy. He flew a couple of air tests and took his gunners up to practise their marksmanship over the coast at Filey.

When the nights darkened again, ops returned with a vengeance. A trip to Duisburg was followed by another to Berlin. Two days later, on a wet and very windy morning, Jack's name was on the battle order again. He was short of a bomb-aimer and Bert Beck, the Squadron's bombing leader, stood in. He also needed a navigator, so telephoned the Nav Section to see if they could find him one. Archie Paxton, newly commissioned, asked to go. His wife was expecting their first baby and he wanted to get as many ops behind him as he could so he could go on leave. Twelve crews ran through the pouring rain to the briefing room, where the map revealed the target: Berlin again. This time the route would take them over the North Sea, across Schleswig-Holstein more or less along the line of the Kiel Canal, and out over the Baltic, before turning south-east to attack Berlin. As an experienced captain, Jack would be in the van of the attack.

Did he have a premonition about this one? Who knows? I imagine I'd have had a premonition every time. As he waited in the officer's mess, the wind rattling the windows, he scribbled a letter to Peggy at the Hilliams' farm. "I'm glad your mother's staying with you," he wrote. "It will make things easier for you." Then the drive through the rain to the aircraft waiting in the dusk. The usual pre-flight checks. Start the engines. Contact.

A red flare soared into the night sky, signalling cancellation – the scrub everyone had anticipated because of the weather. But it was only a postponement. Two hours later, having repeated the process, they were off. Each aircraft battled slowly upwards through strong winds and lightning, hail stones rattling like shrapnel on the wings and fuselage. Large chunks of ice, breaking off the propellers, were caught by the slipstream and crashed along the side of the aircraft. One Halifax from Jack's squadron never took off. Another, overturned by the storm, managed to jettison its bombs and land safely. Five more turned back before they'd crossed the North Sea. Jack's and four other crews fought their way above the weather and pressed on.

As they approached the German coast, the clouds cleared completely. Because the bombers' best defence was swamping the German defenders by passing a lot of aircraft across any one point at any one time, Jack now found himself in a very vulnerable position. His aircraft was out in the lead of a very depleted and greatly dispersed bomber stream in clear visibility.

It's here Leutnant August Geiger enters our story. You don't know him. I don't know him and, given what he was about to do, I'm glad I didn't. But, ironically, you and I owe our existence to his brief, violent, tragic intervention. Relatively new to night fighting, Geiger was patrolling his radar-controlled box in north-west Germany when he was directed to attack a solitary British bomber. He found it, attacked, set it on fire and saw it fall before disappearing back into the darkness to find another prey. He'd find four others that night and two score more during the rest of his short but eventful career. Six months later, the British night fighter ace Bob Braham sent his Messerschmitt 110 spinning into the Zuider Zee.

For now, Geiger left Jack's K-King blazing and her captain struggling to maintain control. We can't know for certain what happened because no one survived, but it's clear that someone tried to land the burning aircraft in a field at Tellingstedt. Perhaps there were wounded on board and the crew decided to stay together to try a landing. K-King circled the village, approached low over a barn and touched down in the field beyond. Just as it hit the ground, it exploded.

At the Hilliams' farm next morning, the weather had cleared and Peggy was hanging Anne's nappies on the line to dry. She and her mother were going to catch the bus into Grantham to do some shopping. Before she went, she decided for the first time ever to telephone Linton and check that Jack was all right. She was put through to the officers' mess and asked for Flight Lieutenant Wetherly. After a long pause, the padre came on the line. Meanwhile, in the orderly room one clerk was typing a letter to Peggy for the CO's signature and another was closing Jack's pilot's logbook, opened during the pre-war weekend days of 1936, with a single word: "Missing".

In many ways, Jack was right. He did come back. He never really left. He was always with her, and, after her marriage to my father, he remained with our family for the rest of her life. His sapphire engagement ring switched hands, the RAF eagle brooch alternated with a Hampshire Regiment one and the coloured, portrait photograph of him in his new pilot officer's uniform stood on the china cabinet in our dining room.

If Len and Wally were our unknown soldiers, whose names evoked an aura of tragedy, Jack's was a living presence, recalled, more often in humour than in sadness, as brave, boisterous and always young. Although his loss was just as tragic as theirs, my mother never doubted the justice of the cause for which he died. But that didn't – and doesn't – make it much easier to bear.

With love,

Christopher

18: Fair stood the wind

Odiham

Sunday, 29th January 2006

Dear G,

The photograph of my father which my grandparents kept on a tiny table behind an armchair in their sitting room always puzzled me. As an eight-year-old, avid collector of army cap badges, I couldn't understand why, when my father was an infantry soldier through and through, in this picture he was dressed as a second-lieutenant in the Royal Artillery. It was the traditional portrait photograph taken on being commissioned as an officer: cap on, head erect and staring rather seriously into the middle distance. But why was he wearing the wrong badges? He was in the Hampshire Regiment, not the artillery.

One Sunday when we were visiting my grandparents at Ilford, I asked him how this had happened. He explained that, when first he enlisted in the Army in mid-1942, he found himself sharing a barrack room with a large number of boys, most of whom seemed to have come from youth prisons (known as Borstals). This worked to his advantage in two respects. Having survived Chigwell, he found he had more in common with them than he might at first have thought possible. Then, in comparison with his contemporaries, he shone as a star of unusual military brilliance and enthusiasm.

At the end of eight weeks' basic training, he was sent to an Officer Cadet Training Unit to train for a commission. However, he'd rather overdone the shining and the boy who at school had done so remarkably badly had so impressed the army with his intelligence that they sent him not to the infantry OCTU he anticipated, but to the more demanding gunner OCTU. This Royal Artillery OCTU – pronounced 'octoo' – was in Ilkley and was commanded by a colonel with a large white moustache and the imposing features of Sir Edward Elgar. His name was Sebag Montefiore and my father remembered him as a kindly and thoroughly decent old man, the epitome of the Edwardian gentleman. A hero of the Great War, he was now doing his best in the second one. According to my father, it was a good best, as professional as it was kindly. I wonder how, as a Jew, the Colonel regarded what was going on in Germany. Did he realise that his Wehrmacht equivalents, who had fought for their country in the trenches, instead of running OCTUs were locked in murder camps being starved, beaten and gassed?

Royal Artillery OCTU Ilkley 1943
Sydney is centre front row standing. Seated second from right is
Lieutenant-Colonel Sebag Montefiore DSO MC RA

Understanding my father's predicament, the Colonel advised him to stay at the gunner OCTU, which offered a longer and fuller course than its infantry equivalent, and then switch after he was commissioned. Sydney did just that, switching to the Hampshire Regiment simply because one of their battalions had been stationed near Ilford early in the war and he'd liked the look of them. He was posted to their 12th Battalion in Sussex where, attending a great many courses and battle schools, he awaited the forthcoming invasion of France.

Sydney's experience at battle schools followed the pattern of his time at school. Because of the need for experienced soldiers elsewhere, they tended to be staffed by warriors of a theoretical, rather than a practical bent. He didn't meet their standards. He wasn't aggressive and didn't shine, and many doubted his ability to command a platoon in battle. Meanwhile some of his contemporaries cultivated moustaches, took pot shots at various forms of unsuspecting wildlife and looked much more impressive in their new uniforms. One enormous young officer, deciding his bed was uncomfortable, walked into town, bought himself a replacement and carried it home on his back.

At this stage in the war the south of England was one enormous armed camp, containing a British group of armies and an American one, everyone waiting for the off. The beaches had been mined and fenced off for four years. Even off duty, officers carried side arms and behaved as though they were in a theatre of operations. In May 1944 leave was cancelled and the whole of Sussex was sealed off. It was clear the invasion of Western Europe was imminent. Where would the Allies land? The Pas de Calais? Normandy? Only the senior generals knew.

D-Day and the following month found my father waiting in Sussex, listening intently to the news on the wireless – Americans had radios, the British had the wireless – and awaiting his turn to join one of the Hampshire Regiment's battalions as a reinforcement. When it came, like so many long-awaited events in life, it didn't quite happen like that. Landing on Sword Beach from an American landing craft which lowered its ramp too early, Sydney jumped ashore and disappeared under deep water. This inauspicious baptism by total immersion was followed by the base depot sending him not to a Hampshire battalion, but to the 4th Somerset Light Infantry, who had just lost most of their officers in a morning trying to take a single hill. He must go and join them temporarily and then transfer back to his regiment later. After a short spell with the Somersets' anti-tank platoon, which gave him a seat in the stalls from which to observe the battle of Briquessard, he was allocated a rifle platoon.

The gods smiled on Sydney Jary the day he was allocated 18 Platoon. He didn't just have one good NCO, for whom many young officers would have given half their pay. He had three: Jim Kingston, Doug Proctor and Owen Cheeseman. He also, which he doesn't mention in his book, had a very bad platoon sergeant. Both the sergeant and the platoon's previous officer had made themselves scarce during the last battle and responsibility had fallen on Jim, Doug and Owen. Now, the officer had been removed but the sergeant remained. Fortunately, he had little taste for the task and for much of the time Jim stood in, officially or unofficially. So, although my father's book *18 Platoon* is technically misleading in this respect, it's true to the spirit of what happened.

Above them, their company commander proved as useless as the sergeant, but his higher rank provided even greater scope for getting people killed unnecessarily. Here again, *18 Platoon* doesn't quite tell the whole story. My father describes how his company commander has led them up a sunken Normandy lane to a position where, despite digging in, they are getting heavily shelled. Despite Sydney's protests, he won't move them and his behaviour is nervous, snappy and critical. Finally he announces that he's tired and needs to sleep. Bedding down in a slit trench, he takes no further part in proceedings. Meanwhile, shells are still falling and soldiers' lives are at risk.

It's an inexperienced subaltern's nightmare in his first battle. What would you do? Although he didn't put it in the book, Sydney decided to shoot him. He planned to wait until the next stonk of enemy shells, to run up to the slit trench, put three or four bullets into his sleeping superior and then announce he'd been killed by shellfire.

He was saved by the decisive intervention of Dennis Clarke, a gunner forward observation officer, who simply told him to take command. Meanwhile, Dennis reported what was going on to his battery commander, who was with the Somersets' colonel. If I know Dennis, he will have described the company commander in colourful, memorable and persuasive terms. His intervention was certainly effective: my father took over, the position was vacated and the company commander was removed for good – in both senses.

I can say "If I know Dennis" because I *did* know Dennis. I met him several times and spoke to him often after Alex and I first stayed with him in Hamburg when he was an old man. Because she was then at Leeds Girls' High School, he called her "Leeds United". He called me "dear boy". He was eccentric, outspoken, cultivated, acerbic and, I found, enchanting company. But I was lucky to know them all: Owen, Doug, Jim and other survivors. I probably owe my existence to the NCOs and soldiers of 18 Platoon – and so do you – because they kept their officer alive for eleven months when his life expectancy in Normandy was three weeks. They're good men to know as well as being important to our story, and I'll introduce you to them properly in my next letter.

Meanwhile, we'll leave twenty-year-old Sydney to lie awake pondering the lessons of his chaotic, inconclusive and very difficult first battle. He'd already survived longer than the young giant who'd hauled the bed home on his back. Running up the beach as he landed in Normandy, he'd had his balls shot off.

With love,

Christopher

19: To Arnhem on foot

Odiham

Monday, 30th January 2006

Dear G,

By the time he'd survived the battle of attrition that was Normandy, skirmishing from hedgerow to hedgerow as the Germans clung on to every defendable line, Sydney had learned his trade. He'd learned the virtue of speed and momentum in the attack, of bypassing pockets of resistance and of the sudden, controlled display of concentrated firepower. All these were ways of winning battles while keeping his own casualty rate as low as possible. He'd also got to know the men who were his platoon, whose friendship and professionalism had silently persuaded him to stay with the Somersets and not return to his own regiment.

There was Jim, the thirty-two-year-old corporal from Bristol. His father had been shot accidentally by his own officer in the First World War, leaving Jim's mother a widow with several children to raise with virtually no money. Jim had won a place at grammar school but his mother couldn't afford to let him take it up. He'd gone to work at fourteen. Lunch for him, when he came home in the middle of the day, was a highly polished apple on a plate. His mother could afford no more. He never swore, never raised his voice and was a model of Christian selflessness and patience. Because he thought young soldiers needed more sleep than he did, he took extra hours of watch to allow them longer rest. He asked nothing for himself but expected a great deal from officers and other NCOs, who he thought were there to lead. Although he'd been denied an education, somewhere along the line he'd acquired something greater still: wisdom.

Doug, from Nottingham, was younger, more direct and self-confident. At some point he'd upset the prickly new colonel and been removed from a fairly safe job and sent to a rifle section, where he excelled. Sharp, quick-witted and a leader, he ran a tight section and dealt forcefully with any backsliders. One of his men vanished from the battlefield and came back, via an American hospital, having persuaded them he was suffering from battle fatigue. Doug wasn't fooled. He knew that before the war the man had been part of a criminal gang with a reputation for violence. Now he was on the receiving end of some. Tapping the magazine of his Sten gun, Doug assured him that if he hung back for one moment in action, there was a bullet in there for him. The soldier didn't dare stop to tie his bootlace. He survived.

After one of their tiny battles, Doug and his section found themselves guarding a group of Germans who had just surrendered. All had their hands up when one suddenly dropped his arms to reach inside his tunic. Doug, who was closest, shot him with his Sten gun. Fifty years on, he was still agonising inside about whether he'd killed a man unnecessarily. Had he been reaching for a grenade, a pistol or a packet of cigarettes? Such are the unavoidable decisions created by war, and Doug's lasting doubt and regret are the equally unavoidable response of civilised man turned warrior.

Among the books on my daughter Alex's shelves, two have pride of place. One, *The Wind in the Willows*, is inscribed "To Alex, my little friend, with love from Uncle Jim". The other, a collection of Kipling's stories for children, comes "with love from Uncle Doug and Auntie Jean". The gentlest of men, it was hard to see either as one of the victors of the bloody campaign of attrition that followed the invasion of Normandy. During the campaign they faced elite German formations, including Waffen SS and parachute troops. Often, on the spot, they were outnumbered. But they never lost a battle.

Now, the German defenders withdrew from Normandy or were captured. Their survivors retreated to the line of the River Seine. On a day in late August, while the Americans and Free French paraded through liberated Paris, the Somersets boarded storm boats to cross the Seine at Vernon. The crossing was as chaotic as any battle: the leading companies landed by mistake on islands in the middle of the river. My father's company therefore found themselves leading the attack, rather than supporting it.

Their advance was checked by a German machine gun firing straight down a lane. Its first burst had already wounded the commander of the preceding platoon. Sydney noticed, however, that across the lane was a gate which, if open, would let him into the walled orchard beyond. Protected by the wall, he might then be able to get level with the machine gun and toss a grenade over the wall. He ran across the lane, hurled himself through the gate, which, luckily for him, collapsed, and ran up the other side of the wall towards the machine gun. As he got near it, it fired again, enabling him to pinpoint its position. Taking the pin from a grenade, he let the lever fly off, counted three – he didn't want to give them time to chuck it back – and lobbed it over the wall. A loud bang was followed by the clatter of boots on cobbles as the German machine gun team ran away.

The advance could now continue, with my father taking command of the platoon which had lost its officer. He tried to maintain the pace of the advance, keeping the defenders on the hop. Ignoring battle school doctrine, he led with one platoon, consolidated and then ran back to lead the next forward. In this way, working their way up the hill, they steadily cleared the town. En route, by the side of the road, they found the bodies of the two members of the German machine gun team who had bled to death. Even in close infantry warfare, it's rare to confront so immediately the human reality of your personal actions. It doesn't take much imagination to realise, despite his success, how twenty-year-old Sydney must have felt.

The Germans were in headlong, disorderly retreat, withdrawing from France, through Belgium, faster than the British and American armies could pursue them. Between the advancing allies and the German industrial centre of the Ruhr lay several rivers and canals. Field Marshal Montgomery's plan, which would end the war in 1944, was to isolate the

Ruhr by dropping parachute troops ahead of the infantry advance to capture the bridges over these waterways. Remembered as the Battle of Arnhem, the plan was called *Market Garden*. *Market* was the airborne plan, *Garden* the ground operation. Sydney's Somersets were involved in the latter.

Their early role in the operation was easy. Guards Armoured Division led the advance with their tanks and infantry. 43rd Wessex Division, including the Somersets, simply followed the advance up the road. Finally, after the Guards and American parachutists had captured the penultimate bridge at Nijmegen, immediately south of Arnhem, the Somersets and the rest of their division crossed the bridge and were unleashed to fight their way north to relieve the British airborne troops who were holding the final bridge at Arnhem. What they didn't know at the time was that, before they had crossed Nijmegen bridge, the beleaguered parachute troops who had captured the bridge at Arnhem had been forced to surrender. The battle was already effectively lost.

Advancing north from Nijmegen, the Somersets found themselves in very different country from the close farmland of the Normandy bocage. The land here was flat and open, interspersed with neat villages and towns of prosperous looking houses. It seemed disconcertingly like fighting a battle round Epsom until, in one silent house, they found the bodies of a mother, father and children, each riddled with machine gun bullets. My father describes it in his book and ascribes the murder to the SS, but once again *18 Platoon* doesn't tell the whole story.

Between Nijmegen and Arnhem is a small town called Elst. Here, just north of the town by the railway line, the advance ground to its final halt. Ahead the Germans had a screen of artillery and machine guns which, in this flat, featureless landscape, prevented tanks or infantry getting any further. It was tantalising. From Elst churchtower they could see the bridge at Arnhem, which had been the final, clinching objective of the whole operation. But they couldn't reach it.

The Somersets went to ground, lining the dykes that criss-crossed the farmland on either side of the Arnhem road, digging in and keeping their heads down as the German gunners fired periodic airburst over their heads. Machine guns traversed the ground and to raise one's head spelt death. Feeding and relieving the troops in the forward positions were hazardous operations which could only be done stealthily at night. By day, they lay low. Bill Faux would have felt thoroughly at home with the experience.

The sustained tension of trench life was broken by the abrupt arrival of a German halftrack, which skidded into the Somersets' positions from the rear. Out tumbled two drunken SS soldiers, both curiously wearing make-up. In the back of the half-track was the family silver they had looted from the Dutch family they'd gunned down. For obvious reasons, my father omitted the end of this story from his account written in the 1980s. What actually happened was that an uncle of the family identified the silver and the men, was given a Sten gun and shot them both.

Thus ended the Battle of Arnhem, which had liberated swathes of the Netherlands at great cost but had failed in its strategic objective. The arms factories of the Ruhr remained productive and in German hands. The war, which Monty had hoped to end in 1944, would drag on indefinitely. Sydney and the Somersets now faced the dismal, dangerous prospect of approaching winter, an assault crossing of the Rhine and having to fight their way into the German homeland.

With love,

Christopher

20: Bulge, Bedburg, Bremen and a Nazi

Odiham

Tuesday, 31st January 2006

Dear G,

I always feel every battlefield should be haunted, but they aren't. Some, where there may have been the most terrible carnage, seem to retain no atmospheric memory of what happened there. The present landscape is unmoved by its history, there are no ghosts and it's become merely the spot where something unpleasant happened long ago. The ground itself of other battlefields – Agincourt, Isandhlwana and Rorke's Drift among them – explains what happened and why. A few, though, seem to be imbued by echoes of the fighting that happened there. In my experience, this tends to happen more often with smaller battles on more compact sites. The tiny stretch of preserved trenches near Montauban where Bill fought is a case in point. So is the railway crossing at Bedburg. But perhaps this is simply because both of these are so personal to me, to our story – yours and mine – and to our existence.

I'd grown up with the story of Bedburg. On the palm of my father's hand was a small scar, where a bullet had ricocheted off the road and hit him. A small pot on the mantelpiece in my parents' bedroom, where my father kept his shoelaces, held another bullet, scuffed down one side. In the ottoman on the landing, my father kept his camouflage smock (which he used for major dirty jobs like cleaning out the garage) and a webbing strap. If you put the strap over the shoulder of the smock as both would have been worn, you'd have found two neat holes in each. A bullet had passed first through the strap at the front, then through the smock – two holes, in and out – and then through the strap behind. In between, miraculously, it hadn't touched my father, who was wearing both garments at the time. The bullet in the porcelain pot had been fired at the same time and had hit the road beside him. A fourth bullet had gone straight through the beret he had been wearing, making two more neat holes. These were four bullets of thirty-two – an entire magazine of a Schmeisser sub-machine gun – fired at him by a German parachute soldier. None of them hit my father, although a corporal behind him was killed outright by another bullet from the same magazine. Out of ammunition, the German soldier then surrendered. The incident had taken place on 12th February 1945, on the railway crossing at Bedburg, near Cleves, just over the German border from Holland.

Thirty-five years later, Lois and I went to Bedburg and found the crossing exactly as my father had always described it. Young trees had grown to reduce the gap between the woods and the crossing, but it was unmistakeable. Just up the road through the Reichswald Forest is a war cemetery, where we found Corporal Porteous's grave. Perhaps it's simply because I grew up with this story but for me the railway crossing, the scene of a single tiny skirmish in a massive campaign, seemed still to have an air of brooding menace. What led up to the tiny battle at Bedburg?

After Arnhem, the Somersets had spent a month on the Dutch-German border near the Reichswald Forest. For 18 Platoon, this was a period of cold autumn nights, spent in trenches, enlivened by night patrols "to keep the Germans on their toes" or to gather intelligence about their dispositions. The Somersets didn't know, but Montgomery was planning to advance through here to move up to the Rhine, crossing which might be their next big battle. Sydney enjoyed patrolling and was good at it. He usually took Doug and Jim with him. They had been together now for so long that they didn't need to speak to communicate: each knew instinctively what the others were thinking and what was required.

Monty's plan was now delayed and the Somersets' immediate future decided by two German attacks. The first was on the Americans in the south of Holland, where the battalion was sent to help restore the situation. November and December were therefore spent fighting their way through the villages and woods north of Geilenkirchen. One place my father always described with a shudder was Hoven Woods, cold, sinister and littered with the putrefying corpses of the Cornwall troops who had tried to capture it. Here, they returned to a grim trench existence in a desolate winter landscape reminiscent of the First World War.

They were suddenly relieved from this existence by the second German attack. Remembered as the Battle of the Ardennes (or the Bulge), it began just before Christmas. Its result for 18 Platoon and the rest of D Company was Christmas spent guarding the bridge over the River Meuse at Visé in Belgium in the congenial company of Dennis Clarke. The Germans never reached them, but on Christmas Eve news did. The Colonel's third attempt to get Sydney a Military Cross had succeeded. Geoff Neale, Dennis's battery commander, thoughtfully produced a spare piece of ribbon for Sammy Snook, my father's batman, to sew onto his battledress. Although two or three other Somerset officers had won the MC, none had survived with the battalion to wear it. Sydney's longevity was already remarkable.

After a brief but horrific return to the snow-covered trenches around Geilenkirchen, the Somersets moved north again to take part in Monty's delayed plan to clear the west bank of the River Rhine. Having captured Cleves, the army turned south-east towards the Rhine. 18 Platoon found itself the lead platoon of the lead company of the lead battalion as Owen Cheeseman's section led their very rapid advance down the road to Bedburg.

Here, clearing a house, Jim fell downstairs and dropped his Sten gun. A single bullet was fired which hit Doug in the groin. The man whose father had been shot accidentally by his officer now shot his best friend in similar circumstances. The irony didn't appeal to Jim, who hurled his Sten gun away and tormented himself with guilt until Doug reappeared after the war, completely mended.

In an operation where the Army's average daily rate of advance was just over a mile, Owen and his section advanced three in a morning down the straight, tree-lined road towards Bedburg. By keeping up the pace and never allowing the Germans time to regroup, they suffered no casualties. Just short of Bedburg, Owen asked Sydney if another section could take the lead: his soldiers were tired out.

The advance was quickly renewed with Corporal Porteous leading what was usually Jim's section. Reaching a spot, just short of the forest, where the railway crossed the road at an angle, my father sprinted ahead and onto the crossing. He hadn't realised that the crossing was defended by a company of German parachute troops, one of whom now leapt out of a trench, levelled his machine gun and fired a long burst at my father. Corporal Porteous, who had followed my father onto the crossing, was hit and killed instantly by a single bullet. My father, as we know, was unscathed. The German threw down his empty gun and surrendered; his comrades fled back across the fields behind them. Jim and the rest of Porteous's section hit the ground and shot a number of them as they ran. Sydney's luck, which had held since Normandy, was still holding.

The Somersets' Colonel later received a Bar to his Distinguished Service Order for his leadership in this battle. The advance, which was remarkable by the standards of Operational Veritable, deserved recognition. It's ironic, however, that the honour should go to the Colonel, whose only contribution to the operation had been to visit 18 Platoon afterwards to criticise Jim Kingston for not having shot more Germans as they ran away.

After capturing Siegfried's birthplace, Xanten, and crossing the Rhine in late March, the Somersets fought their rapid way – a hundred miles in a month – north-east across Germany. Their advance was a series of small victories over pockets of fierce but unco-ordinated German resistance. Alternately exhilarating, tiring and frustrating, it was paid for with blood. Whether armoured car, tank or infantryman, the first to bump into the expertly hidden German defenders rarely survived the encounter.

Finally, in late April 1945, after some vicious street fighting, they captured Bremen. Here, so long had Sydney been around that his Corps Commander, Brian Horrocks, and his Brigadier, Joe Vandeleur, both haled him as an old friend. I mention this because you may have come across both these names: in Richard Attenborough's film, *A Bridge Too Far*, Horrocks is played by Edward Fox and Vandeleur by Michael Caine.

Half a century later, visiting Dennis Clarke in Hamburg, my father and I were walking in Bremen's Burger Park. I'd just seen a red squirrel and dashed into the bushes to watch it scuttle away, when a runner stopped and asked me what I was doing in the bushes. He looked about seventy and spoke excellent English with a strong German accent. I explained that I'd seen a squirrel and remarked that we didn't have many red squirrels in England.

"German squirrels are better," he replied. And then, quite unconnected with anything else, he began to rant about the Turkish workers in Germany. (For some time Germany had deliberately attracted immigrant workers from Turkey.) "We have these people here. They are scum. We'd have known what to do with them once."

My father, a similar age to our new-found friend, was quicker off the mark than I was. Smiling, he enquired: "You were in the Wehrmacht?"

"I was in the Hitler Jugend. Then in the Army. They were great days."

Pointing to one of the Gothic concrete bunkers that still tower over the Burger Park, my father asked: "Do you know what happened there?"

"No."

"That's where, fifty years ago next April, my battalion took the surrender of General Siber when we captured Bremen."

Less keen on the turn the conversation had taken, he bade us a perfunctory farewell and continued his run. I've never met another Nazi before or since. And I'm rather glad I haven't.

With love,

Christopher

21: Victory in Europe and Bognor Regis

Odiham

Wednesday, 1st February 2006

Dear G,

How did people feel on 8th May 1945 when, after nearly six years of rationing, hardship and loss, the war against Nazi Germany was finally won? You'll have seen the black and white newsreels of the cheering crowds in Trafalgar Square, the soldier with the beer bottle atop the lamp-post, and Churchill joining the royal family on the balcony at Buckingham Palace to wave to the jubilant thousands massing below.

But how would you feel if you'd lost your husband in the process? Pleased and relieved to have won, certainly. But you might not have felt much like celebrating. For twenty-seven-year-old Peggy, VE-Day was a day of mixed emotions shot through with tragedy. After Jack's death was confirmed, she'd spent most of her time living with his parents. Jack's bossy, bright-eyed little mother dominated Peggy's life, involving her in domestic chores and keeping her occupied and secure. Of her own, very considerable loss she never spoke. When Peggy was finally due to return to her own parents, at the last moment her mother-in-law found her in tears. She didn't want to go home. Gertrude quietly went and told Bill and Dora that it would be better for Peggy to stay with her a bit longer. They didn't argue. One didn't with Nanny Wetherly.

After D-Day Peggy had gone with her cousins to a funfair at Southport, where a fortune-teller had told her – it was a fairly safe statement to make to any woman wearing a wedding ring – that a young man was fighting in Europe but would be back safe. Unsurprisingly, the news brought her little comfort. If she and three-year-old Anne were to stay together, she saw her future as a live-in housekeeper for perhaps an elderly couple. It was essential Britain had won, but for her the prospect of peace was not an attractive one.

VE-Day found Sydney and the Somersets poised to attack Bremerhaven. They never did. The order came to stand down: their war was over. Despite the tragic precedents of his uncles, the dismal portent of that schoolboy photograph and the odds against it, he'd survived. Some veterans came to feel guilty about having survived when their friends hadn't. My father never did. In the last ten months he'd given the fates ample opportunities to pick him off, but they'd missed their chance. His attitude, in the schoolboy language he used when describing it to me, was always: "Yippee! I got away with it."

He'd learned a lot. All traces of that introverted boy in the school cap had vanished, but neither he nor his friends in 18 Platoon felt much like celebrating. They were too tired, had seen too much and had lost too many good men to throw a party. Instead, they started to catch up on their lost sleep. There was a lot to catch up on.

The horrors and tragedies of their battlefields shrank into insignificance compared with what they confronted next. The battalion was sent to help clear up the concentration camp at Belsen. Although Belsen was not a murder camp in the sense that Auschwitz was – it had no gas chambers – the effect was the same. Here, Jews and people of many other races and religions were starved, beaten, worked and neglected to death, rather than gassed or shot. Is there a difference? Here, just three months earlier, the young diarist Anne Frank and her mother had died of typhus. Thousands more had met similar ends while those that survived were reduced to tottering skeletons clad in rags. American troops, discovering such horrors, had shot the guards (and, sadly, some of the wrong people) in anger and out of hand. It's understandable. What is the correct human response to industrialised genocide? The Somersets' professionalism was tested to the full when they found themselves guarding the unrepentant German guards, some of them women who now offered their guards sex in exchange for cigarettes. The experience had one advantage: at the end of it none of them could question, as Bill questioned for the rest of his long life, either the propriety of, or the need for, the war they had just fought.

Now Sydney was coming home, but only temporarily. He was to join Tiger Force, which would be sailing for Burma to ensure the final defeat of the Japanese. Arriving in London, he found his parents away on holiday on the Sussex coast, and caught a train to meet them there.

In July 1945 Jack's father, who knew Fred Jary slightly through the freemasons, took his wife and daughter, Beryl, on holiday to Bognor. He also took Peggy and Anne. Staying at the same boarding house were Sid and Winnie. The Wetherlys' connection with Sid's older brother had emerged somehow in conversation, and today the Jarys – especially Winnie – were excited. Their son had arrived home unexpectedly from the war. They hadn't seen him for a year and he was coming down to stay with them.

Peggy was standing in the hall when she first saw him coming down the stairs before dinner. Having met Sid, she'd had a clear picture of what his son would be like. He wasn't at all what she'd expected. Later they talked. Later still, despite the older generation's efforts to steer him towards Beryl, they spent time alone. They walked on the beach and heard each other's stories. My mother told me it was the first time she had been able to talk properly about Jack to someone who understood. It was probably also the first time Sydney had spoken about his experiences to anyone outside the Army. She had no idea he was just twenty-one. She thought he was her age. He looked it.

They met again in London and Sydney came to her parents' home in Crossways. Anne, touchingly but embarrassingly, introduced him to some local children as her daddy. Two atom bombs were dropped and the prospect of the trip to Burma vanished. The war was over. But Peggy felt Sydney was too young to take on the responsibility of a wife and ready-made family, while he still thought of himself as a soldier with a career ahead of him. She went with him to London while he badgered the War Office for a posting to the Hampshires in Libya. By the time he had got what he wanted, he was deeply in love and wished he hadn't asked. Peggy told him they should break up: she was too old for him. The evening she said this they went to see the new film *Brief Encounter*, a cinema classic which I imagine you'll know. Under the influence of Noel Coward, Trevor Howard, Celia Johnson and especially Sergei Rachmaninov, the separation didn't take. While Sydney was in Libya and Palestine, where, ironically after his experience at Belsen, he was trying to prevent Jewish terrorism, they wrote to each other every day.

Peggy's letters kept Sydney in touch with news from home. A notice in the newspaper announced that, more than two years after his death, Jack had been posthumously awarded the Distinguished Flying Cross. At a sad, next-of-kin investiture at Buckingham Palace, Peggy noticed that the King was resorting to make-up to hide his illness. (He died of cancer five years later.) Jack's father, too, died suddenly of cancer. She tried to reciprocate her mother-in-law's kindness and spent a lot of time at the hospital but by chance, when Harold Wetherly died, only his wife was at his bedside. Upset, Peggy said how sorry she was that Gertrude had been on her own at the end.

"But I wasn't," she replied. "Jack was in the room with his father. He was there."

On 8th May 1947, two years after VE-Day, Sydney returned from Palestine to execute the order he had telegrammed to Peggy: "Leaving Army. Returning England. You will marry me." She did. They met at Woking Station.

A month later they were married in Old Coulsdon Church and were inseparable for nearly fifty years. You and I are just two of the many consequences of their long and very happy marriage.

If you look at the wedding photograph, however, you'll notice that the event itself was far from happy. Sydney and Peggy look strained and nervous and both sets of parents grim and disapproving. Winnie was good at silent disapproval. She'd disapproved of my mother from the outset. Whether it was simply the usual mother's disapproval of an only son getting married, the seven-year age gap between the couple or some primitive objection to her son marrying someone who'd been married before, she never revealed. She was silent when told of their plan to marry and, on the day, she and Sid arrived late for the service and sat throughout in granite silence. Whether because they disapproved of Winnie's disapproval or simply caught the atmosphere, Bill and Dora look almost equally gloomy in that photograph, taken on a day in mid-June 1947. Before the wedding Dora had told Peggy that, if she invited Bill's mother Alice, she (Dora) wouldn't come. Peggy often regretted not having given Dora's ultimatum the response it deserved.

Ironically, the only parent-in-law who greeted the event cheerfully was Jack's mother, who welcomed Peggy's re-marriage. Twenty-five years later, when she lay dying, she held my father's hand and said: "We've always been good friends, you and I, haven't we?"

Sydney and Peggy bought a tiny house in Carshalton where, eighteen months after their marriage, my sister Elizabeth was born. In fact, she was the unconscious cause of a reconciliation between them and my grandparents Jary. After the frosty wedding there had been little or no contact between Sydney and his parents but when, just before Christmas 1948, Elizabeth was born, Sid and Winnie arrived unannounced to see their first grandchild. Sid, who always had a soft spot for girls, fell in love, I think, there and then.

With love,

Christopher

22: Nobby and me

Odiham

Thursday, 2nd February 2006

Dear G,

When I was seven, my sisters were fourteen and twenty-one. They seemed a lot older than me and, through most of my childhood, I felt pretty much an only child. Except, that is, for Nobby, our wire-haired fox terrier. A year older than me, Nobby was my friend and companion. In fact, he'd voluntarily assumed this role long before I came to consciousness. When Jim Simpson, Auntie Lily's son, visited us from Cape Town and asked if he could slip upstairs and look in at the new baby asleep in his cot, Nobby guarded the staircase like Horatius his bridge. No one was going up those stairs unaccompanied. So, instead of an older brother, I had Nobby. I can remember sitting beside him on a low wall in our back garden, hugging his silky neck – which most dogs hate – and saying: "He's my brother."

When my father returned from Palestine, he left the Army. With no training or skill beyond infantry warfare, for which there was little demand in post-war Britain, the job opportunities were not exactly endless. Bill tipped him off about a job on the *Daily Mail*. Although, like most such tip-offs, this one didn't materialise, it set him off in the direction of publishing and advertising where he would spend his entire career. He was ill-equipped for the business world, had no time for pointless hierarchies and politicking, and was unprepared for insincerity and deceit. His first ten years were turbulent, involving sackings, resignations and unhappiness. Finally, soon after I was born, my mother suggested he set up on his own. He did, forming a one man, one woman (my mother) business, publishing journals and selling advertising space, which started operating from the table in our dining room. His first major contract in 1958 was to produce the catalogue for the forthcoming Moscow Exhibition. He made a good living but had no real taste or ambition for the work. From start to finish, however successful it was at times, Sydney Jary Limited was never more than a source of income to finance the sort of family life Sydney and Peggy had chosen.

Like quite a lot of 1950s and 1960s Britain, their home recreated the 1930s. If you were to walk into their house perhaps on an autumn day in the mid-1960s, you'd find the hall deserted. On the far wall, over a low wooden table, is a print of Annigoni's recent portrait of the young Queen. Let my ten-year-old self show you round.

"Those are the stairs that Nobby guarded – but he's in the garden now, so you needn't worry. That door on the left is the dining room."

Beyond the door my father's working in there at a desk by the window. A cloth covers the table and his secretary, Marjorie Watling, has her typewriter on it as she's typing some letters.

"Her husband, Ron, flew in Beaufighters over Burma and his cousin, Jack, is an actor. He's in a television programme at the moment about business.

It's called *The Power Game* and my father watches it, though I think it's boring. But they look busy so we'd better move on."

A vacuum cleaner hums through the door of the next room, our sitting room. A woman with tightly curled black hair, turning grey, is in there cleaning. She's wearing a long, flowery apron and looks up as we peer round the door.

"That's Mrs Keen. Her husband has just died and she must miss him. He was a soldier for many years and then became a postman. He was a nice man. I remember meeting him when he was on his round and his bicycle shone like his boots. Mrs Keen looks after me when my parents go out. She and I get on well and she usually gives me ten bob on my birthday. You'll see her at Nanny Faux's house as well because she helps her too. She looks busy now and she can be a bit shy so let's go into the garden."

As you approach the kitchen you're hit by a wall of humid heat and the smell of hot, wet washing. A small white spin-drier is rattling noisily in the corner and gradually propelling itself across the kitchen floor with the force of its spin. My mother, in a short, yellow apron, is handwashing some pullovers at the sink. Washing hangs from the airer that's suspended from the ceiling, and on the wooden table are my pencils and colours and a half-finished drawing of a Spitfire which I left when I came to let you in.

"My mother says it's too wet to dry washing outside but, if we put on our coats, we should be all right. Here's the back door. Mind the steps and watch out for Nobby. He's out here somewhere with Arthur.

"Mind the holly. It needs pruning. Here we are. Arthur's down there beyond the birdbath."

A small, elderly man, dressed in a grey suit over a thick navy pullover, is stooping over some Michaelmas daisies in a flowerbed. He stands up, stretches his back and grins at us, revealing strikingly blue eyes and a pink nose above a clipped white moustache.

"He tells me about butterflies and fish and animals. I ask him what things I've seen are and he always knows. He's even seen a Purple Emperor. He gave me a book the other day about British mammals."

Domestic scenes like this could as easily have been played out in 1932 as 1966. The people, their language, their relationships and their attitudes were no different. When, for example, I was born in October 1956, instead of going into hospital, my mother engaged a nurse, Lumley, and stayed at home. Not surprisingly, I have no memory of Lumley, but I'm told her short-lived presence caused chaos. As a family – with the proud exception of my grandparents Faux whom she respected – we did not, it seems, measure up to the standards established by her previous employers. She looked after me effectively (except when *The Archers* was on the wireless when she ignored me completely) but looked down her nose at everyone else. My mother breathed a sigh of relief when, with barely concealed hostility on both sides, she finally left us.

The seven year gap between Anne and Elizabeth was the work of Man: it was Hitler's fault. The slightly longer gap between Elizabeth and me was the work of Nature, and it wasn't until 1955 that my mother found she was expecting her third child. With two girls, they were vaguely hoping for a boy. Then, one day in September when my father was up in London, my grandfather Faux called in. Peggy and Sydney had only been in this house about a year and a new bedroom carpet had just been delivered. Bill suggested they should put it down. All they needed to do was to move this wardrobe a bit. If Peggy took that end, they'd have it done in a moment.

Whether the miscarriage that followed was in any way caused by this enforced furniture removing, we don't know. Bill, I think, thought it was, and so did my parents. But the doctor who attended Peggy that night made things a hundred times worse. Handing Sydney a bloody bundle to dispose of, he first showed him the contents.

"Look, it's perfectly formed. A little boy."

The seasoned infantry soldier and liberator of Belsen couldn't confront the reality of this tragedy. Twelve months later, I came along and he was able to persuade himself that the dead baby wasn't dead at all. It had just been me, trying to arrive a year early. Meanwhile, Bill went out and bought Peggy a wire-haired fox terrier pup. So when I sat on that wall and announced that Nobby was my brother, I was a lot nearer the mark than I knew.

With love,

Christopher

PS It strikes me you won't know what a spin-drier was. Separate from a washing machine, which you might or might not have as well, it was about the size of a large kitchen bin. It spun clothes to remove most of the water and it seemed to have a life of its own, lurching across the kitchen making a very loud noise.

23: The shadow of war

Odiham

Friday, 3rd February 2006

Dear G,

Some pictures, whether they're good or bad, somehow captivate you. Whenever I visited my grandparents Faux I used to stare at the one on their wall. It was a large, painted, wooden carving of a coach arriving at a coaching inn in, perhaps, the eighteenth century. In the rather dark hall where it hung it didn't look much and you might easily have passed without noticing it. But, when you switched on the hall light, the whole image came alive as light and shadow were thrown across it. The dog in the foreground by the huge coach wheel, the hunched man with the trunk on his back, carrying it into the inn. Everything suddenly became three-dimensional. As I've tried to remember events and people I saw and knew personally, a similar thing has happened in my memory. Small, insignificant images, long in my mind, have expanded into much larger ones as light flooded into the original picture, illuminating dark corners and highlighting detail long forgotten. Take Christmas.

At one end of our Christmas dinner table stood my father, concentrating hard on carving the turkey. At the other sat my mother, passing vegetables and making conversation. Behind her on the china cabinet stood the portrait of Jack in RAF uniform. Either side of the table, interspersed with my sisters, cousins and me, sat my four very disparate grandparents and, exerting his subtly unifying presence among them, sat little Uncle Jon. Jon and his two sons, David and Robin, started to join us for Christmas after Jon's wife's death in the early 1960s.

Their company leavened the atmosphere because my grandparents didn't really get on. I suspect Winnie found Dora overpowering – who didn't? – while Sid would have thought Bill morose or heavy-handedly sarcastic.

Dora would have thought Sid common, and Bill may have considered Winnie reserved and a bit prim. While Uncle Jon rapidly got on Christian name terms with my grandparents Jary, twenty years after they'd met Bill and Sid remained "Mr Faux" and "Mr Jary". Jon would always have done his research and have a comment or two to make or a question to ask about a horse running in a Boxing Day race. Sid relished this while Winnie kept quiet. But Jon was so considerate to her too that she couldn't really take umbrage. He could also reminisce with Bill about the grandfather they shared, William Faux, and about Fairmead, where Jon had spent much of his boyhood. But this would have been of no interest to the Jarys while Dora wouldn't spend thirty seconds talking about the Faux family. What could they all talk about?

Many grandparents in this situation would have chosen to talk to and about the grandchildren they shared, but this wasn't possible. Their interest in, like their affection for, their grandchildren varied. Dora openly favoured and spoiled Anne, whom she had treated since birth as a favourite doll. Bill alternately joined in Dora's spoiling or reacted resentfully against it, muttering some cruel observation about her. Sid and Winnie favoured Elizabeth and tended to sideline Anne and me. So the activities of their grandchildren provided no safe ground for dinner-table conversation.

Just as my father had finished carving and the vegetable dishes were being passed around, I remember my grandfather Jary abruptly enquiring: "Were you ever lousy in the trenches, Jon?" I remember it only because of the laughter evoked by its unprompted incongruity. The trenches were an experience they all shared because, like my grandfathers and great-uncles, Jon, who was actually a cousin, had also been there. He'd been an infantryman with our local regiment, the Queen's Royal West Surreys, on the Somme sector from 1917 until the Armistice.

On the Faux side I had Uncle Jon, widowed and living in Worcester Park with his two bachelor sons, David and Robin. And on the Fletcher side I had Auntie Gladys, widowed and living in Bayswater with her two unmarried daughters, Pat and Wendy. They were my favourite uncle and aunt.

Uncle Jon had endeared himself to me for all time by pouring me a glass of Calvados at the age of six. It made my eyes water. It was Uncle Jon who encouraged me to collect regimental cap badges. After his wife's death, he and my cousins visited us often, and usually he gave me a generous ten bob note (50 pence) as he was leaving. Better still, sometimes he would produce from his pocket a new addition to the collection. I remember particularly the highly polished brass lion of the Leicesters or, most memorably, the huge silver stags' heads of the Gordon or Seaforth Highlanders. He never asked me what I wanted, but he never duplicated anything: he knew and remembered our collection. This Christmas he'd encouraged me into a more serious league of collectors by giving me the newly-reprinted definitive book on the subject.

Left to right: Dora, Gladys, a friend of Dora's and Bill

Auntie Gladys, who always patted my hand or rested her hand on my forearm while she spoke to me, exuded warmth and always made me feel loved and welcome. She'd said to my mother long ago: "You should have been one of my daughters." Unlike Peggy's, hers was a long widowhood. She'd married her childhood sweetheart, Joe, who carried her satchel for her home from school. When he died she was not yet forty. My mother said Gladys had refused to accept he was dying. When the nurse had said he was slipping, she'd seized his arm and said "Well, help me lift him up." She never remarried. When Lois and I got engaged one of the first people we visited was Auntie Gladys, who welcomed her with a warmth none of my grandparents would have found possible. As far as I could see, her heart never failed her.

Any encounter with Auntie Gladys or Uncle Jon was always a treat. They both took an interest in what I was up to and made me feel that they were somehow on my side. Looking back, I wonder if independently of each other they'd noticed my grandparents' favouritism and were trying to compensate for it. They were certainly perspicacious and warm-hearted enough to do it. The result is that I remember them with unequivocal affection and gratitude and so, now, will you.

The memory of that Christmas lunch grew in detail and colour as I remembered it, but other memories come unbidden. Driving home in the car the other day a tune came into my mind which I couldn't place. It was a persistent, lilting tune – a song – perhaps sung by a woman. And then the whole picture returned. A winter's evening, my mother lying on the sofa with her feet on my father's lap, a dog curled up beside her. On the radiogram one of her favourites, the musical *Robert and Elizabeth*, about Robert Browning and Elizabeth Barrett. And this song, sung by an attractive soprano voice, adapted from one of the poems, *I know now*. It wasn't an especially good musical; it was probably more than a bit corny. It certainly wasn't the sort of thing I liked as a young boy. And yet somewhere in my memory was that song, which has now conjured for me a vivid picture of that otherwise utterly uneventful, unmemorable evening at home.

By the time I came to consciousness Anne was an adult and was away teaching at a girls' school in Sussex. Elizabeth grew up quickly, left school at fifteen and, by the time I was eight or nine, was either out at work or out with the boyfriend *du jour*. I therefore spent a lot of time with just my parents. What were they like as parents? Affectionate but sentimental, generous but indulgent, unselfish but egocentric.

While I was in no doubt of their love for me at any stage during my childhood, the atmosphere was often dramatically – even melodramatically – emotional. The feeling of the moment obscured all common sense. If my mother was cross, whoever had caused it was entirely without merit of any kind. He or she (and it was often me) probably strangled dogs, beat up old women and voted Nazi as well. There was no good to be said of them. Once reconciled, all was right again and the person concerned was now canonised and could do no wrong. My father also conducted his business on this basis, which is how many years later he came to give a Rolex watch to an associate. He'd wanted to give the same man and his wife a substantial shareholding, but I just managed to dissuade him at the last moment. This was fortunate as the relationship ended, not long afterwards, in the law courts.

With similarly impulsive generosity and without telling me, my mother once sold a ring to enable me to buy a very expensive group of medals for my collection. But, when I was unhappy and unsettled at school, although they were sympathetic and often took immediate action of one sort or another, neither of my parents offered sensible advice based on my needs. Whatever my problem, big or small, their conversation always reverted within two or three sentences to their own lives. Sometimes it was their childhoods and how their parents had treated them. More often it was the Second World War, which was never far away.

Perhaps, because of age and sheer chance, my family had been affected more than many, but every family I knew was to some extent affected. The fathers of most boys in my form at school had been in the Second World War and most of their grandfathers had been in the First. But, although in many cases it was a source of deep sadness, it could also be a strongly unifying force, transcending the classes and creating an unspoken mutual bond of respect between people who today might have few points of contact. My father, for example, had far more interest in and respect for Mr Matthews, our postman, who had fought his way across the desert with the Queen's, than he had for the most elegantly tailored of his business associates. When he and one of the removal men who had organised our house-move once discovered that they had both been in the 43rd Wessex Division in Normandy, neither could do enough for the other. My father's attitude to Anne was founded on the same sense of chivalry. Some men might have hesitated to bring up another man's daughter or have found it difficult to treat her identically with their own children. He regarded it as a privilege to look after the widow and daughter of someone he saw as a heroic brother in arms who had been less lucky than he had. He also felt he owed a very personal debt: if Jack and his Bomber Command comrades hadn't continued their sacrificial offensive, the armies invading Normandy would have suffered much higher casualties and he might have been among them.

If, on your way to my house from the station, you'd called in at Mr Quattrucci's off-licence, you'd have met its kindly proprietor. A large-built cockney with an engaging smile and gentle manner, Ted Quattrucci was a devout Roman Catholic who sent his daughters to the same convent school my sisters attended. Sometimes he would give my sisters a lift to school in his van and I remember my parents' disgust at the cheap snobbery of a neighbour who wouldn't let her daughter be seen in a shop van. As a conscientious objector, Ted had joined the army as a stretcher-bearer. His last job had been to help clear up the murder camp at Belsen. If it was a hot day, Mrs Quattrucci might be wearing short sleeves, in which case you'd see the prisoner number tattooed on her arm. She'd been a fifteen-year-old runner for the Polish resistance in Warsaw until she was captured and sent to Belsen, where she met her kindly, courageous husband. I remember her telling my father one day that she was considering having the tattoo removed. And I remember his reply: "Don't. It's worth a VC."

At the bottom of the hill, if you'd called in at Taylor's newsagent to buy a paper, you'd probably have seen John Taylor, whose rather flashy Ford Zephyr convertible was parked outside. His sons were at prep school with me and they told me that their dad had won the Distinguished Service Cross for his bravery serving on motor torpedo boats. Across the road and a few doors to the right, looking through the window of Church's toy shop, you might have seen its owner, Major McCarthy, who had served in the Royal Corps of Signals, or his wife. They had met in Kenya, where Mrs McCarthy had been a stenographer at the trials of some of the Mau Mau leaders. She'd had to record their atrocities and, ten years on, was still unable to talk about it without weeping. Our butcher was a

Royal Ulster Rifleman. Mr Bottrell, who ran the garage where my father bought his Cleveland Discol petrol at six bob a gallon, had been with the Royal Tank Regiment in the North African desert. Jack Skilton, the father of my sister's latest boyfriend, had been on Lancaster bombers and, like my mother's Jack, had won the Distinguished Flying Cross. And there, in our pulpit on Remembrance Sunday, stood elderly, bespectacled Tubby Clayton, wearing on his cassock the Military Cross he'd won many times over as a padre in Flanders.

And so it went on. Behind the safe, rather dull suburban façade, these very ordinary people around us had seen and done some extraordinary, often very dangerous and important things. After Belsen, the dull ordinariness of Carshalton Beeches must have seemed a perpetual paradise for the Quattruccis as they raised their daughters and son in peace and safety. Their standards and expectations, and those of our other neighbours, were formed in another world and were quite different from the standards and expectations of the neighbours who surround me now. And all of this I inherited and absorbed, consciously or unconsciously, for good and ill. On this life-and-death scale of values, most things didn't seem to matter much. While some of my contemporaries left university and seemed to expect careers which interested and fulfilled them, I had no such expectations. I was just very glad to be safe and free – and escaping from school probably strengthened this feeling. Although I've always enjoyed my work and have been strongly committed to particular jobs or people, I never expected to have much choice in the matter. It's always seemed to me a positive privilege just to live in peace and comfort and to enjoy my family unthreatened by wider world events.

It's easy for any aging generation to harp on about the past. It can be fascinating or it can be very boring indeed. Alex and Vicky may have a different view but, prompted by my own experience with my parents, I've tried to discuss my daughters' various problems in practical terms and without being deflected onto autobiographical reminiscence. The politician Tony Benn, a year younger than my father, recently told some students at the College where I teach: "Old men remembering the past are a bore. Old men complaining about the present are intolerable. Old men trying to run anything are a disaster. The function of the old is to encourage the young."

Looking back, I realise my parents dwelt too much in their heroic, tragic past to be wholly effective parents in the present. Given what had happened to them both, it's understandable. From my perspective now, as a fairly experienced parent approaching fifty, I can see that both of them were damaged. They did their best. Most of the time it was a good best. No one can ask more.

With love,

Christopher

24: At The Gallop

Odiham

Saturday, 4th February 2006

Dear G,

If you're familiar with goats you'll know why it amused me, as a child, to find I had a grandmother I called Nanny who had a husband she called Billy. Each could be good company, but I don't remember them both being good company: they didn't seem to bring out the best in each other. Especially with younger children, Dora could play the part of affectionate grandmother with gusto. I remember her bouncing me on her knee as she sang:

> *This is the way the lady rides*
> *Trit-trot, trit-trot.*
> *This is the way the gentleman rides:*
> *Gallopy- gallopy, gallopy- gallopy and… over the fence*
> *This is the way the farmer rides:*
> *Hobbledy-hoy, hobbledy-hoy and ….*
> *Down into the ditch!*

And I'd fall into the folds of her long skirt before she caught me again. Later, when I learned to draw what I thought was rather a good elephant, I'd give her a pile of my latest artistic creations. She was good at simulating interest and admiration.

Bill sang too, but his songs tended to the ironic and were often aimed at passers-by as we drove along in his grey Rover.

> *Tumpety-tumpety-tumpety-tum,*
> *Here comes the galloping Major.*
> *Tumpety-tumpety-tumpety-tum,*
> *Sitting so high on his charger.*

All the girls declare
That he's a gay old stager.
Hey! Hey! Clear the way!
Here comes the galloping Major.

Or, if we passed a dog of any kind – particularly if we were stationary at traffic lights – he'd pass the few available moments stirring it into what E M Forster called "a howling wilderness". He could over-excite any dog in seconds simply by leaning out of his window and, in a high falsetto, enquiring: "Who's a little willy-wog-dog, then?" He was an appalling driver, who had learned before there was any form of driving test. On hills he switched off the engine and coasted down to save petrol. The rest of the time he didn't believe in changing down so, at low speeds, his car jerked and juddered on the point of a stall.

He was very impatient indeed and everything was done in a hurry, with extra little tasks inserted to fill up any spare time. (I recognise this trait in myself and have to make conscious efforts to curb it.) Bill always had a better way of organizing things than anyone else. My father once made the mistake of having breakfast with him at his house. I wish I'd had a ringside seat for this one because my father was a morning person; Bill was not. Silent and morose, Bill had timed his breakfast routine to minimise the number of steps required to reach the kettle and switch it on, to fetch the bread from the larder and put it under the grill, to put out cups and plates and to get the milk from the fridge. He never ate marmalade but had apricot jam instead – a taste I've inherited from him. My father had to keep out of the way while this carefully timed, silent, choreographed performance took place. His presence disrupted the routine. Describing this scene sixty years on, I suddenly realise Dora was absent from the kitchen. She would have been. My grandmother would never have got up to get Bill's breakfast and, given his mood, it's perhaps as well she didn't try.

Grandpa sometimes took me to the zoo at Chessington, and we went on the little train that chugged round its perimeter, and he once took me to the cinema at Purley to see *Lawrence of Arabia*. It was a long film with an intermission and, when the first half ended, Grandpa thought it was over and started putting on his coat. At the end, as we drove home, it transpired that he thought the whole thing had been about the Second World War. Although they were almost exact contemporaries, Lawrence's experiences bore no relation to the First World War Bill had endured.

When I was ill and home from school – which happened as frequently as I could reasonably contrive it – Bill would sometimes arrive at my bedside with a book or some grapes.

"Hello, pudd'n-head. Not dead yet?"

And he'd give me the latest collection of Fred Bassett cartoons from the *Daily Mail*.

He'd worked for Associated Newspapers, who owned the *Mail* and the *Evening News*, for most of his career – even during the mid-thirties, when the proprietor, Lord Rothermere, was pro-Nazi. At work he seems to have been a company man, who did as he was told. My father could never understand this and used to explode from time to time: "How, after the Somme and Ypres, can he possibly allow himself to be bossed about by these little toe-rags in Fleet Street?"

But perhaps it was his experience in the trenches, combined with his upbringing and his life with Dora, that had knocked the stuffing out of him. At work and with Dora, Bill took the line of least resistance.

To some extent it worked. In about 1950 he was promoted to become Advertisement Director for the group of newspapers. He told my father: "We're in the money now." He was earning two and a half thousand pounds a year. It seemed a lot but my mother remembered that his predecessor in that job had earned thirteen thousand before the war. He was being used as a caretaker to fill the job until the person they really wanted was available. Within two years he was told to retire and they gave him one of those big city lunches where egos are stroked and promises are made. I once saw a photograph of him making a speech at that lunch, cigar in one hand and an expression on his face I didn't recognise as Grandpa.

After thirty years on their papers, he'd made no friends and never heard from any of them again.

He bought a bungalow in Carshalton Beeches in a road called The Gallop. It was an odd hybrid: a bungalow with two bedrooms upstairs. Downstairs it had a lot of smallish rooms, including my grandfather's tiny study, through which one reached first a conservatory and then a very large garden. If I called in to see them, I'd find Nanny in the small sitting room they used when they were on their own. She'd be reading or sometimes knitting. If it was raining, Grandpa would be sitting opposite her doing the crossword, but if it were meteorologically possible, he'd be out in the garden. Out of the tiny sitting room you'd turn right along a dark corridor. If you carried on along the corridor you'd reach the dining room, which was cold and dark.

"My sisters think it's haunted. But don't go up there. Turn left instead, through the study and past that small bookcase on your left. Look, there's the picture of an elephant in orange felt pen I drew for Nanny last Sunday."

Step through the open door into the conservatory, which smells strongly of soil and geraniums, and out into the garden. Outside in the bright sunshine, a long lawn stretches ahead of you, flanked by well-tended flower beds. On your right is the garage, where my grandfather keeps his Rover. Behind it's an enormous willow tree.

"I can't see Grandpa. Sometimes he's digging in one of those flower beds over there, where he grows lupins. They're nearly as tall as me and bright blue. He must be in the vegetable garden through that gate over there. See that stump on the left? It was a plum tree and we used to get lovely Victoria plums off it. But it got the blight and Arthur had to chop it down."

The tall iron gate squeaks as I open it. "After you… There he is."

Over in the potato patch beyond a line of runner bean plants an elderly man is bending to pull up a weed. His tie dangles in front of him as he stoops. Straightening up a bit cautiously, he rubs his back in exaggerated pain.

"Oooooooh! Me lumbago! Look what the wind's blown in. Hello, Horace. You're looking as ugly as ever. Who's this with you?"

I was mostly sure of my welcome with Grandpa Faux, but never entirely. He once told me off very strictly for pointing my toy gun at him. For years afterwards I assumed this was an echo of the war. Who knew what accidents he'd witnessed in the trenches? But one day my father told me what had happened. Between the wars, Dora and Bill had gone to tea with another family. They were sitting in the garden when a small boy appeared beside Bill with a toy gun. In party mood, Bill picked it up, pointed it at the cat and pretended to fire. The gun did fire. It was an air gun and Bill had shot his hosts' pet cat stone dead.

He could sometimes be cruel. Once, when my sister Anne was wearing something unwise, my grandparents were sitting round in general disapproval. Winnie was silent. "You look like something the cat's brought in," Dora and Bill chorused. Only Sid dissented. "I think you look very nice, girl," he said. Whether his remark was prompted by Jary cussedness, bad taste, his affection for girls, or simple human warmth, it was the right thing to say.

In private with his own sons, my Uncle Jon always irreverently referred to Bill as "Old BF". As well as being typically Faux, this faintly disparaging nickname based on Bill's unfortunate initials exactly captured Jon's affectionate but realistic view of his cousin, about whom he had no illusions. He once told him bluntly: "You shouldn't be unkind to young ones, you know, Bill."

One evening Bill heard Uncle Jon and me talking about my cap-badge collection and how I was branching into medals. "You can have my medals, if you like," he said. "They're still in the envelope they arrived in. I don't think I ever opened them."

The next evening I cycled round and called in. I didn't mention the medals, but they were much on my mind. No one else mentioned them either so I sat in the large sitting room making slightly stilted conversation. I wasn't sure why, but there seemed to be an odd atmosphere. Finally, the light began to fade and I thought it was time I must go. My grandfather saw me out through the conservatory and I retrieved my bicycle.

"Sorry about the medals," he shrugged. "Your grandmother thinks I should keep them."

After his death, my mother gave them to me. They were still in their unopened envelopes. They meant nothing to Grandpa who, some time between the spring of 1917 and September 1939, convinced himself that the whole ordeal had been worthless. When Hitler's War came, unlike my grandfather Jary, who improbably became a sergeant in the Ilford Home Guard, Bill refused to play any part at all. From my present perspective – I'm now the age Bill was when Nazi Germany invaded Poland – I can understand his response to both world wars, but I think he was wrong about both. Although the second war embraced genocide and Nazism, both were about stopping bullying German expansionism, which I believe had to be stopped on the Somme and at Ypres just as it had to be stopped at Alamein and at Stalingrad. But I wasn't on the Somme or at Ypres. Bill was.

My mother always felt there was a loving father in Bill, often glimpsable but just out of reach. She said he was like a nice dog who'd been kicked once too often. Forty years on, this strikes me as an astute analysis. If he was wagging his tail, he was fun to be with, but sometimes he had a look in his eye I didn't quite trust. And, when you get bitten, however sorry you may feel for the dog, it still hurts.

With love,

Christopher

25: A Sunday at Ilford

Odiham

Sunday, 5th February 2006

Dear G,

Adults can usually find some form of escape from extreme boredom. Children can't. I remember as a child the claustrophobic, physical discomfort of it: being unable to sit still, feeling too hot, stifled, my legs and arms aching through enforced inactivity. My happy experience, however, is that, once you're grown up, you're never as bored again. I wish I'd known that on the Sundays when we visited my grandparents Jary in their flat at Ilford. It would have provided some comfort.

My grandfather would sit in his armchair by the china cabinet, on the table beside him a bowl of the pink and white coconut ice we used to buy for him, which my grandmother would chop into thick slices. I hated it. It was sickly sweet, had what my mother called a nasty consistency and left a lingeringly unpleasant taste in the mouth. But he liked it, and so we always stopped on our way to see him to buy a huge bag of the foul stuff and a box of chocolates for my grandmother.

"Would you like a Spion Kop?"

For tea my grandmother sometimes produced some small cakes, sprinkled with grated coconut, that stood quite tall on the plate. The name was an echo from another century of a hill near Ladysmith, where 350 soldiers died trying to capture it from the Boers. Winnie and Sid would have been a year old when that happened.

Their sitting room was always too hot. Conversation was heavy going and sporadic and didn't involve me. Displayed around the walls and on various bits of furniture were large photographs of my sister Elizabeth at various stages of development. On the window sill was a wedding photograph of my sister Anne, who had married in the spring. On a small table, hidden behind a large chair in the far corner, stood the picture of my father in Royal Artillery uniform and, behind a curtain in the side-window, was a snapshot of me, taken in a canoe a few summers ago when we'd had a holiday in Italy.

Sometimes I'd take some toys to keep me occupied or I'd badger my father to take me for a walk in the park opposite, where my grandfather spent most of his time playing bowls. In term-time I even took my homework and would disappear into their dark dining room, still redolent of my grandmother's roast lamb, and sit at the heavy table supposedly working but actually listening to *The Navy Lark* on their wireless.

My grandfather had just come out of hospital having had both hips replaced. He was one of the first in the country to have this new operation and it had cost a fortune. After a lifetime's gambling, he didn't have a fortune but, one afternoon, my mother and grandmother returned from a shopping expedition to find him looking very pleased with himself.

"Had a bit of luck, girl," he confided in my mother when Winnie was out of earshot.

"Have you won some money?" Peggy enquired.

He grinned.

"Have you won enough to have that hip operation?"

He had. A series of bets, known as *an accumulator*, had produced the thousand or so pounds he needed. My mother steered him to the telephone and he booked an appointment with the surgeon. He went into the London Hospital as a private patient and had the operation.

In the next bed was a publican from the East End who had a friend who was a bookie. By the time Sid was discharged from hospital, he'd lost all his winnings. My grandmother, who was staying with us, was furious and worried sick about where the money would come from to pay the hospital's bill. When he and Winnie arrived home and sorted through their post, they found a letter from a company Sid had forgotten he'd had shares in. The company had been taken over and the shareholders bought out. The writer enclosed a cheque for a thousand pounds.

There's a real classlessness about horse-racing. Whether dukes, bookies or punters, most real devotees are much the same: common. Sid fitted right in, which is why his sister-in-law Dolly memorably described his social circle as "Sid's assorted toe rags". But Sid ascribed to all these friends superhuman powers and achievements.

If my father had just bought a new car, one of his friends – Albert Wilson – would just have bought a better one. If I did well at school (unlikely but it happened occasionally), Albert Wilson's grandson would have done better. For a time we were fooled by these stories but, whenever we met his friends, we realised that they, like the rest of us – perhaps even more than most – had feet of clay. What we were confronting here was not reality but a public relations campaign. But it was a very powerful and effective one. Sid would ignore any evidence you could produce to disprove his claims or to prove the scale of your own achievements. We called it "Bert Bog Status" and it works like this.

Anything Bert Bog buys, does or says is perfect. He may be arrested for indecent exposure, convicted of murder, certified as insane or found to have been a leading member of Mosley's blackshirts: none of that can ever damage or even reduce his reputation. The corollary, of course, is "Anti-Bert Bog Status". Anything someone awarded this status buys, does or says is worthless. He may be canonised, elected Prime Minister, establish a worldwide network of homes for terminally ill children or win the VC: none of those things can ever prove that he's done anything of the remotest value. My father and I both had Anti-Bert Bog Status.

Once you've defined Bert Bog status – and I've encountered it in other environments, although my grandfather was a past master in its application – life becomes easier because you know there's no truth in the claims being made. And you also know that there's absolutely nothing you can do about it. Only once, as a boy, did I temporarily triumph over it.

My grandfather Jary had been to visit my father's cousin Gordon (Fred's boy) and he was extolling the virtues of his young sons (Fred's boy's boys). This in itself was an unusual departure for Sid, who much preferred girls and seldom noticed small boys. I suspected the story had a point to it and was being told for my benefit, and my father's.

"And we sat in their lounge all afternoon. It was a lovely lounge. Twenty-five feet long with French windows into his back garden. Big garden, he's got there. Gordon's got a good job, you know. Pays two hundred pounds for his suits. He's a clever chap. And all this time, his two boys were in their play pen in the corner. And we didn't hear a peep from them. So, after a couple of hours, I went and had a look in the play-pen. And, do you know, there they both were…."

"Dead," I said, completing his sentence for him. Everyone laughed – except Sid. And my grandmother. But it was a unique victory. Because it was unaffected by reality, Bert Bog Status was ultimately untouchable.

Once, during one of our Sunday visits, my grandmother leapt from her chair, darted to the window, hid behind the curtain and hissed: "Jews." A couple with two children were walking past the park along the pavement on the far side of the road.

"They're looking at the houses," explained my grandfather. "There are lots of Jews moving in. They like it round here. You can tell which ones they've bought. They all have the same type of curtains."

The ten-year-old me couldn't make head or tail of this. I asked my mother about it later: "Who are Jews? Do we know any?"

It appeared we did, but not many. The nice old couple who ran the wool shop in the arcade off Sutton High Street apparently were Jews. The next time I went past their shop I peered in. They looked just the same to me as they ever did and no different from the rest of us. I don't think my attitude to anti-Semitism has changed much since then. It always strikes me as not only one of the nastiest forms of prejudice but also the silliest. Purely practically, unless they're wearing some sort of costume, how on earth are you supposed to know who's Jewish and who isn't? If, for example, you identified people on how closely they resembled some sort of Shylock or Fagin stereotype, you certainly wouldn't have spotted the old couple in the arcade but you'd have classified my grandfather Jary, with his hooked nose, dark hair and olive skin, as a prime specimen.

I was ashamed of my grandparents' prejudice and wished my grandfather's independence of mind had asserted itself on this subject, prompting them to take a different view.

My grandfather's birthday was in January. My grandmother had made a special cake, which was in the kitchen awaiting tea-time. On its iced surface she'd spent hours recreating a bowling green, complete with a white jack and several brown woods.

Because it was a special occasion, my mother had warned me not to go wandering off but to stay in the sitting room, so I'd come prepared, bringing my box of soldiers. I'd recently discovered the desert war and my battles around this time usually involved the 8th Army and Rommel's Afrika Korps. There were some highly-prized new additions among them as I had just found a shop that sold plastic model tanks from the same period and in the right scale. I'd assembled two Mark III German tanks and a single Mark IV and two Sturmgeschutz self-propelled guns to face a single Sherman tank, which my father and I had made together in a kit, supported by a troop of Royal Artillery 25-pounder field guns. Painstakingly these had been arranged on the carpet, surrounded by a couple of hundred tiny soldiers as I recreated the kind of battle that had taken place in Libya a quarter of a century earlier.

With surprising nimbleness for a man who'd just had two major hip operations, my grandfather suddenly sprang to his feet. Through the window he'd glimpsed a teen-aged girl he often spoke to on his walks. She was summoned and my grandfather led her, shy and slightly red-faced, into the hot room, clearing a path for her through my soldiers and plastic tanks by sweeping them aside with one of his walking-sticks.

"Get the girl a bit of my cake, Win."

It wasn't teatime and Winnie's creation had yet to be produced and cut. My grandmother looked at my mother.

"Go on," he said. "You'd like a bit of cake, wouldn't you, girl?"

My grandmother returned from the kitchen with a slice of his birthday cake which the poor girl ate awkwardly in front of us. Later, at the tea table, Winnie's painstaking creation was displayed: a perfect bowling green with a large wedge cut out of it. She said nothing, but she never made him another birthday cake.

Meanwhile, I quietly picked the scattered remains of my soldiers and tanks off the carpet and put them back in their box.

With love,

Christopher

26: No relations of ours

Odiham

Monday, 6th February 2006

Dear G,

If you're who I think you are, whether a great-grandchild or a great-great-niece or great-great-nephew, we're related by blood. What does that mean? Clearly, it means something or I wouldn't be wasting my time trying to tell you about a lot of people whose only connection to you is blood. I'm told all my genetic and instinctual programming is designed to ensure the supremacy of my bloodline. The strength of my feeling for my children is supposed to derive from that primeval compulsion to survive and propagate. It all sounds very Darwinian and logical, but I remain unconvinced. Proximity, protectiveness and natural human affection seem to me to be stronger forces still. Family are family firstly because they are around us, and secondly because we share a common ancestry. So it's a doubly strange thought that one of the strongest influences on my life has been someone unrelated to me by blood, whom I never met.

People often struggle to define my family relationship to Jack. Someone once tried "posthumous step-father", but it doesn't work. Step-fathers replace fathers; they follow, rather than precede them. In any case, I had a perfectly acceptable father who filled the role admirably: I needed no substitute. But there he was, and his spirit presence has broadened my view of life and enriched me. How can I explain it? The facts are simple: my mother was married in the first month of the 1939-45 War; her husband was killed three and half years later, leaving a baby daughter; my mother married my father in 1947; he brought up Jack's daughter as his own; I was born in 1956. The facts alone – except perhaps my father bringing up Jack's daughter as his own – offer no explanation at all. For that, one must look to experiences and feelings.

It began one evening when I was about six or seven. I'd had my bath and, pyjamaed and wrapped in camel-coloured woolly dressing gown, I came downstairs to sit on the sofa between my mother and father. My mother took out a large box and showed me my father's medals: the Military Cross and his war medals, mounted for wearing. Then she took out a small black box and showed me Jack's Distinguished Flying Cross, which she told me was the Royal Air Force equivalent of my father's MC. In a tiny cardboard box addressed to Mrs M A Wetherly, Jack's four war medals were wrapped, separately from their carefully folded ribbons, in clear paper envelopes and there, loose in the box, was the little bronze oak leaf that showed he had been mentioned in Despatches. Jack, my mother explained, had never worn any of his medals. He died before he knew about any of them, except the mention in Despatches. The DFC had been given to her by the King at a very sad investiture for *next of kin* after the war. Perhaps unwittingly, there and then she created a direct link between Jack and the young boy who was me.

"He'd have liked you," she said.

Suddenly things fell into place in my mind. Nanny Jary was Nanny Jary because she was my father's mother. Nanny Faux was Nanny Faux because she was my mother's mother. Nanny Wetherly was Nanny Wetherly because – she was Jack's mother. I shared her just as Anne, Jack's daughter and my older sister, shared my father. It was rather special to have three grandmothers.

The immense tragedy of it all didn't hit me immediately. A while later, again late at night, I remember standing and looking at Jack's picture in our dining room, and realising for the first time that some things happened in life that could never be put right or made fair. I suddenly realised how young Jack was and how much sadness his loss must have given, and still give, my mother. Had my seven-year-old mind seen a bit further, I could have produced a list of others permanently saddened by this single loss, starting with his mother, my Nanny Wetherly. I began to feel strongly how unfair it was that a young man should lose his life, his young wife and his baby. The feeling has never left me. Indeed, as I have got older and had first one daughter then another, and enjoyed watching them both grow to adulthood, it has got stronger and stronger.

This feeling may originally have been strengthened by the fact that Anne evinced little interest in her own father: my father seemed enough for her. We never talked about it but she seemed to have a very different view from mine. When the war ended and fathers were returning, another child had teased her that her father would not be coming home. My father, who had only just met my mother, happened to be in the sitting room. Three-year-old Anne had run into the house, grabbed this stranger's hand and pulled him out into the street. "This is my Daddy."

"I never knew him," she said much later, explaining to my mother why she never seemed to ask about Jack. "And I can't remember anything about him."

Perhaps, from Anne's perspective, this was a psychologically healthy approach. My father said it made his job a great deal easier because, whether she treated him well or badly, she never treated him any differently from how she would have treated a real father. So the substitution – a gallant one on my father's part – worked, and maybe Anne's attitude was understandable, healthier and more convenient. But I have to confess it has always struck me as deeply unfair.

And so, just as my father adopted Anne, I adopted Jack and he has been with me, and more recently my family, ever since. A generation on, Jack has become my daughters' third grandfather. 29th March 1993 found eleven-year-old Alex with me at his grave in Kiel to mark the fiftieth anniversary of his death. On the sixtieth Vicky joined us. To us all it's a debt of honour, repaid willingly in sorrow and affection. His isn't a tragic presence but he does serve as a very personal, insistent reminder of just how lucky I am to be here to enjoy the various stages of my life, especially a marriage measured in decades and a quarter century of parenthood. Were it not for August Geiger's intervention, had things gone as they should perhaps have done, he would have had all this instead of me. I have long felt a great obligation to make the most of it. For us both.

A year or so ago Lois, Vicky and I went to the Imperial War Museum. While Lois and Vicky were looking at something else, I followed the signs announcing "The 1940s House". There had recently been a television programme where the production team had recreated a typical 1930s semi-detached suburban house as it would have been during the 1939-45 War. A modern family had volunteered to live in it as they would have done during the war, and the cameras recorded domestic life in wartime in a London suburb. I'd watched the programme and knew that the house was from the road Nanny Wetherly had lived in: Braemar Gardens, West Wickham in Kent. The one chosen was not identical to hers, but the mirror image (that is, the other semi- of the pair); so everything pointed the other way and was in reverse.

By chance that floor of the museum was empty as I approached the back door and stood in silence, looking into the tiny kitchen with its walk-in pantry and primitive gas oven. And at that moment smell, sight and memory conspired to return me to a long-forgotten chilly Sunday evening in winter in the mid-1960s. Little Nanny has spent the day with us and my father and I have just brought her home in the Standard Vanguard. She stoops to rifle in her handbag and produces a set of keys to unlock the kitchen door. From the other side of the door there's great barking, scratching and canine rejoicing.

"Down, Raf. I'm coming."

The door opens and a large yellow mongrel leaps up at my tiny grandmother. Then at me. Then at my father.

"You'll have a drink before you go back." A determined lady, and perhaps a lonely one. We can't refuse.

She disappears into the pantry and emerges with a can of lemonade shandy for me. On the lid the makers have stuck a free beer-mat. On the beer-mat is a very bad reproduction of the face of Ringo Starr of the Beatles. I've never had shandy before but I drink it, pretending I like it. And then we leave her, in her little house with her boisterous dog, his name a leg-cocking, barking, tail-wagging but living and proud memorial to her dead son.

One Christmas Nanny Wetherly – known in the family as Little Nanny – sent me a present that was shaped like a tube. On Christmas morning, sitting in bed surrounded by lots of presents, I was intrigued by this one. You can often guess from the shape of a parcel what's inside it. In this case, I had no idea. It was quite heavy but very thin and quite long. I could have sat there till lunchtime and still not have guessed. So I tore off the wrapping paper and found it was indeed a tube, inside which were lots and lots of brass threepenny bits. I counted them. There were forty – ten shillings' worth, or four weeks' pocket money. Nanny, who had been left with very little money, had saved all her threepenny bits throughout the year. She'd then split them three ways: between her grandsons John and Paul, and me.

Why have I remembered this so vividly for forty years? Is it because it was such an unusual present, which it was? Is it because it was a generous one from an old woman on a tiny income, which it also was? Or is it because – even at the age of ten – I appreciated what Little Nanny was trying to do by treating me the same as her "real" grandsons? How, after all this, could I not make sure that her son, however undefinable the relationship between us might be, was remembered as he and she deserved?

So when someone says "blood's thicker than water", perhaps you'll understand why I hesitate. Love and loyalty, it seems to me, are thicker than both.

With love,

Christopher

27: A remembered landscape

Odiham

Tuesday, 7th February 2006

Dear G,

Summer came early in 1969. In mid-April, a fortnight before I was due to start at boarding school in Sussex, I remember playing badminton on the lawn of our new house. My sister Elizabeth was there and her then fiancé, Michael, and my grandmother Faux, who had just had her 80th birthday. She was staying with us while my grandfather was in hospital. We'd fixed up the net halfway down the lawn between the open French windows and the walnut tree, and Michael, a keen player, was showing off by hitting the shuttlecock hard and low, beating Elizabeth and me. When my grandmother asked if she could have a go, we assumed she'd play Elizabeth, but she chose Michael. He started with a few patsy shots, which she returned accurately and effectively. As he increased the pace and velocity, the same happened to them. Finally, he was playing at full stretch and found he had to fight hard to win a single point. My mother wasn't remotely surprised.

"She wasn't as good a tennis player as my father," she said. "But she was like a brick wall. She always got everything back over the net."

She certainly did.

A day or two later my father took me for a day out in Winchester. We walked round the city, had lunch and went to the Hampshire Regiment museum. On our way home, I remember remarking for the first time in my life on how nice the countryside looked. It was the cautious understatement of a pre-adolescent male. The English countryside had actually, for the first of countless times throughout my life, made me catch my breath. Either side of the road, caught by the early summer sun, the gently sloping fields shone different shades of green and light gold under a blue sky.

"Where are we?" I asked.

"Just past Alresford."

The name rang no bells in my mind and it wasn't for thirty years that I realised that the country that had first moved me in this way was where generations of my Westbrook ancestors had spent their lives. Do we inherit a vague memory with our genes? Can vivid impressions or experiences become imprinted on our genetic code, or is this nonsense? All I can claim is that the picture of those Hampshire fields has stayed in my memory for forty years, thirty of them without my knowing of the Westbrook connection. The reason, by the way, that I can date this visit to

Winchester so precisely is that on our return my mother came out to meet us and said – I remember her exact words – "My father died today."

Memory can be shaped by landscape. Landscape is shaped first by geology – Nature – then by history – Man. Our landscapes in turn shape us. They surround us and are our home, and, unless we spend too much time indoors, they are constantly in our line of sight, framing everything we do and see. How do we evoke landscapes? In paintings, which, in my view, seldom successfully catch what they tell us. In poems, which tend to concentrate more on the poet's own response to the land. And in music. For me, music has always been the most powerful of the three. Perhaps because it's more abstract than paint or words, it comes closer to my feeling of what landscapes say and are. And at this point you'll have to forgive me if I become chauvinistic and sound a bit prejudiced. This is personal stuff, and I can only say how it feels to me.

Mention pastoral music and people will often think of the *Pastoral Symphony*. "Beethoven" they'll say. I'm fond of it – not least because, thirty years ago in the summer of 1976, Lois and I heard Sir Adrian Boult conduct it at a Prom. The 87-year-old legend with his impressive moustache, erect as a major-general in his white mess jacket, barely moved his baton beyond beating time, but he lit Beethoven's familiar music with freshness and colour as I've never heard before or since. For me, though, the pastoral aspect of it is incidental; it's just beautiful music. It conjures no landscapes and says nothing to me about my relationship with the country. Sibelius's depictions of the watery wastes of Finland work better, while Copland's music tangibly evokes New England's fields and neighbourly, non-Conformist culture. But I've never been to Finland or New England. They are not my countries and not my landscapes. They are evocative and they move me, but not half as much as some music that depicts my own country.

To find music that does just that, you might turn to Vaughan Williams, who used English folk music to evoke the English landscape. His *Pastoral*

Symphony and his *5th* capture for me the voice of the land itself and the feeling of being on it, in it and of it, while the second movement of his *London Symphony* paints in subdued tones the impressions of Edwardian evening in a London square. Although a lesser composer, the miniaturist John Ireland evokes the gentle landscapes of southern counties, occasionally providing a glimpse of their primeval past. When the time comes when I can't take the dog for a walk in the countryside, I imagine I'll listen to the music of Ralph Vaughan Williams and John Ireland, and the songs of George Butterworth and Ivor Gurney, even more often.

And then there's Edward Elgar, whose music, quite simply, is in my bloodstream. By this, I mean his serious music and some of his smaller pieces (*Sospiri, Elegy, The Wand of Youth* and *Mina*), rather than *Land of Hope*. The *Pomp and Circumstance* marches are brilliant and memorable and portray one aspect of patriotism, but for me they are less powerful than his quieter, greater pieces. *The Kingdom* brings me closer to God than any church service has yet. Much of his music is imbued with sadness about time passing – which, it occurs to me, at a far more parochial level is a recurrent theme in these letters.

He once said: "I have written out my soul in the *Violin Concerto*, the *Second Symphony* and *The Music Makers*." He seems to have written mine out too. Once, some years after Lois and I married, I had a dream in which I was walking, humming quietly to myself the slow movement from his Second Symphony. Gradually I became conscious that the music was also coming from outside me. As I walked on, it got louder and louder and I couldn't hear my own humming. I realised I must be surrounded by an invisible orchestra. The music steadily obliterated all other sensations until, as the brass reached their massive, sad *fff* crescendo, there remained only the music, which had possessed and consumed everything else. It was a vivid, slightly scary dream, which perhaps is why it's stuck in my memory for twenty years.

A few years ago we spent a weekend in Cheltenham and went to see some of Elgar's houses around Malvern. He moved house often and had all sorts of homes, which seemed to have nothing at all in common – until we realised that each of them offered a different but spectacular view of the Malvern Hills. One in particular, Birchwood Lodge, has an unbroken view from its front door. Beside the small house are the woods where Elgar walked in the hot summer of 1900 as he composed *The Dream of Gerontius*: "I don't like to say a word about these woods for fear you shd feel envious but it is godlike in the shade with the snakes and other cool creatures walking about as I write my miserable music." A century on, I could hear his music in my head as I walked in his woods. I found two birch branches to take home to make into walking sticks. I gave one to my father and still use the other on long walks myself. And, such is the sense of communion his music has created in me, all the time I was in the woods I expected to turn a corner and see his erect figure, leaning on an axe and looking up into the trees.

Although none of us played an instrument, music was around me in my home as a child. My father, as I've mentioned, loved Delius. My mother did not like Delius. She loved Rachmaninov. My father liked Rachmaninov. But they both loved Elgar. His music was played so often from so early in my consciousness that I can't remember a time when I didn't know every note of the *Enigma Variations* and his overture *Cockaigne* and both the symphonies. Then, in my teens, I imprinted the rest of his music equally deeply on my memory. I went recently to hear Sir Colin Davis conducting *Gerontius*, which I hadn't heard for years, and still knew every note and every word. If my voice weren't so awful, I could have sung along.

Elgar used no folk songs, yet his music embodies Englishness. Don't ask me how. I'm not musical and I've no idea. Don't ask me what Englishness is – trying to answer that lies far down the lane past the signpost marked "Pomposity". You'll have your own ideas and perhaps they aren't too far removed from mine. Perhaps, though, they are. It's possible in four generations that you may not be primarily English, or that what I regard as the acceptable face of nationalism may have changed utterly. Whatever your view, I imagine my own ideas of Englishness will emerge from these letters, and I hope it still seems to you mostly humane and generally benevolent.

Whatever Englishness is, Elgar's music and Sassoon's prose define it for me. No one gets nearer than Elgar to how I feel about my landscape and my country, and this has reached an extent where the two have merged in my sub-conscious. I can't listen to Elgar without conjuring images of the countryside; I can't walk in the countryside without hearing his music in my head. It's a frequent and potent experience for me. And I trace it all back to that warm day in April 1969 when my father and I returned home from Winchester to hear that my grandfather Faux had died.

With love,

Christopher

28: School

Odiham

Wednesday, 8th February 2006

Dear G,

I'd known from the outset it would be a ghastly experience and I was right. My three-year-old self bounced up and down on the bench front seat of our grey Standard Vanguard, shouting: "Start it up! Start it up!" We'd just arrived outside Seaton House Nursery School on my first day. It was a warm day in 1960 and I'd already decided school wasn't for me; home was preferable and I wanted to return thither as quickly as possible. I therefore urged my father in the strongest possible terms to start the engine so we could go home. He didn't, and I remember a thoroughly miserable morning spent sitting on a teacher's lap as she tried to persuade me that everyone else was having a good time. This was patently untrue. I knew then, and I've never doubted for an instant since, that any child with an ounce of sense would always rather be at home than at school. Thus began my long, largely unproductive and frequently unhappy relationship with compulsory education.

In time Seaton House, which at least had a sandpit, was replaced by a prep school called Homefield, which did not. Like my suburban homelife, Homefield belonged in the 1930s. We wore maroon blazers, grey shorts, long, grey woollen socks with a maroon stripe round the top and maroon school caps. On my shoulders I carried a leather satchel, heavy with textbooks – including Kennedy's *Shorter Latin Primer*, its blue and grey cover dutifully defaced to read Kennedy's *Shorter Eating Primer* – and exercise books filled with large, rounded handwriting. We went to school six days a week and played gruesome amounts of sport – uncomfortable soccer in the winter, interminable cricket in the summer – on Wednesday and Saturday afternoons.

We called all the masters "Sir" and we often called Matron "Sir" as well, even though she was a very attractive brunette in her late twenties. We avoided the irascible headmaster and I avoided the prefects – pompous thirteen-year-old jacks-in-office – even more assiduously. But a lot of the time I failed in this endeavour and most Friday lunchtimes were spent standing, with other felons, outside the headmaster's study while the prefects reported my misdemeanours of the previous week. They were many, varied but unremarkable. I was just a bit awkward and played them up, but they didn't appreciate it. Neither did the headmaster. As a consequence, I soon held the school "whacking record" – I was beaten (caned or slippered on the bottom) more often than any other pupil. It hurt, but had no other effect on my behaviour. I was set on the sometimes painful but often amusing road to being a thorough nuisance.

On the train the other day a guard remarked that she wished we'd bring back corporal punishment to deal with some very stupid boys who had been annoying her. I told her that I'd held the whacking record at school and she replied: "Didn't do you any harm, did it?"

"Oh, I think it did," I said. I may have overstated it. I'm not at all sure it did actual harm. I'm quite sure it did no good. But it was, I suppose, an element in keeping me in a perpetual state of anxiety throughout my time at school. At any one time I never felt relaxed and always out of place and ill-prepared for whatever we were doing.

Little things loomed ridiculously large. I remember arriving on the day of the carol service to find, when I removed my raincoat in the school cloakrooms, that I'd forgotten to put on my school blazer underneath. Greatly distressed by this, I asked the duty master, Mr Jones, what I should do.

"You must go and tell the Headmaster," he replied grimly, clenching his cadaverous jaw in ominous disapproval.

And so I set off, choked with anxiety, towards the headmaster's house. Turning a corner, I almost cannoned into my form master, Mr Worton, and blurted out my sad story.

"Go back to the others," he smiled. "Keep your coat on. I'll phone your parents and fix things."

He did. My blazer was delivered to the church. The headmaster was never told. The world didn't end. Trevor Worton earned my undying gratitude. I also remember Mr Jones, but rather differently.

I remember too a blazing hot Saturday afternoon of compulsory cricket in early July 1966. I'd managed to manoeuvre myself into my favourite position – fielding at long-stop – from where the game impinged infrequently on my thoughts, which seldom had much to do with sport. This afternoon they were about dogs. My good friend Nobby had recently died. I'd arrived home from school one Wednesday afternoon to hear the news. It was my first bereavement and the shock had knocked the breath from me. Nobby had always been there and I couldn't imagine life without him. His successors, two brown and white Jack Russell pups, were arriving that afternoon. In fact, here they were now with my parents, coming across the field towards me. Barney and Rusty captured our hearts on that afternoon and would hold them in thrall until Rusty's death nearly fifteen years later.

Then came the school holidays – eight and a half weeks in the summer – and that incomparable feeling of release when I woke up on the first morning with the prospect of sixty free days unshadowed by the cares and worries of school, stretching unthreateningly before me. Of days spent on long cycle rides miles from home with my friends, of walks in Oaks' Park or on Banstead Downs with the dogs. Of reading Richmal Crompton's William stories that made me laugh out loud. Of holidays in Cornwall and butterflies and fishing and target practice with my new air rifle. The prospect gave a sense of freedom on a scale I've seldom experienced since.

The holidays ended and, in September 1966, I started at a new school, King's College Wimbledon, which coincidentally Kit had attended in the late 1870s when it had been in the Strand. Here my English master encouraged us to develop an extensive vocabulary by the simple expedient of violence. If anyone didn't know a word, Mr Warburg would instruct the boy behind to "Give him help", whereupon the Oxford Concise Dictionary would be brought crashing down on the back of his head. Nice man, Mr Warburg. I remember you too.

Every Sunday brought a migraine attack as I dreaded the next morning and the week that followed. Mystified because I didn't like King's, the kindly headmaster suggested to my parents that I might need psychiatric help. Looking back, such treatment would have been appropriate only if I *had* liked the school. Instead, my parents concluded that a smaller, boarding school might be the answer. They chose Hurstpierpoint in Sussex. They were wrong again.

I began there on 25th April 1969, an unusually hot spring day soon after my grandfather Faux's funeral. That had been an odd experience. My grandmother had been too gaga to attend the service and treated the occasion as a family party. She'd been so excited at seeing so many of her sisters and other relatives that we'd had to take her out to dinner. As she went to bed, she thanked us for a wonderful day. A few weeks later the headmaster, a man called Heslop, singled me out to tell me my grandmother had died too. Apparently she'd had a clot circulating for some time which finally reached her brain while she was fast asleep. I didn't go home for her funeral.

I lasted at Hurstpierpoint for one term and three weeks. Bullying was rife and institutionalised. (Since Tom Brown's father it's been traditional for each generation to claim that's how it was in their time, but that now, of course, it's much changed. I have no evidence to suggest that this is the case but, if it has, such a change is a century and a half overdue.) Boys with too much time on their hands, unsupervised by complacent, often incompetent, masters, behaved like savages. My time there ended on 5th October, when I returned home for a Sunday *exeat* and my parents discovered I'd been beaten up a day earlier because it was nearly my birthday. I never went back.

The whole experience provided only two things that have proved of lasting value. First, my determination, resolved upon there and then, never, in any circumstances, to send any child of mine to boarding school. However incompetent I may have been as a parent, I could not do a worse job at rearing a child than that hopeless, neglectful bunch at Hurstpierpoint did. Second, it provided me with a yardstick of misery which I still apply when the going gets rough. No matter how bad anything may have been since, nothing has ever approached the level of desolation I felt throughout my mercifully brief time in Mr Heslop's depressing institution. About a decade after I left Hurstpierpoint – two or three years after I was married – Lois woke me from what proved to be the last nightmare that took me back there.

The clouds lifted on 13th October, when I arrived at a new, not very good day school for boys in Ewell. As I walked into my new classroom on that Monday morning, my new form master smiled and said: "Come in, Christopheles." Until I met him I didn't know it was possible for a teacher to call me by my first name. This man knew all our names. His own name, God bless him, was and is John Andrews. He was tall, undisciplined, very kindly, deeply emotional, and talented both as a teacher and a writer. He became my friend in that moment and he still is. And he still calls me Christopheles.

Despite John, I still hated school. Five or six years ago I was walking down Stamford Street towards Waterloo Station. I'd had a reasonably enjoyable day teaching an agreeable group at Customs and Excise

Headquarters, it wasn't raining and I had plenty of time to catch my train but, as I turned a corner, a massive wave of despair engulfed me with all the physical symptoms – heart and stomach – that accompany such an experience. After a second or two my brain caught up and I began wondering what I'd remembered that had caused this dramatic mood-swing. But there was nothing in my mind – apart from that smell. It was wafting through the open backdoor of a university and it was the smell of an institutional kitchen. As I strolled past it had wrenched my sub-conscious mind back thirty-five years, awakening in a contented, confident, middle-aged man his primeval fear and hatred of school.

While John encouraged and developed my love of language, another master, a priest called David Swarbrigg, encouraged me in what we now call Religious Education. In other subjects, though, my progress was dismal and my behaviour consistently awkward. Three years later, just as I was about to take my O Levels (which one took at sixteen), the headmaster wrote to my father, asking him to take me away. Thanks to John and David, three of my O Levels were good; the rest were quite dreadful.

My last two years of education were spent at the City of London Freemen's School at Ashtead, where I made a number of good friends – girls and boys because it was mixed – didn't do a stroke of work, had a thoroughly enjoyable time and left with a solitary A Level in English. I hadn't the foggiest notion of what I wanted to do with my life but I'd finally emerged from school. And that was enough for the seventeen-year-old me.

With love,

Christopher

29: Lois

Odiham

Thursday, 9th February 2006

Dear G,

Some of the more organised aspects of modern life don't always seem to me an advance. Couples discuss marriage and producing children with the same dispassionate financial calculation they apply to getting a mortgage or buying a car. Although I accept that it's better not to have more children than one can support, I worry about a society which treats heart and head decisions of this scale of importance as ones that are primarily about one's purse. I remember some friends of my younger sister Elizabeth reaching thirty and feeling it was time they got married. Each then cast around to find suitable candidates to fill the vacancy of wife. It didn't seem to me to be what marriage is about and, for me, it wasn't a bit like that. I met the right person at the wrong time. It was far from convenient, especially financially, but it involved no conscious choice at all. We married because there didn't seem anything else to be done.

The sequence of these letters suggests that I left school and got married but, although I married absurdly young, this isn't quite true. After leaving the City of London Freemen's School in the summer of 1974, I spent a year working in the family business. My task was to manage the advertising for the journal of the Royal Town Planning Institute. It provided an undemanding interlude, allowing me time to relax and consider the future as well as to read a great many books and listen to more music than I have managed ever since. My parents exerted no pressure on me to do anything and I think it reflects some credit on them and me that, after a few months, it dawned on me that I couldn't simply step from school into my father's company; I needed to strike out on my own.

My father arranged for me to see the recently retired chairman of a major publishing house who offered to give his advice. Donning my weddings, funerals and interviews suit, I called in to see him at the company's office in High Holborn. I don't know what I expected and I certainly don't think I was naïve enough to think he'd spot me as just the sort his firm needed, make me an offer, hand me a cigar and sit back to discuss books. Nor did I expect what actually happened. We sat together in the foyer of the firm while he told me all about himself. From time to time he'd break off to greet a passing colleague and, in between, his eyes darted over my shoulder to see if anyone else of interest was approaching. It wasn't a helpful interview and I don't remember a single piece of his advice. It's quite possible he didn't give any.

Some psychologists ran tests on me and pronounced that I had a facility with words and a propensity to be over-assertive with people in authority. Beyond these two conclusions, which had been crashingly obvious since my prep school, their suggestions became hazy. One of them, I recall, seemed strongly in favour of my sleeping with my then girlfriend – a piece of advice I felt fell outside his frame of reference.

Equipped with adult guidance of this calibre, I decided to go to university but, to get there, I would need more A Levels than the one I'd scraped in my last year at school. When I was eighteen, I signed up at a very expensive "crammer" in Croydon to take some A Levels in a year. One of my English teachers was a young Oxford graduate with long dark hair and green eyes. I didn't entirely approve of her at first. She seemed to me to be a touch too familiar with the students, but I supposed most of us were only five or six years younger than her, and she did seem to know her stuff. Her teaching was up to John Andrews's inspirational standard, but she was more consistent and better organised. Any essay she returned had more comments from her than there was essay. Her comments were crammed all over the page, making them almost impossible to decipher. But there were lots of them. You got your money's worth from Lois Lightfoot. In fact, she was the only person at the College to realise, when my mother was ill in a private hospital for a long time, that my family's finances might be hard hit. She noticed that, when Bristol University offered me a place on the basis of two A Levels, I dropped the third one to reduce the expense. Now, she thoughtfully suggested I should join her special S Level English class. She'd already made sure none of its other members minded my joining unofficially and without paying the extra fee they had paid.

I took her out for a drink to say thank you, and found I enjoyed her company. We met again, and again, and talked for hours. This was tricky. Seeing Lois was suddenly becoming the most important thing in my life, but she was my teacher and to her I must have seemed very young.

"If you're not busy this week, perhaps one evening we might go out for a meal?" I took care to keep the invitation vague and allow her an easy escape route.

"Monday, Tuesday, Wednesday, Thursday, Friday, Saturday or Sunday?" she asked, smiling at me.

We met often and I found myself planning days and evenings to spend as much time as possible in her company. When I came to pay the bill in the Chinese restaurant, I found a thoughtful five pounds waiting beside my coffee cup. She knew I had no money but knew also I'd be sensitive to not paying the whole bill. We discovered we both had an excellent relationship with our parents, and it's just possible I may have dropped casually into conversation that my mother was seven years older than my father, as Lois was seven years older than me. She told me there was a similar age gap between her parents. She stayed a weekend with us and met John Andrews, who came to dinner. They got on admirably. That night I found her sitting on the stairs outside our bathroom, plaiting her long dark hair. She turned to look over her shoulder at me. I didn't touch her. I said nothing. But I knew. This was it.

It's inconvenient to fall in love with your teacher when you're just nineteen, she's twenty-six and you have neither income nor the prospect of a job. I was painfully, embarrassingly slow in telling her how I felt. I'd had a couple of girlfriends but this was different. Late one night as we walked on the heath at Walton-on-the-Hill, I finally kissed her. Seven days later, on 8th May 1976, I asked her to marry me. It was lucky I did.

Unknown to me, my mother telephoned her later that day and said: "If he's going to marry you, he must get his A Levels."

She needn't have worried: I did get my A Levels, and a Distinction in the S Level Lois had taught me unofficially. She offered to move to Bristol while I was at the University, but the time for that seemed to have passed. I didn't take up my place and, instead, applied to the Civil Service's junior management entry scheme.

Our parents' response was characteristically unconventional. Having intuitively grasped remarkably early that I wanted to marry Lois, my mother then kicked up one of the biggest emotional storms of my life. She didn't seem to disapprove of Lois, she didn't – as any parent might quite reasonably have done – express her concern about the practical and financial aspects of our decision. She quite simply made a great big fuss. After a few months the fuss ended and to this day I've no idea what it was about or why it suddenly, as storms often do, blew itself out. She then gave us her mother's diamond ring to use as our engagement ring.

Lois's parents' response was much less violent but equally unexpected. When we became engaged, I hadn't met either of them. In July we went to Yorkshire to stay with them for a week and, after a day or two, I broke the news. There was a long silence. Then Lois's father said: "Oh blow you." I've no idea what he meant either. He seemed all right about it afterwards. Strange things, parents – as Alex and Vicky will confirm.

Just after my twenty-first birthday, Lois and I were married in Yorkshire by my old teacher, David Swarbrigg. That was a curious experience because, on the way to the church, the three of us – David the priest, my cousin David my best man, and I – found the road blocked by an overturned lorry. It had been laden with whisky bottles, which had smashed across the asphalt, making the chill autumn air reek of alcohol. Inside the cab, trapped upside down with the steering wheel embedded in his chest, was the driver. David Swarbrigg climbed in beside him. While receiving the last sacrament, he told David that he had six children and they discovered that they were both Irish. After the ambulance had arrived, we pressed on to the church, where a white-faced David married us with blood stains on his cuffs. During the reception we telephoned the hospital and heard that, after massive blood transfusions, the driver had survived. When David went to see him they discovered that each had pretended to be Roman Catholic because he thought the other one was. While the hooded figure of Death waited with his scythe beside the lorry's cab, sensitivity to each other's feelings had prevailed over denominationalism. And so, in my view, it always should.

While David was at the hospital, Lois and I were on our way to honeymoon in Malta. A week later we returned, very poor and very happy, to start our life together in a tiny one-bedroomed flat in a small, modern block in Bromley.

With love,

Christopher

30:   A pair of Lightfeet

Odiham

Friday, 10th February 2006

Dear G,

In-laws are the only important relationship one neither is born with, nor chooses. They just come with our spouse as perhaps the least considered part of the package. And yet it's a relationship fraught with the potential for resentment, jealousy and bitterness. My parents did not do well with either their parents-in-law or their sons-in-law. They handled the relationships badly, but they were also unlucky. I was luckier: both in terms of what Lois's parents were like and of the effect they had on our married life. Lois's father, for example, was the unconscious reason for our moving from the London suburbs to the Peak District.

My first encounter with my father-in-law was arresting. A very short, stocky man with a tightly clipped moustache, he emerged from their kitchen, holding a teapot and wearing an orange, quilted, woman's winter dressing gown from Marks and Spencers. Memories of this so far agree, but now they divide. I maintain he was also sporting a pink, woollen tea-cosy on his head; Lois holds that it was on the teapot. It's possible that my memory has embellished this aspect of the picture but both of us agree that, if on this occasion he wasn't actually wearing the tea-cosy, it was just the sort of thing he might well have done. He took a utilitarian view of the world and, if a woman's dressing gown or a tea-cosy kept him warm, he would happily have worn either.

There was a surreal quality to both Lois's parents. It was perhaps a touch more disconcerting in David than in Joyce because, when dressed normally, he looked deceptively unremarkable: a small man in late middle-age who bore more than a passing resemblance to Captain Mainwaring in *Dad's Army*. In public Joyce was less reticent in her eccentricity. Very tall for a woman, she had black dyed hair, the freckled complexion of a redhead and a very loud voice with a marked Smethwick accent. Listening to David speak, you could spot his Birmingham origins; Joyce's were more immediately obvious. They'd moved to Yorkshire a few years earlier after David had been made redundant, and they had settled comfortably and with a sense of great good fortune in Boston Spa, near Wetherby.

Theirs had not been easy lives. They were both the youngest child of elderly parents and their older brothers and sisters were contemporaries of my grandparents Jary. David was the last, most intelligent and most responsible of nine children born to an elderly clerk and his wife. His father, who was from Carlisle, was an invalid and belonged to a strange Christian sect who seem to have believed that everyone except their tiny membership would burn in everlasting hellfire. He beat his children with a belt and, unsurprisingly, they kept out of his way. David was thirteen when his father went to join the elect and, although he had older brothers as well as sisters, he seems to have been the one who assumed immediate responsibility for his mother, the family and the home. Pausing only to pitch his father's religious books into the canal – an uncharacteristically extravagant gesture for him – he took over as head of a poor family, made unusually close by poverty and adversity. He grew up fast and won a place at university before his seventeenth birthday.

He once remarked to Alex after he'd mentioned some incident in his childhood: "It must seem like history to you." I detected no resentment, only satisfaction, as he sat in an armchair in our centrally-heated, clean, carpeted, comfortable little house in Derbyshire and recalled how he'd scraped together the money to instal electricity into their bleak terraced house in Camden Street, Birmingham. That had been a good memory. He had others. Of sharing boots which didn't really fit. Of queuing at the butcher to get the cheapest off-cuts of meat which would be painstakingly picked over and conserved to enable the family to extract the maximum protein. Of copying out text books because, even when he'd got to

Birmingham University, the money wasn't there to buy them, even secondhand.

Joyce's childhood was financially more secure but emotionally less so. She seems to have been the unwanted last child of a Welsh printer and his wife. Hers is a story of neglect, which she didn't ever tell. Whenever her parents were mentioned, she became vague and evasive. "They died during the bombing," she said. But it was clear that, long before the war, she had disengaged from her family. David's straitlaced Methodist sisters thought her flighty, and they disapproved bitterly when she and he married in January 1942. He was just twenty-three, Joyce nearly twenty-nine – although she had inexpertly doctored her birth certificate to knock a year off.

Theirs was an odd match. Perhaps because his father had been born in the 1860s, David's cast of mind was Victorian. A scientist by training, he had the perfectionism of a craftsman matched with an immense capacity for hard work, an encyclopaedic thirst for information, a love of word-play and a whimsical sense of humour. He was painstaking, industrious, methodical and – despite the orange dressing gown – intensely rational. His was what I always think of as an Anglo-Saxon brain, which made steady progress from one point to the next. Joyce's was Celtic, making frequent, instinctual, sometimes wild, leaps. Her judgement could be very sound indeed or entirely wide of the mark. In Lois's childhood, her father provided calm, measured, affectionate encouragement in her steady progress towards an Oxford scholarship; her mother provided a noisy, sometimes slapdash environment in which she yet made sure that her younger daughter was fed, healthy and sure of a mother's love. Perhaps their contrasts made them effective parents but, given their own casts of mind, how they tolerated each other is a mystery.

Precluded by his double vision from serving in the forces during the war, David was commissioned in a South Staffordshire battalion of the Home Guard. His war and Joyce's was one of Birmingham being bombed, of rationing, of marriage and of losing their first child, a daughter, at a few months old. When some of his sisters objected to Joyce as a sister-in-law, he simply refused to countenance any sort of family breach and waited for better sense to prevail. It did. They had two more daughters: Elaine, born in 1946, and Lois, three years later.

Throughout his life David was entranced by animals and the countryside. When Whipsnade Zoo opened in the early 1930s, the fourteen-year-old had walked all the way there, camping out in a tent, stayed nearby so he could spend enough time there to see every animal, and then walked home; when his money and food ran out, he sustained himself by eating raw cereals picked from the fields he passed. Now his young family spent most weekends and every holiday in the countryside.

They were not well off. It was not the sort of thing he would talk about but I suspect a proportion of his salary went to support his mother and his sister, Mary, who remained at home as a companion for his mother. And, just as money was becoming a bit less of a worry, the family were hit by two disasters. First, the firm David worked for was taken over and he was made redundant, and then Joyce suffered a severe stroke. Told she would never walk again without a stick, she was inspired by Douglas Bader's example to keep trying. Like him, she had boundless determination and, like him, she succeeded.

By the time I met them, although they were happy to be settled in the Yorkshire countryside, they had retreated into their own world. Their conversation was quite different from any other I've encountered. Over a cup of tea they were far more likely to discuss the practicalities of negotiating with invading Martians than the weather or the effectiveness of the health service. And people spoke concurrently, rather than consecutively, which made it hard to follow. But theirs was a kindly, if slightly off-beat, world and their deep pleasure in reliving childhood with their grand-daughters was a joy to see. David appearing suddenly at our window clutching a small suitcase and dressed as Paddington Bear. Joyce telling us that we gave the girls too many sweets and then pressing acid drops on them as they left for home. Joyce's voice shrieking from her bed: "Don't bring buckets of hedgehogs into my bedroom, David!" And both their faces lighting up when we arrived, unexpectedly, as a family and appeared in their garden.

Just as he was about to retire, David was admitted to hospital. When the diagnosis seemed almost deliberately unclear, I telephoned to speak to the specialist. The news was bad. He had inoperable lung cancer and was unlikely to survive more than a year or so. It was then I applied for a transfer north to be near them, and we moved to Derbyshire. David and Joyce never knew why we moved. They never knew he had cancer. David never asked and, deciding that he would have asked had he wished to know, we didn't tell either him or Joyce. Whether this was the right decision, I don't know. It was certainly the correct one: David enjoyed another thirteen, reasonably active years and finally died of something else.

They weren't my parents and, as with any elderly people, they could sometimes be irritating, but I still miss their human warmth and amiable eccentricity. In January 1995, when David died, I cleared out his tiny bedroom, like a teenage boy's full of the equipment of his various hobbies, and had the sad job of taking down the Christmas decorations he'd put up only a fortnight before. He'd carried on with characteristically fierce independence for two years after Joyce had slipped quietly away in her sleep, which was probably the only thing she ever did quietly in her life.

Recently – just in these past six months – Joyce has worked a miracle from beyond the grave. Last July, my cousin David, Uncle Jon's son, was admitted to the Royal Marsden Hospital suffering from prostate cancer, which had run riot and permanently damaged his back. Told he would never walk again, he decided to follow what he called "Joyce Lightfoot's example". He set himself a gruelling regime of relentless exercise and physiotherapy, which he pursued with Joyce's single-mindedness and courage. Last Sunday, Lois and I drove down to Dorchester to see him discharge himself from the nursing home and walk out. Joyce's seems a worthwhile legacy.

With love,

Christopher

31: Dogs and Derbyshire

Odiham

Saturday, 11th February 2006

Dear G,

Have you got a dog? Of the twelve or so souls I've been most profoundly glad to have known, several have been dogs. To adapt *Twelfth Night*: some achieve dogs; some have dogs thrust upon them. In Derbyshire both happened to us. We achieved Monty, our Jack Russell who came to live with us as a pup. His father was on the farm at Foolow, near Eyam, high on a hill just west of the valley we lived in. His mother was a farm dog from Darley Dale, near Matlock. Monty, named after my father's field marshal who often looked and behaved like a Jack Russell terrier, was all his name suggests: sharp nosed, bright eyed, mock aggressive and with the biggest ego any dog ever possessed. We visited his mother and her litter, and he was the dog we chose in the normal way. Well, perhaps not quite. There were four bitches and a dog, and I was holding and about to choose one of the bitches when I glanced down at the floor and saw that Monty had already chosen eighteen-month-old Alex in her pink and white striped dress. He was standing on her lap, his tiny paws on her shoulders, licking her nose. That settled it. It was the best choice I never made.

Sandy, who came a lot later although we'd known him for years, was thrust upon us. He was an old mongrel with an Alsatian's body and colouring but a Labrador cum terrier head: a real mix. He lived in our village, belonged to an old lady and led a double life: a sedate indoor one with his owner, and a wild one alone, loose in the village and surrounding countryside. He took a shine to Alex, who encouraged him, and Monty, who tolerated him, and he often added himself to the strength when we went for walks.

Over the years the tide of his owner's Alzheimer's disease advanced and, as she retreated into a world of her own, Sandy increasingly spent his days with us. Then we'd send him home to spend the night with her.

Finally, one morning Lois found the old lady's home help on our doorstep. She had arrived at work to find Sandy badly injured and locked in the cottage. His owner's niece, who lived opposite her, had been awakened late at night by a man carrying the injured Sandy. After he'd left us that night, Sandy had wandered onto the main road and been hit by a car. His head was cut, his side bruised and his tongue bitten through. Sandy had limped off towards our house but, not knowing where he was heading, the driver had carried him back to his official home. Rather than call the vet, the niece had simply locked him in with her aunt overnight and in the morning had gone to work, leaving him for the home help to find.

By the time I arrived home from Sheffield, Lois had organised everything. Sandy had been with the vet all day. I collected him and paid the vet's bill, brought him home, carried him into the garden for a moment and then brought him into the house, where he clambered awkwardly onto an armchair, looked around him to reassure himself about where he was, relaxed with a loud sigh and fell deeply asleep. He'd come home.

An hour or two later his owner's niece's son arrived, brandishing a lead and asked to take him home. I told him Sandy couldn't walk. He demanded I return the dog. I refused. Having spoken to the RSPCA, I had the perfect formula, so when his mother arrived later, I was able to say. "If he is your dog, the RSPCA are going to prosecute you for cruelty. If he isn't, there's no reason why he can't stay here." He stayed. Within a month he'd recovered and become a handsome dog with glossy coat and bushy tail. His days sleeping rough were over.

He repaid us tenfold. First by saving Monty from an unaccompanied Alsatian who came over a wall and attacked the little Jack Russell without warning. Sandy, who was not an aggressive dog, hurled himself at the Alsatian and bowled him into an enormous bush of nettles. His protection was especially welcome because Lois was alone with Monty and heavily pregnant with Vicky. Later he did the same again when a Rottweiler attacked Monty and the children as they came back from school. But, most of all, Sandy repaid us as most dogs do: with love and loyalty. And the odd dead rabbit.

Our house in Calver looked out across the pub car park and village cricket pitch to a hill. Beyond the hill was the valley cut by the winding River Derwent. Then the land rose steadily to the rocky escarpment of Froggatt Edge, which we could see from our bedroom window. Our favourite walk was up that hill towards the edge and then down to the river. I still walk it here in Hampshire when I can't sleep. I could take you on it now, if you're ready.

Once out of the village and across the Baslow road, there's a path that climbs the hill at an angle. Nowadays some tidy person has removed some of the trees but, when we were there, the trees and hedges met over your head, forming an enclosed tunnel of branches. In winter, when it snowed, this shone white in the bright sunshine, overhanging hawthorn berries glowing red against the white snow and blue sky. Lois once tried to photograph it but found it impossible to capture the real impression of it. In this, as in all other family photographs, the scenery was secondary. Monty stood four-square in the foreground, tongue lolling, eyes shining, ears erect, and tail vibrating at 90 degrees to his back.

At the top of the hill, the path turns sharp left but, if you step forward a few paces, you can see right across the hill towards the Curbar Gap on Froggatt Edge.

On a clear day, over to the right you can see the tall fountain in the grounds at Chatsworth. In the autumn the bracken on the ground leading up to the edge turns to brown, contrasting with the dark green conifers below the edge. This was how we first saw the Peaks when Lois and I came house-hunting on 13th October 1982. Having seen the colours on Froggatt Edge, we looked no further.

Back on the path, you walk away from Chatsworth parallel with the dry stone wall enclosing the field beyond. Here Monty once caught a stoat. Luckily he killed it instantly because I looked at its teeth and, had it had a chance to sink them into his face or eye, the end might have been very different. Here's the stile on our right. You climb up, over the wall and jump down some way into the field. Once, after a very heavy snowfall which prevented my getting the car out and going to work, I'd strapped the young Alex on my back, and Monty and I strode up the hill through the white tunnel. Here Monty had jumped off the stile and skittered about in the snow. I followed him and disappeared up to my waist. I'd forgotten how far down the step was into this field, where the heavy snow had drifted in the unchecked wind. Stand just here and you get another marvellous view across to the edge. And in late spring this field, between here and the barn over there, is a mass of yellow buttercups.

From the barn, the field beyond slopes down into the valley and there's a very steep path down to the road that crosses the bridge over the Derwent. I always put Monty on his lead near the bottom in case there's any traffic on the bridge. Nothing coming? Pause a moment on the bridge and look to your right. There's the weir. When it's been raining hard, it can be full, fast and impressive. The Derwent is a serious river. And then down some steps to the left of the bridge. In summer the whole river bank reeks of garlic or sweet vanilla from the pink balsams. If the dogs are quiet we may hear a sudden plop as a water vole takes to the water. They're scarcer now, but when we were here there were lots of them.

Walking up to the next bridge you pass the backs of the long gardens of a few houses close to the river. One of them floods often and has a small wooden bridge to reach the river path. And then you have a number of choices. You can cross the next bridge and come back down the river the other side. If you do this, you'll pass Monty's tree, which he climbs, jumping up to where the trunk forks and sitting there panting – or is he laughing? Or you can go on and walk through Froggatt village or back towards Curbar on the road. Or you can just do a 180 degree turn and go back the way you came. That's what I usually do because this is my favourite version of my favourite walk, and I'd rather do the same thing twice than go somewhere even marginally less beautiful just for a change.

After we moved away, I returned there some years later on my own. I took our usual path up the hill, stepped down from the stile and stared out across the field to the edge beyond. It was just as I remembered it. But today I was alone. Lois was at home in Hampshire. The family we'd been here no longer existed. Alex was a young woman and Vicky a girl, far from the toddler who lived and played here. Sandy and Monty were dead. Memories overwhelmed me. There were too many ghosts – friendly ones, happy ones, but ghosts nonetheless – and I spent the entire walk with tears in my eyes. Remembered happiness can sometimes be just as poignant as sadness. I've learned my lesson: when we return to Derbyshire now, we go as a family and match all that past happiness with plenty from the present.

If ever you visit Calver, do try our walk. I'll look out for you because, if I'm given any choice, I'll be spending quite a lot of eternity up on the hill there and down by our river.

With love,

Christopher

32: Some family snaps

Odiham

Sunday, 12th February 2006

Dear G,

Two days after Alex was born, I went to my grandparents' flat at Ilford for the last time. They were eighty-four and my grandmother was becoming very forgetful and starting to wander. My father was trying to persuade them to move into sheltered housing, and he asked me to go with him for moral support. He needed it. We found Sid at his most aggressive, Winnie quietly evasive. When my grandfather shouted at my father, I ticked him off – which, I suspect, was a novel experience for him. He ordered me from the house. My grandmother sat, silent, immobile and expressionless, as if someone had flicked her off switch. During our brief visit neither even mentioned their new great-grandchild. A day or two later my grandfather cut me out of his will.

I never saw him again. When, six months later, my father told Winnie that Sid had died in hospital, she replied: "Comes to us all." She lived another five years, never mentioned him again and asked to be buried in her parents' grave at the parish church with the window remembering Wally and Len. It seemed appropriate.

But my last memory of her is a much happier one. I'd taken Alex, aged five, to visit her in her nursing home and we all sat round an institutional, formica-topped table. I'd been dreading what promised to be a difficult conversation, but Alex planned otherwise. She was at her most talkative and humorous. While Alex held forth I saw Winnie laugh more that afternoon than in the rest of her life put together. It was good to see.

It's not surprising that Alex seemed to succeed where the rest of us had failed. Looking back on their childhoods, I've enjoyed every stage but among my favourites was when they were four or five. They seemed at that age to inhabit a Paddington Bear world of forthright and sometimes unerringly accurate honesty, enthusiasm for experience, simple fun and companionship. One of the advantages of having a seven-year gap between the girls was that, soon after Alex left a particular stage, Vicky arrived at it. So we had several years of having a small child about the place and, I must confess, it's something I miss and that makes me look forward to the prospect of our own grandchildren.

I remember the five-year-old Alex looking thoughtful and saying: "I wish I could do magic." We were at the Chatsworth farm shop and it took a moment for me to realise what she meant. Then I saw the bodies of the six or seven ducks and pheasants, strung from a hook on the wall by their necks. We can't and shouldn't protect our children from the ugliness of life – and as a family we're far from vegetarian so ours is an emotional, irrational stance – but just then I wished very much that I could have done.

When Vicky was born, just before Christmas in 1988, we were a bit worried about how Alex and Monty might react. Alex had been an only child. How would she feel about sharing our attention? She was thrilled. Her friends at school had brothers and sisters; now she had one of her own. From the day I taught her to tie her own shoe laces and we went to see our new baby in the hospital in Sheffield, I never detected a moment's jealousy.

But what about Monty? People warned us dogs could be very jealous of a new baby. Monty followed Nobby's admirable example. On the first night, when Vicky woke us crying, Monty sat bolt upright and nudged Lois. "Come on, Mum. The baby's crying." Within a couple of nights he'd lost interest. He'd wake up, open one eye to watch Lois set off towards Vicky's bedroom and then relax back into untroubled sleep. When, soon after Vicky's birth, we went to stay with Joyce and David at Boston Spa, Lois found Monty and Vicky cuddled up, fast asleep on an eiderdown. To Monty, she was another puppy to play with and look after.

Perhaps because of the age difference, perhaps by chance or perhaps from simple affection, the girls have always got on well. Vicky's first word was "Ee-ah", which we deduced, from her gestures, was an attempt at "Alex". As a toddler she raced around the sitting room, sitting astride her gallant "Ee-ah" who, like many horses, was patient most of the time but prone to lose interest and wander off to pursue her own interests just when her rider was getting really interested.

Both girls loved animals and played and slept among a pile of fluffy animal toys. There were tigers, bears, hundreds of dogs, lions and cats. Among Alex's favourites were some furry hand-puppets, which included a raccoon. She wants to bring them with her this morning because an expedition is planned. Dad's at work and Mummy's taking us all for a picnic.

It really is a bit of an expedition. First there's eight-year-old Alex, carrying the lunch bag in one hand and holding Monty's lead in the other. Then there's Lois, over her shoulder a bag of clean nappies, baby-wipes, baby drinks and other essentials, pushing the one-year-old Vicky in her pushchair with Sandy's lead round one wrist. Luckily where they're going isn't far. Just over the main road – that's the tricky bit – and half-way up the hill opposite. The last bit will be a bit of a struggle with the pushchair, but it should be all right.

And there, in the sunshine, Lois and the girls and the dogs play in the sloping field. Sometimes they find themselves roped into Alex's game but mostly the dogs amuse themselves. While they're off investigating some interesting smells fifty yards across the field, out come the skunk and the raccoon and a pretend game begins.

Lois is good at these. She makes them imaginative and funny, and the girls love them – although Vicky's a bit young yet to catch the subtler nuances of the animals' dialogue. And suddenly Alex realises that a brown stoat has stuck his head out of the dry stone wall to watch their game. His head disappears, then comes popping out again to watch them with his bright little eyes. He's obviously interested. Until now, this description could apply to many similar expeditions but the advent of the stoat marks it out as a particular day, still mentioned quite often: the day the stoat came and watched our game.

Important though our fluffy animals were, they were no match for the real thing. The badger Alex encountered unexpectedly down in Dorset when, absorbed in his own business, he crossed her path one evening on his way towards the river. The grey fox cub I nearly trod on in Derbyshire whose fieldcraft was still so poor that, instead of diving into the tall grass either side, he ran hell for leather straight up the open path ahead of me, his brush sailing behind in his slipstream like a schoolboy's satchel. I could almost hear him shouting a worried "Mu-u-um!" The startled roe deer we often meet here in Hampshire in the fields or in the woods by the canal. The red squirrels and the osprey we saw in the Lake District a couple of summers ago. The colony of rare crested newts Vicky and her friend found, and the Purple Emperor butterflies I spotted on our canal bank that made me remember Arthur the gardener and wish he were here so I could tell him about them. And, foremost among all this fauna, the dogs with whom both girls shared their childhoods.

In one of the *Winnie the Pooh* books there's a picture of Pooh and Piglet, walking away from us into the sunset. It's one of Sheppard's simplest drawings and, for me, it's always captured the essential relationship between Alex and Vicky. It's the impression Lois and I have often got when out for a walk – whether in Derbyshire, Hampshire, Dorset, Venice or, as in this picture, Gozo – we've looked ahead at the rear views of Alex and Vicky walking together.

Whatever age they may be – whether Alex is telling the infant Vicky a Manglepandy story or they're discussing the intricate love-life of one of Vicky's college friends – there's an entertaining conversation going on. Both are enthralled and, even if they're squabbling a bit, each is enjoying the other's company.

Piglet and Pooh formed an important part of both their childhoods. In their turn each had a hardback copy of *Winnie the Pooh*, which was red, and *The House at Pooh Corner*, which was green. Both had been mine when I was a boy. But Alex and Vicky also had the two books of poems, which I didn't know at all. And, because I read them to them aloud, we all got to know them together. Just a handful of words – *There once was a dormouse...* or *King John was not a good man...* – transport me back to bedtimes of one or two decades ago. Like most of us at bedtime, I was often tired. Like many fathers, just home from work, I wasn't always keen to get out of my chair and go upstairs to read to them. But Milne's words and characters usually worked their magic. By the time I'd read a page or so, I was enjoying it just as much as they were.

Another favourite was Kipling – especially *Rikki-Tikki-Tavi*, which was exciting and whose eponymous hero reminded us a bit of Monty. And there was *The Elephant's Child*, whose main characters, the Elephant's Child himself and the Bi-Coloured Python Rocksnake, by the rhythms of their speech suggested voices to me. The first, with his piercing *'scuse me!*, was my mother-in-law Joyce. The second, with his rolling Johnsonian prose, was Winston Churchill. Vicky told me the other day that it was several years before she realised that all Bi-Coloured Python Rocksnakes – and all Elephant's Children – didn't really speak like that...

This letter's a snapshot and is frozen in time just like that picture of Lois, Alex, Vicky and Monty on the hillside in Derbyshire. Once it's been written, life will move on and, by the time you read this, you'll know so much more than I know now. You'll know how both my girls spent most of their lives. What did they do? Did they marry happily? Did Alex live in the country and keep a great many dogs, which is her current plan? Which university did Vicky choose? Did she run a charity as she plans now?

I only wish you could tell me, but you can't. Rest assured, though, I'll find a way of keeping an eye on what they do, wherever I may be. That, as A A Milne undoubtedly would have put it, is how it is with dads.

With love,

Christopher

33: Dorset, daughters and dogs

Odiham

Monday, 13th February 2006

Dear G,

A sunny day on the River Frome, near Muckleford, just north of Dorchester. Here the river, little more than a broad, shallow, swift-flowing stream, ripples under a grey stone bridge. An eight- or nine-year-old girl with long blonde hair stands mid-stream, cotton skirt tucked firmly into knickers, fishing-net poised for action, peering with rapt concentration into the sparkling water in front of her. She's spotted a miller's thumb lurking on the river bed and, tongue pressed into sun-blushed cheek, is advancing upon it with silent determination.

A sudden bark and a splash, and a black, tan and white Jack Russell terrier crashes headlong into the water in manic pursuit of a stone he's dropped down the steep bank.

"Oh Monty!" Anyone else allowing the miller's thumb to escape capture would have faced serious anger. Monty gets away with it – just – and, with a heartfelt sigh, the girl resumes her fishing.

On the bank which Monty just left so precipitately a blonde toddler, wearing only a sun-hat, runs barefoot through the grass towards her mother, beaming and yelling at the top of her voice: "Aaaaaaaaaaaaaaaah!"

It's August and we're spending three weeks in the cottage at Muckleford. Judging by the girls' ages, it's either 1990 or 1991, but it could be any year in the 1980s or 1990s, when we spent most of our summer holidays in Dorset. We've walked up the long lane from the cottage, collecting dogs as we've gone along: an elderly golden retriever from the house opposite the end of our drive, a couple of loopy sheepdogs – Kim and Tigger – from the farm and Moley, the whippet, who is Monty's special holiday friend. All the dogs get along splendidly because they recognise that Monty's the leader. Mole, who's the fastest dog I know, will beat Monty to any thrown ball, stone or apple, but always politely stands aside and gives Monty the prize. He's so fast that he can almost do a Percy Grainger.

Have you seen Ken Russell's film about Delius? Grainger, the young Australian composer, hurls a cricket ball high in the air over the roof of a house, then runs straight through the house and neatly catches it in the garden before it's bounced. Moley's so fast he easily catches it on the first bounce – and he has to run all the way round the cottage, which has no backdoor. He attaches himself to the strength throughout our stay, during which he neglects his own family entirely. Luckily, they have other dogs and don't seem to mind. In fact, one year, when we mentioned the thought that we might one day like to go abroad on holiday, his owner looked horrified. "If you didn't come here, Moley would be distraught," she said.

We chose this type of holiday for two reasons: because Dorset's a beautiful southern county by the sea and we lived in a beautiful, northern, inland county, and because we couldn't afford much else. Once installed in the cottage, we recreated the sort of life we lived at home in Derbyshire but without the interruptions of school and work, and with the additional thrill of different country and accessible beaches. From about 1990 onwards we sometimes went abroad, but foreign holidays always had to be on top of our Dorset visits, which both girls much preferred. We all did – especially Monty, whose vibrating tail registered maximum levels of enjoyment from arrival to departure.

We've hundreds of snapshots of Monty on holiday, perhaps eating an ice cream at West Bay, chasing a stone on Chesil, walking on the hills above Abbotsbury or looking for fossils on the beach at Charmouth. Although Monty was obviously the centre of any picture, a few of them also include one or both of the girls. Unless they're together, at some stages of their development – between about four and eight – it's hard to tell them apart. So when I come across a picture of a small blonde girl, I sometimes have to work out who it is by peering closely at Monty, who inevitably will be standing beside her, beaming into camera. Does he look young or is he beginning to go a bit silvery round the muzzle? The girls told him this just made him look even more distinguished, but he needed no reassurance on that point.

As I write this, Alex and Vicky don't look as alike as they once did but, even now, any description of either could be applied to the other. Long blonde hair (like that lock of Kit's hair in the drawer behind me), blue eyes, small nose – they're made of the same ingredients, but the effect of those ingredients is different. Throughout, Vicky has been one size smaller, weighing half a pound less at birth and maintaining that differential so she's now a couple of inches shorter than Alex. Like my mother, Vicky is five foot four. Both favour my mother's side of the family. Alex, I suspect, is how my mother might have turned out had she had the benefit of a secure, loving home. During her childhood Vicky was more confident with her own age group, but perhaps this simply reflected the greater confidence of a younger child. Both – and I think this is attributable to Lois's blood – are much cleverer than any of my forebears.

What I wasn't prepared for was how much more enjoyable our children's successes are than our own. You've read how my grandmother Faux treated my mother and how my grandfather Jary treated my father. Both seemed scared lest their child might outshine them in some respect. Dora's defence was to keep Peggy out of the way to ensure that she didn't compete for Bill's attention or money; Sid's was to ignore, belittle and ridicule anything my father did. After nearly a quarter of a century of parenthood, this is beyond me. It seems unnatural. Our children are not our competitors; they are our future. It seems to me natural for us to want to lay foundations on which the next generation can build higher than we could in our time. If the human race is to make progress, this surely is how parents must be programmed. I chose to make my way without the ticket of a good degree from a respectable university; I'd like Alex and Vicky to have any advantages of this kind that may be available to them. Compared to Lois's parents, we didn't have a tough time when we first married, but money was tight and our first flat and first house were very basic. We'd like Alex and Vicky to be a bit more comfortable and have rather more choice than we had. If along the way they can leave things a bit happier and fairer than they found them, even better.

Alex did very much what Lois had done thirty years earlier. She read English at a women's college at Oxford, won an exhibition and emerged with a high second. Despite being less willing to devote hours of study to something of little interest to her, Vicky's already exceeded even Alex's total of GCSE exams. Although she didn't get quite the same astonishing consistency of top grades, hers were all As and A*s. Their school careers thankfully bore little resemblance to mine except that, like my father and me, Alex was bullied. It was this that spurred her to irritate her tormentors by achieving the best results in the school, which she did. Vicky was luckier and had a strong group of pleasant friends who protected each other through secondary school.

We can't take credit for intelligence, which is God-given. We may be able to take credit for applying it, but even here it's arguable that, along with the brain, God simply gave us a capacity for using it. We can, though, take credit for courage and determination, which both girls have shown at various times. Both when very small by hanging onto a dog's lead even though they were being dragged across gravel and their knees, chins and noses were being cut. Alex by coming out of an important exam to be sick with nerves, but then going back in to finish it (and pass). Vicky by publicly sticking up for an unpopular girl against friends who were bullying her. Lois and I have always taken pleasure in their academic achievements, but these are the aspects of Alex and Vicky in which we take a real pride. Lois and I know that both of them, whatever they do and wherever they find themselves, however high the cost, will always be a force for good.

Our last holiday at Muckleford was in the summer after the elderly Monty had died. We were joined by his very young successor, Harris. When we arrived we were warned that Moley was almost blind and very old, and that he barely ventured outside his house. It was a sad start to a holiday but, on that first evening, we heard a scratch at the kitchen door. The ancient Mole tottered very slowly into the sitting room, his tail wagging almost imperceptibly as he paused to greet each of us and sniff our hands. He didn't stay long and I saw him back to his house. It felt what it was: a farewell visit. But he'd come to see us for friendship's sake, and we felt honoured. A few months later his owners wrote to tell us he had died.

We didn't go back to Muckleford. Our holidays there belong in their time, when the girls were still small and Monty and Mole played in the summer sunshine.

The memories are so vivid that sometimes I wonder if they're all still there somewhere, in one of those big green fields or down by the river, if only I could find them.

With love,

Christopher

34: In Government

Odiham

Tuesday, 14th February 2006

Dear G,

I wasn't going to mention my work, but Lois insisted I must because it's an important part of my life so far. So this letter's a bit different from the others, but I hope still reasonably interesting. For the past thirty years I've played various tiny, walk-on parts in different aspects of government. During half of that time I've known some of the well-known politicians of the time. It would be an interesting test to see which names mean anything to you. I can certainly remember sitting in the office of a particular Cabinet minister, who was very worried about something that had happened or might happen, and thinking silently to myself: *In fifty years' time you'll be a footnote in a specialist history book.* I wonder if this rather sceptical assessment has proved correct?

Because of Hitler and the Kaiser, mine was the first generation for a long time to have to choose a job straight from school or college. Financial pressures caused by Lois's and my decision to marry made the decision urgent, but I really had no idea what I wanted to do. The past four generations of my family had made their living in publishing in one way or another, but it was the writing, rather than publishing, aspect that attracted me and, even at nineteen, I wasn't daft enough to believe I could earn a living writing. After my father's switchback career in business, I found the private sector less than attractive and I was confident that my life's ambition did not rest in becoming managing director of the Metal Box Company or Andrex Lavatory Paper. The last two generations of my family had risked or given their lives for this country; now I wanted to do something that, however small in scale, made it a slightly better place. I joined the Civil Service.

Looking back, it was an odd choice. Among our family papers we have a letter from Gladstone thanking some distant relative for sending him a copy of his book on Irish history, and a commission signed by William Pitt appointing a distant ancestor of Winnie's mother to a post in the Port of London. But we have no recent history of either government or public service in the family. Pat, Auntie Gladys's daughter, told my mother she thought it would last six months. This year it's lasted thirty years. Pat was wrong, but I still think the evidence at the time supported her judgement. I am not a natural civil servant and have spent most of my career feeling out of place. I regard most rules as things to be bent or ignored, I detest systems and processes, I prefer the practical to the theoretical and the outdoors to indoors, I dislike hierarchies and I get bored senseless sitting at a desk. The last thirty years have been a challenge to my bosses and to me, but I like to think the tension created by my unsuitability has sometimes been creative. I've never planned my career or pursued promotion, I've avoided office jobs – and especially those controlling money – with the enthusiasm with which I avoided maths and organised games at school, and I've worked with some extraordinarily nice people doing some very interesting things.

My first job was not interesting but I was lucky with my immediate boss, Alan Stagg, a veteran of Slim's Burma campaign whose kindly interest kept me going during the only two years of my entire career when I worked in London and commuted daily. Without him and the very cheery group of other young ones I worked with, Pat's prognostication might have proved correct. Now in his late eighties, Alan's still going strong and still in touch. When Alex won a place at Oxford, she received a card from Alan and his wife, Kathleen, enclosing a cheque for two hundred pounds. It's not often a present takes your breath away. This one did. A characteristic note explained that, when Kathleen had joined the ATS in 1942, an uncle and aunt had sent her a fiver and she'd felt very rich indeed. The Staggs had done their sums and reckoned that the current equivalent was two hundred.

Two years later I moved to an office in south east London to manage a team paying benefit to unemployed people. I arrived there just as Margaret Thatcher became Prime Minister. In the next two years, as harsh economic reality hit us, unemployment trebled to top three million. Politically there was a massive debate about whether this pain was necessary or not. In the front line of the unemployment benefit service, my role wasn't to consider cause but to help treat effect.

I learned a lot. I saw teenaged single mothers struggling to keep small children on skimpy state benefits. I saw professional middle-aged men, like my father-in-law, rendered hopeless first by redundancy and then by being thought too old for re-employment. I saw petty criminals working as painters and decorators while claiming benefits others needed. And I saw a lot of people who'd struck unlucky and would have given anything to have a job and to be self-supporting again. Meanwhile, the left wing press regarded all our claimants as hopeless victims of Thatcherism, while the right wing press painted them all as scroungers and frauds.

I remember the *Daily Mirror* phoning me up once to ask if they could come and photograph the endless queue of jobless school-leavers signing on for the first time. I told them they were very welcome to take pictures outside my office but that they wouldn't find any queues because we'd already arranged with the local schools a registration system that would avoid anyone being kept waiting. At this point the reporter lost interest.

Perhaps the biggest lesson I learned during my three years in the benefit offices was from my junior colleagues. Working for very low pay in a job with very little kudos and few thanks, housed in a building that was frequently smelly and sometimes infested, their behaviour was often gallant. At the end of the day I used to have to chase some of them to get them to go home. And, for some, their gallantry didn't stop there. Working mothers with children and husbands who didn't reckon to do much round the house, some of the women were effectively doing two full-time jobs at once. And they did them well.

It was in their cheerful company that I learned a little about leadership and a lot about what life was like for a less fortunate part of the population. I caught their practical sense of public service and developed a healthy scepticism for political -isms, which served me well when later in my career I worked closely with our political masters, government ministers.

I wouldn't have left the benefit service had David Lightfoot's cancer not intervened: I enjoyed managing people and had been lucky enough to get my first promotion before I was twenty-five, but Lois needed to be near her parents. I applied for a transfer north. Nothing happened for a long time and then, one day when I was telephoning our personnel people to chase them up for the umpteenth time, my call was misdirected and I found myself talking by mistake to a chap I knew vaguely. He asked why I wanted personnel and I explained I'd applied for a move to Yorkshire.

"But I'm arranging people's moves to the new Manpower Services Commission Head Office in Sheffield," he said. "Why don't you come to us?"

I did. We moved at public expense to Derbyshire, where we spent ten of our happiest years. The first seven involved me working with different sectors of industry and helping to develop a new form of vocational qualifications. After a couple more promotions I spent the last three years managing the organisation's ministerial and parliamentary work and writing a great many speeches. I didn't realise it then but I was actually learning skills that would form the basis of my work for the rest of my career. All I knew then was that it was hard, exhilarating work with a team – my Secretariat – I was proud to be allowed to be a member of, let alone its boss.

We dealt with all the MSC's letters (of which there were scores of thousands per year), all the Parliamentary Questions asked by MPs, and all major briefings and speeches required by our ministers. During three years I wrote for some thirty ministers and (very occasionally) for two prime ministers, Margaret Thatcher and John Major. But the minister I knew best was Michael Howard.

This was Howard's first Cabinet post. Later he became Home Secretary and then, in the long years of opposition that followed 1997, he was Shadow Chancellor and Leader of the Opposition. But this was late 1990 and he was forty-nine. His short career had been meteoric since his election as a Kentish MP in 1983. His bottom had scarcely brushed the back benches before he was first a junior minister, then a minister of state. Now he was our new Secretary of State. As a very successful and wealthy barrister, he had a reputation for a forensic, humourless capacity for analysing and dismantling other people's logic. He was seen as a brain, rather than a heart, and perhaps respected rather than liked. Certainly I have seen him, in relentless, terrier-like, barrister mode, deconstruct some argument, jabbing repeatedly and painfully at the flaw he'd exposed. But, although there was this side to his political persona, like many personae, it turned out to be a bit of an act. Inside, there was a much nicer man than he often seemed prepared to reveal. It was the side of him that he reserved mostly for his family, to whom he was devoted, and to friends and colleagues who were in trouble. Many officials never saw it. I did.

When I'd been writing for Michael for just about a year, I awoke one night in a sweat with a pain in my chest and tingling up one arm. I drew the obvious conclusion but the doctor reassured me it was a panic attack, the consequence of stress. I'd just written *Portrait of a Bomber Pilot*, Lois had mild but prolonged post-natal depression, Vicky wouldn't sleep, a close colleague had been devastated by the sudden suicide of a partner and my mother had been diagnosed with Alzheimer's Disease. There were plenty of reasons for stress. So I asked to see the Secretary of State to explain and to ask to be relieved of the job of speechwriter, which I'd been doing on top of my usual job. Michael's immediate response was to ask what he could do to make my life easier to enable me to continue with him. He then reorganised his diary so we could meet by video-conference to save me travelling to London so often. He never kept me waiting, never broke an appointment and never met me again without first enquiring after Lois and my mother. When, years later, he was elected Leader of the Conservative Party unopposed, I was less surprised than many. Like me, a lot of his colleagues had also glimpsed the real Michael and my impression was that twenty years of personal good will, as distinct from political rivalries, handed him his party's leadership on a plate.

By chance I met him the other day, shortly after he'd resigned as Leader of the Opposition, and I was able to tell him that I thought no party leader in my lifetime had assumed and resigned its leadership with better grace. Of his politics, I say nothing; as a civil servant, my view is irrelevant. Whether he'd have made a good prime minister, who knows? But of one thing I am sure: he was a much better man than he allowed most people to see.

Following a job of that kind is nigh-on impossible. After a brief, rather dull spell in another job in Yorkshire, I fell on my feet, joining the Civil Service College at Sunningdale as a lecturer. A small, dedicated community in beautiful surroundings, the College has allowed me to teach what I learned working for and around ministers. This is my twelfth year and I still love it as much today as I did at the start. The products have been a couple of books, one called *Working with Ministers* the other *Joining the Civil Service*, and thousands of teaching hours helping thousands of very dedicated people (senior and junior) to play a tiny role in a demanding, rewarding and immensely valuable task – the democratic government of a country.

Lois works part-time with the same organisation, teaching civil servants to write clearly, briefly and with precision. Sometimes we work together, which we do very happily indeed. (Curiously, we can teach together without argument. If ever we divorce it will be because we tried to write something together. That always leads to argument because her mind and mine, like her parents' before us, work so very differently.) Next month we're running a course together in one of the state rooms in 10 Downing Street, helping the Prime Minister's Direct Communications Unit. Then, in April and May, we're off to train Department for International Development staff in Delhi. Nearly half the people in the poorest states of India where the Department concentrates its main efforts have an income of less than one American dollar a day. The role of the international development agencies is therefore a matter of life and death. Meanwhile, I'm helping newly appointed ministers here in Britain to get to grips with their new roles more quickly, and working with a team across the Service to turn my two Civil Service books into electronic modules that will be accessible on all the departments' internal websites.

Shortly before he retired as Head of the Home Civil Service and Cabinet Secretary, Sir Richard Wilson button-holed me at a drinks party and said: "I want you to go on doing exactly what you're doing." I hadn't the foggiest what he meant, but in the years since I've always interpreted this message from on high in the broadest possible sense…

Because at the most I've ten working years left, I'm concentrating my efforts on three subjects where I think a difference can be made: how we introduce new entrants, junior and senior, to the Civil Service, how we work with ministers, and how we communicate – with each other, with ministers and with the public. It's a fascinating and rewarding job, never the same one day after another, I have some of the nicest colleagues imaginable and I know I want to stick with it until I retire.

As I read through this letter, I'm sitting in a roomful of students who are occupied on an exercise, writing a complex briefing paper for a minister. We're sitting in a ground-floor room in the Treasury building at the end of Whitehall, opposite the Houses of Parliament. It's just midday and Big Ben has struck twelve. After thirty years in government service, I'm left with no party political beliefs but an abiding faith in democratic, accountable government. I believe that government and Parliament are full of mostly decent people doing their best in increasingly demanding jobs, that cock-ups (of which in three decades not surprisingly I've seen several) are much more common than conspiracies (of which I've seen none), that a few politicians are unattractively ambitious and some civil servants scared of their own shadow, but that most have a thirst for public service and do a difficult job well.

Looking back, I can wholly understand why Pat thought the Civil Service and I wouldn't last, but she was wrong. There's nothing I'd rather do, and no one I'd rather be doing it with: a happy position to be in.

With love,

Christopher

PS   Two abbreviations may fox you in this letter. The ATS were women soldiers, who did everything their male counterparts did except actually fight in battle. The MSC was a non-departmental public body created in 1973 to relieve unemployment and improve the skills of the working population. Staffed by civil servants, it was re-absorbed into central government proper in 1990.

35: My friends pictured within

Odiham

Wednesday, 15th February 2006

Dear G,

Why are we friends with some people but not with others? Shared interests? Similar opinions? Common backgrounds? I don't think so. There are some people who share similar interests and many of my opinions and perhaps come from a similar sort of family, but I don't get on with them at all. There are others, diametrically different from me in every discernible respect, and we get on like sailors on shore leave. My grandparents' generation would have described this as *chemical*. *There's something chemical between them* could mean that two people hated each other with a deadly loathing or that they were head-over-heels in love. It was an interesting take on human emotion, entirely discounting rational choice, but I think it's quite near the mark. We don't choose our friends consciously. We just like them. And we're no more likely to like them because they're like us than because they're different from us. We just enjoy their company and feel happy with them.

Soon after I first met Lois, she went north to spend Easter with her parents and I found myself at a loose end. Another student at the crammers, a lively red-haired lass called Nicky, invited me to her house in Cheam to meet some of her friends. They were very much my sort – spoke nicely, behaved well and had been to local minor public schools. Conversation palled. We just weren't on the same wavelength at all. We all meant well. I tried. They tried. But the only thing we shared was class, which seemed to me then – as it does now – just about the silliest basis one can imagine for forming a friendship. Episodes of this kind still happen from time to time although they surprise me less now than they did. What I don't know is if my outsider's response to the more conventional aspects of being middle class is a genetic echo of Alice or of my peasant Jary antecedents, or if it's simple bloody-mindedness on my part.

At school people thought I was odd because I rubbed along amicably with the ancient Squadron-Leader Bliss, the Science master, and was still friendly with John Andrews, the youngish English master. They hated each other, and I can see exactly why they did. John was undisciplined, scatty, talented, irreverent and humorous, the Squadron-Leader rigid, methodical, serious-minded and conventional. My background, you might think, would have made me more comfortable in Bliss's company, but you'd have thought incorrectly. Although both men had a hidden vulnerability, I detected in John a magnanimity that ultimately I thought the older man lacked. John might have been capable of silliness – who isn't? – but he was not unkind. I was less sure about the Squadron-Leader.

But some of my best friends have been squadron-leaders. Just after I'd finished writing *Portrait of a Bomber Pilot*, I encountered one of them for the first time. His name was Jack Currie and he'd written a number of books about Bomber Command, with whom he'd flown as a Lancaster pilot. On television he'd seemed relaxed, humorous and thoughtful. I wasn't quite sure whether my book was any good, and I needed a dispassionate opinion. I found Squadron-Leader Currie's telephone number and telephoned him at his home in Easingwold. I explained why I was calling him.

"Sure," he said. "I've just finished writing something, so it'll be good to read something by someone else."

His speech patterns were unique. Born in Yorkshire, he'd learned to fly in Georgia, flown with three Australians and finally done a course in speech and drama. The effect of all these influences was a richly resonant baritone which made listening to him a joy.

We became good friends. I don't know why he liked me, but I know why I liked him. A keen golfer and cricketer, Jack came over as cocky, handsome and slightly selfish – none of which were likely to recommend him to me – but I found him thoughtful, sensitive, a talented writer and amusing company. Although he was thirty-five years older than me, he behaved with me as an equal. I remember roaring off from our house in Derbyshire in his Ford Escort Cabriolet to try to find a house he'd lived in as a boy in nearby Grindleford. I remember him teaching my girls to fly on a flight simulator at Elvington and how he forgot to put his undercarriage down before landing.

"Johnny Walker used to do that for me," he replied loftily when I pointed this out. (Johnny was his flight engineer on Lancasters.)

And I remember him inviting us to East Kirkby to meet the legendary Leonard Cheshire, who a year earlier had written the foreword to my book and whom Jack described as "the nearest thing we've got to a saint". And then, quite unexpectedly, the call came from Jack's wife to say he'd died very rapidly but painfully from lung cancer. I wept. He'd never seemed old, always so vital. I hadn't known him more than six or seven years and we probably hadn't met more than ten or twelve times. We spoke on the phone and wrote, and his friendship lit up my life. I gave the address at his funeral with Jim, his navigator, and Johnny, his flight engineer, sitting in the front row. I read a piece from his book, *Lancaster Target*, and reflected on Jack's humour and his capacity for friendship. And I'm jolly glad I did because the idiot vicar who conducted the service had no idea who Jack was, referring to him as "John" throughout. Nine years after his death, things still crop up and I find myself thinking: *I must tell Jack about that*. But he's not here, and I miss him. That conversation will have to wait a while.

And then there are my Uncle Jon's sons, David and Robin. Physically they are Fauxes, slight of build and not very tall. Accuse them, though, of being Fauxes and you'll be in for an unpleasant surprise. To them the word is synonymous with troublesome. They were fond of their father but suspicious of the family as a whole. Reluctant to meet more of the family, they nearly went out the evening Uncle Jon came to meet my parents. I'm very glad they didn't.

Our first meeting, in the early 1960s, began unpromisingly when I emerged from behind a sofa and shot them both. After that, things improved. During my childhood and adolescence they encouraged my interest in history and music and used to take me out occasionally, often with their father. I remember once having lunch at a restaurant in Sussex with Robin and one of his teaching colleagues and their fathers, both veterans of the First World War. Uncle Jon sat one side of the table, Herr Stranz the other, as they worked out if they'd faced each other before – on the Somme in 1918. It was a historic occasion. Something, in fact, to tell one's great-grandchildren about!

Academic by career, training and inclination, David and Robin both went to Cambridge and both spent their lives teaching, first in schools, latterly in higher education. They don't especially like animals, although they tolerate my dogs. Neither shares my interest in things military; in fact, their dreary experience of 1950s compulsory National Service made them both positively anti-military. And yet they're probably my closest friends.

Robin made the speech at my coming-of-age party (when I didn't use Wally's knife to cut the cake); David was best man at my wedding. Lois and I have holidayed with them in France, Belgium and the Netherlands but, most importantly, it was in each other's company that we all discovered Dorset. When, two years ago, Robin retired from Liverpool University, he bought a house in Poundbury, the Prince of Wales's experimental new village near Dorchester. But it all began twenty-five years earlier when the four of us took a cottage in the pump yard at the bottom of the hill in Shaftesbury. Then we tried Bedchester, a couple of miles on near Fontmell Magna, then Sherborne, Kimmeridge and finally Muckleford.

David with coconut, Alex and me

Here on a July evening the cottage door stands open to the kitchen. Inside, Lois, a glass in one hand, is supervising some chips on the old oven while Robin is washing some salad. I'm topping up their glasses with a White Lady from a cocktail shaker. The table's set and a bottle of Harrods claret is open and ready to pour. A cassette-recorder is playing 1930s jazz. Outside, David's singing along, quietly to himself, as he prods some steaks which are smoking on the barbecue. Beside him, a Jack Russell is watching his every move with an almost spiritual concentration. Dinner's nearly ready, which is just as well because these White Ladies are powerful things. Lois swears the barbecue moved across the lawn to trip her up just now. The sun shows no sign of setting and the distant hills shine green and gold in its gentle light. It'd be nice to drive down to Chesil after dinner, but we've all had too much to drink. We'll go tomorrow instead.

A young Vicky and a Christmas Robin

They often come to us at Christmas with other friends who are almost family. Tony, my mother's godson, whose parents were friends of Bill and Dora, lives in Marple now and divides his time between concerts at the Hallé, playing the piano, chess and working as a lay-preacher in his local parish. Like David and Robin, Tony is for me forever in his thirties – which is how I first remember him. Peter often comes too. He was another young tutor at the crammers where Lois and I met. He lives in Streatham and teaches bio-chemistry but is a talented musician. He played the organ at our wedding. And sometimes Steve, my friend from Sheffield, is there with his wife Bev. Bearded, gentle, humorous, utterly unambitious and tolerant to his finger-tips, Steve has been my friend for twenty-three years. I asked him twenty years ago if he and Bev would think about whether they'd be willing to be Alex's legal guardians and take care of her if Lois and I died. I'll not forget his reply: "Yes, we'll think about it. But I can tell you now we'll do it."

And there's Lois's oldest friend – or perhaps she'd prefer to be remembered as Lois's most long-standing friend – Carolyn. In Lois's form throughout their seven years at King Edward's, Birmingham, Carolyn went on to read History at Cambridge while Lois read English at Oxford. Unlike a couple of Lois's Oxford contemporaries, she seemed to have no difficulty extending the friendship to include me when I turned up a few years later. Since then she's managed the same trick with both our daughters, who enjoy her affectionate company and are now both old enough to savour her acerbic observations on life, humanity and herself. Despite being Jewish, Carolyn was the natural choice as Lois's bridesmaid at our wedding, while Alex's middle name commemorates a firm friendship that has lasted more than forty years.

No account, however short, of our lives would be complete without mentioning these friends, who have little in common with us and nothing in common with each other, except companionship, shared happiness and many vivid memories.

With love,

Christopher

36: Fitting in

Odiham

Thursday, 16th February 2006

Dear G,

One of the few attributes I acquired at my various schools that has occasionally been helpful was an ability to look as if I have every right to be somewhere that's strictly out of bounds. One just puts on a slightly busy, pre-occupied face and walks purposefully, but not too quickly, through wherever one isn't meant to be. If one can clutch a small sheaf of papers in one hand, all the better. I did it once quite deliberately during the IRA bombings in London in the late 1970s simply to see how far I could get. I finally reached the very centre of the Royal Courts of Justice in the Strand, having reassured successive police officers and officials by flashing them a glimpse of my public library membership card.

So neatly do I fit some people's stereotype of a safe, establishment figure that I even find myself doing this sort of thing inadvertently. During a debate in the House of Lords, when I was sitting in the officials' box to help our Minister who was leading the debate for the Government, I got lost returning from the lavatory and found myself in a place reserved for their lordships themselves. On the way I'd passed several door-keepers, all of whom had smiled at me and ushered me through. I often feel it was a loss to the guild of confidence tricksters when I became a civil servant.

Foreigners of a more conventional turn of mind love me. I look and sound pretty much as they hope Englishmen will. My appearance seems to reassure them that the world really is as they thought it was while giving them some harmless amusement. Immersed one afternoon up to my waist in the Bay of Naples, I was greeted enthusiastically by a middle-aged gentleman from Milan.

"Excuse me, sir. Has anyone ever told you that you look exactly like Mr Churchill?"

In some environments my face seems to fit, bringing me some light relief and a few minor benefits. In others, with equally little reason, it works against me. People seem to take one look at me, see A, B and C and then deduce all the way to Z. Those who stick around longer than an hour or so, and who are broad-minded enough to do so, usually revise their views, but the initial one is often the same. I can run through the catalogue of adjectives.

Posh – well, if you've read the letters so far, you know that's not true. Southern – as you know, I'm a north-south mongrel who spent twelve of the happiest years of his life living in Derbyshire and Yorkshire. Public school – I was a thoroughly awkward misfit cum reject who has much more cause to dislike public schools than most of the people who take this view. Oxbridge – I didn't go to university at all. Rich – have you seen Civil Service pay scales? I've never had money from any other source. Military – I've had no experience beyond a very short, unsuccessful spell in the Territorial Army when my saluting got progressively more incompetent until finally I knocked my hat off. Conservative – I've long been professionally impartial and personally a political agnostic. It's rather a misleading stereotype, really. Sometimes it makes me laugh; occasionally I tire of it.

You might be forgiven for thinking that, with my background and interest in things military, I would have been a natural fit in the armed forces, but I realise when I'm in the company of serving soldiers, sailors and airmen that, whatever our similarities, I'm cast in a slightly different mould. Their instinct is to respect hierarchies; mine – perhaps a hereditary characteristic, perhaps a response to my school experience – is to challenge them. Although, like them, I value good manners highly, I rate them far below independence of mind and I barely value obedience at all. Ultimately – and this is probably another hangover from school – I'm unwilling to compromise my freedom to make my own decisions pragmatically on issues on their merits. And, unless you're prepared to surrender these things, you'd be wrong to take the Queen's shilling.

At a lunch at the Royal Military Academy Sandhurst I remember discussing with an extremely well-read and free-thinking colonel the news that had just broken that Edward Heath, the ex-Prime Minister, had commanded a firing squad that executed a Polish soldier in 1945. I suggested this was a misuse of soldiers and that, had I been Heath, I would have refused, arguing that I'd enlisted to defend my country, not to be an executioner.

"Then you'd have been court-martialled for refusing to obey a legitimate order," my friend replied sharply.

Does this inability fully to embrace the military ethos stem from what I might regard as moral independence, others as awkwardness or intellectual arrogance? Or does it reflect the experience of the last two generations of my family? It's worth remembering that those of them who surrendered their independence by joining the armed forces did so only temporarily through historical necessity, rather than as a career choice. I remember reflecting years ago during a parade at Winchester that three quarters of the battle honours borne on the regimental colours had not been won by the tailored professionals marching so smartly to the drumbeat, but by ordinary men like Wally and Len, my grandfathers, Uncle Jon, my father, Jim and Doug, and Mr Matthews, our suburban postman.

Although I respect and get on well with a great many service people of all ranks, I'm from a different, though related, species. But I still wanted a career that gave me the satisfaction of serving the public good so, instead of donning some sort of uniform, I joined the Civil Service, where I've worked with people who mostly aren't a bit like me. In the main, it's worked well: they challenge my assumptions; I hope I've occasionally surprised them. We may be different but most of us share a strong desire to serve the public and, although we don't often admit it publicly because it sounds cheesey, to make the country a better place to live in. Even here, given my unwillingness to toe lines, I have long expected some major ruction to end my career in resignation on some decision or point of principle. It's perhaps a measure of the honesty of the environments I've worked in that this hasn't happened, but it may yet.

I sometimes think the pattern was set on that first inauspicious day at school, since when I've never really fitted in anywhere. My schoolmasters often despaired. I looked how they wanted me to look; one pompous old object even congratulated me once on the smartness of my utterly illicit adaptations of our school uniform. I often sounded how they wanted me to sound. But I never seemed, when it mattered, to be what they wanted me to be.

Teenaged rebels who grew long hair and listened to Heavy Metal music conformed to a generational stereotype and announced clearly what they were. Masters were comfortable with that: they could disapprove, secure in the knowledge that, five years on, those same Heavy Metal addicts would be equally committed to training as accountants or surveyors. My version of individualism, which was internalised, was hard to spot and harder to categorise.

Some – like the headmaster who expelled me – thought it subversive. At one school I startled the brick-faced Scripture master, who had just publicly called me a liar, by demanding an apology and adding that, if one were not forthcoming, I'd go to the headmaster. At another I led a deputation to the headmaster to protest at the unfair treatment of a boy who was being punished. I won both rounds but made few friends among the more conventional souls on the teaching staff. There seemed to be two ways to get by at public school. One was to enjoy the fruits of bullying, the other to keep one's head down and carry on regardless. I found I could do neither.

And so it has been throughout my career. Whatever the prevailing wind, I always seem to be walking into it. In my early years I argued strongly that senior civil servants weren't recruited, trained or encouraged to manage or lead. I saw it in the unemployment benefit service, which was virtually unmanaged above the local level, but mine was often an unpopular view in a Service that prided itself on its impartiality, objectivity and intellectual capacity serving ministers. Now everyone in the Service describe themselves as managers I'm seen as old-fashioned for reminding them of the importance of our traditional ethos. When unemployed people were sometimes treated with little consideration or respect, I was seen as starry-eyed in demanding a more humane service for them. Today I find myself viewed with suspicion for questioning the customer ethos which I think debases the accountable reality of our relationship with the people we serve by jamming it into a crude model it doesn't fit. To echo Edith Cavell on patriotism, it seems to me that, in matters of democratic accountability, customer service – however good – is not enough.

I've felt most at home at Sunningdale Park, whose generally tolerant community encourages individualism and where I'm mostly able to be myself. But the only environment in which I've ever felt entirely at home is at home: the one Lois, Alex, Vicky and I have built for ourselves. Everywhere else I don't quite fit.

Ours has been a mobile home: in Derbyshire, Yorkshire and, for the past twelve years, Hampshire. As a family we've put down roots easily and fitted happily into all three villages we've lived in. We've been very lucky with our neighbours here in Hampshire, where Alex's friend Alison and her family, who live next door, have become extended family. But we were lucky, too, in Yorkshire and in Derbyshire, where we quickly felt part of the tiny community which we still miss. One thing we're adamant about: there's no such thing as the north-south divide. The difference is between small communities, where people are usually friendly and behave well, and large ones, where some aren't and a few don't.

Cousin Robin described me recently to one of his friends as a writer *manqué*. I still enjoy writing and for the last few years I've been a regular reviewer for *British Army Review*, the Army's professional journal. On the flimsy credentials of having written *Portrait of a Bomber Pilot*, I was asked to review books about the RAF but I've strayed somehow into the First World War, where Bill's experience sometimes bobs up in my writing. I recently reviewed a new biography of Sassoon, which was a joy, and wrote two pieces about the trench chaplains Theodore Hardy and Geoffrey Studdert-Kennedy, who was known as *Woodbine Willie*. Both men were an inspiration to get to know. Together with the bits and pieces I write at college and for an MA I'm supposed to be working on instead of writing this, this means that the writer is not quite as *manqué* as all that!

Writing, like teaching, seems to suit me temperamentally. I like people and I enjoy communicating. I'm glad to get on with my colleagues and neighbours and hope I'm reasonably sociable. But I'm not a joiner. I belong to no clubs or societies. Once or twice I've tried to join societies concerned with subjects I care about, but it doesn't seem to work. However interested I may be in any subject, I've always found deeply off-putting the single-minded fanaticism of the types who are often the leading lights in these organisations. Once again, I value my independence too much to join anything that may constrain it. So I pursue most of my interests alone. If this is a hereditary characteristic, Alex seems to have inherited it. Like me, she has joined almost nothing and follows her own line. It's not a bad way to be and it's the only sure way to preserve one's independence of action. But it can be hard work and sometimes a bit lonely.

With love,

Christopher

37: More than a disappointment

Odiham

Friday, 17th February 2006

Dear G,

At this point I feel I should admit to having deceived you. I haven't lied as my great-grandfather Kit Faux did when, on his marriage certificate, he gave a false name and described his father as "William Francis, bookseller, deceased". But I've misled you just as deliberately, to the same extent and in much the same way. Until now, my guess is you've imagined my father, like my mother, to have died. He hasn't. Aged 82 this year, he's alive but we don't see him or hear from him, even at Christmas and family birthdays. I've written of him in the past tense simply because it suits me to do so. I'm comfortable with him in the past tense. He was a father to be proud of, as I hope I've described. In the present tense, I regret very deeply that this is no longer the case. In the present tense, I simply don't recognise him as the man I knew.

When people ask after him, I mislead them too. Rather than trying to explain something one can only describe by going into considerable detail, I usually give some vague reply that suggests we're still in touch but that he doesn't get about much these days. Then I change the subject. The explanation Alex invented is simpler: "He's been abducted by an alien." But no one would believe that – even though it's much nearer the truth.

As we approach the last of these letters, perhaps it's time for me to confront the truth. I warned you in my first letter to allow for my subjectivity. In this one you may have to lay off, as they say when shooting a moving target, a bit more still. While they're distant to you, we're dealing here with events that are recent to me, and feelings that remain raw. I expect you love your father. I hope you also respect him. If you're an adult when you read this, perhaps that parental relationship has evolved into a firm friendship. All these things were true of my relationship with my father. To describe dispassionately what destroyed that friendship, love and respect is taxing, but I'll try.

After my father's finest hour, which I think was the patience and care he showed my mother during her final years clouded by Alzheimer's Disease, he moved from the family house. Not surprisingly, he couldn't face living there alone. He told me he'd started seeing my mother around the place, walking up the garden or sitting in her armchair. He moved to our village in Hampshire and bought an elegant ground-floor flat in a recently renovated eighteenth century house in the High Street.

He was good company but, not unreasonably after his recent years, very demanding of our attention. He came to lunch every Sunday, he and I did our weekly shopping together in Alton every Saturday, and we walked our dogs together on Saturdays and Sundays. Most weeks we'd also meet for lunch either at my College or at Sandhurst, where he was a member of the Mess. We spoke on the telephone every day and he came on at least part of every family holiday we had. We went to Tunisia, to Malta and several times to Dorset, where he joined in the life we led in the cottage at Muckleford. Our relationship, always close, became even closer and neither I, nor – much more remarkably because he wasn't her father – Lois, ever resented his demands on our attention. He'd earned it.

Before he'd left Carshalton Beeches, he had got to know a neighbour, with whom he sometimes walked his dogs. She was French, in her fifties, lived with her husband in the next road and her name was Hélène. Gradually it became clear he had bit of a crush on her. He'd rush back from outings while we were in Dorset to get to a telephone so he could call her. At home, he'd spend whole days at her house while her husband was at work. More news began to emerge, bit by bit. Hélène was deeply unhappy. Reg, her husband of sixteen years neglected her. He was reclusive; they had no friends. Would we send them a Christmas card because they didn't receive any others? Hélène wanted to leave Reg but had no money. She wouldn't let him sleep with her. She wasn't married to Reg after all, but had been married to someone else, years before, whose name she still used. She was leaving Reg. She wanted to marry my father. She was staying with Reg while money matters were sorted out – he owed her some money from his business and she wouldn't get it if she left now. She'd decided not to leave Reg after all, but they weren't sleeping together, and she'd offered to sleep with my father. He'd declined. He wanted to marry her.

"I'd marry her tomorrow, old boy, if I could."

I sent Hélène a message via my father inviting her to lunch so we could meet her and gauge what was happening. Our invitation was accepted, then postponed, then declined. Finally, I telephoned her when I knew she would be alone and said we'd like to meet her. She was hostile, guarded and uncommunicative. She didn't want to meet us and wanted me off the phone. Almost immediately afterwards, she secretly arranged for a removal firm to collect her furniture and belongings from Reg's house while he was at work. She then moved in on my father. For a long time, according to my father, she wouldn't answer his telephone in case it was Reg, to whom she hadn't revealed where she had gone.

"But Hélène doesn't want your relationship with me to change, old boy."

And then it changed. Our weekly shopping trips to Alton ceased, his once daily phone calls ended, he was never free to walk the dogs with me, we never lunched together and my children were made to feel unwelcome in his flat. The wedding he'd planned and begun to arrange was cancelled with different explanations given to different people. His bugle played a new tune, quite different from the one we all knew.

"I don't want to degenerate into a *pater familias*."

"It is not for the grandfather to wait upon the grandchild. It is for the grandchild to wait upon the grandfather."

"The boy Blair can't be trusted. President Chirac's got it just about right."

"Peggy was very possessive. Hélène's much easier to live with."

From a second husband whose wife had resolutely refused to make such comparisons between her partners, instead insisting that she'd "married the same type twice", this last remark – which he made several times to several people – seemed to me the ultimate disloyalty.

In March 2000 Alex celebrated her eighteenth birthday. A few days before the birthday Lois and I called in to see him and he tried to give me his present to bring home with me.

"But you'll want to wrap it up," I said.

"She won't care about that," he replied.

"She will, you know." I grinned. "She still likes to have parcels she can open."

"Don't be ridiculous," Hélène interrupted. "She is eighteen, not eight."

As the years passed she became increasingly aggressive in expressing her opinions, which somehow always seemed to contradict mine on small things as well as large. When I suggested that Paris was a big city, she insisted it wasn't. And when, during some now-forgotten political scandal, I made some remark over lunch to my cousin Robin that all the ministers I'd worked with had seemed to me honest, she launched into a voluble tirade about the cynicism and dishonesty of all politicians and the untrustworthiness of humanity generally. Some sort of game seemed to be being played.

Sydney and Hélène lived together in Odiham for six years. During that time we invited them to lunch with us fifty or so times; we lunched there twice. When they visited us, we found her behaviour to us all increasingly offensive. Finally, we ceased to entertain them. Hélène had expressed her unfounded opinions too stridently once too often, and my father had described Lois's Sunday lunch, cooked entirely for his benefit as my mother would have cooked it, as "stodge". Individually these were little more than the thoughtless ups and downs of most family relationships. Cumulatively, however, we were in little doubt about what was happening. Above all, we remembered how much we'd enjoyed his company before Hélène and found it too upsetting to see what he had become in her company.

I'd also caught my father out in a number of pieces of what once would have been utterly uncharacteristic deceit. Meanwhile, he himself had begun to mistrust previously trusted friends and neighbours, who they now insisted were spying on them. His relationships with others close to him, like his relationship with me, were being corroded. During Alex's three years at Oxford he never visited her and telephoned her only once. His behaviour had been transformed and, to those of us who remembered him as he was, he was unrecognisable.

He asked to see me one day and said he was thinking of moving – either into the country or to France. With some of the money Reg had paid her, Hélène had bought a small house thirty miles north of Toulouse, and they might move there. I asked him to reconsider and we talked long and hard about the practicality of an eighty-year-old who spoke no French moving to a hamlet of four houses in the depths of the southern French countryside. He promised to think again and not to do anything without telling us. And then, a few months later, we saw his flat offered for sale in the window of the local estate agents. When I confronted them about this, he said: "I told them not to put it in the window."

He was incapable of grasping that my concern was his deceit, not the fact that that deceit had been unsuccessful. After a long, emotional scene, Lois and I finally managed to persuade them not to move to France. Instead, they promised to buy a flat in Winchester. Six months later, collecting my dog home from kennels, I heard by chance that Hélène's dog was staying there awaiting passage to Toulouse. They'd sworn the kennel-owner to secrecy but he imagined I knew that they'd moved to France two days before. He'd known my father and me in the old days and hadn't realised that the pledge of secrecy they'd extracted from him extended to me. In fact, I was its sole purpose.

And so my father went and I haven't seen him since. Nor do we hear from him. Shortly after he left, it emerged that he had married Hélène secretly at a registry office several months earlier. He will be eighty-two this summer, but for me he died on 28th May 1998, when Hélène moved in on him. His legacy to us? Until 1998, it's a proud one of honesty, courage, humour, decency, fortitude and love. And then, for me at least, there was a period of enormous worry, futile but exhausting efforts to maintain our relationship, sadness and disappointment. But now, having thought as analytically and objectively as I could about it all, I feel differently.

My father was and is the product of his birth and of what happened to him. He was born the son of a casualty of the First World War. His boyhood was spent desperately trying to make up to his mother for the loss of her two brothers and for the all-too-obvious inadequacy of her husband. His marriage – and, remember, thanks to Hitler he had no independent existence between boyhood and marriage – was spent making up to my mother for the neglect of her childhood and the loss of Jack. He had no sisters, no girlfriends and no other experience of the female sex. For him, women were an entirely different, slightly unreasonable, almost alien, species which had to be placated, flattered and pleased. With my mother, who was fundamentally warm, generous and human, this didn't matter. With Hélène, it did.

Finally, a few months after his flight to France, it dawned on me that this whole, tragic experience had fundamentally changed my view of life and of myself. I've no experience of bringing up boys but I'm told they benefit from the presence of a strong male role model. Growing up with two admirable ones – my father and Jack – it had never occurred to me that I could ever measure up to what they were and what they had done. Now, in my late forties, reviewing our lives dispassionately, I realised I'd been wrong. They were admirable role models – their memories still are – but, after eight sad years' reflection, I realised I'm at least as good a husband as my father was, a better father, a more reliable colleague, a more loyal friend and in time I hope to be a better grandfather. In some ways it has been a liberating experience. I'm just rather sad that it took this amount of unhappiness, and nearly fifty years, for me to grasp it.

With love,

Christopher

38: Waiting for women

Odiham

Saturday, 18th February 2006

Dear G,

I've long threatened Lois, Alex and Vicky that, if ever I write an autobiography, I'll call it *Waiting for Women* because that's what I spend most of my life doing. As a father of two daughters, it's probably inevitable; but you have to remember that, before becoming a father of two daughters, I was a brother of two sisters. So I've decades of experience waiting for six assorted women, including my wife and mother, to get ready for this or that. The relationship between the sexes and the complexities of female attire have both changed markedly during my lifetime. It's possible that, by the time you read this, women will take no longer to get dressed than men do, but, although intellectually I can produce this thought, I find it an implausible one. There is, though, a still more frightening possibility: that by the time you read this, men will take longer getting ready than women. Alex has already detected among some young men a fastidiousness of dress which she finds unappealing.

"Never go out with a man who spends longer in front of the mirror than you do," she advised Vicky the other day.

I can see Alex's point. Perhaps it's Darwinism that prevents sensible women from finding attractive the sort of men who are more interested in their own appearance than women's. To celebrate her twenty-first birthday we spent our summer holiday at the Hotel Tramontano in Sorrento, where the narcissism of so many young Neapolitan males, whether in sharp suit or swimming trunks, preening themselves as they strutted purposelessly about, was unedifying. It was a good holiday, though. With both girls and Alex's closest friend, Alison, we did all the usual tourist things: climbed the steep hill up to Vesuvius, drank iced coffee on commercialised Capri, walked around the remains of Pompeii, and stood on the open plain below Salerno to admire the classical symmetry of Paestum. Lois and I left the three girls for one day and drove up to Monte Cassino to visit the rebuilt monastery crowning the hill that cost so many lives in 1944. And after dinner we all sat on the balcony and watched a dramatic electric storm rolling its way round the Bay of Naples below us. Memorable moments.

But we prefer Venice, which Lois and I fell for when we stayed there for our silver wedding anniversary in 2002. I remember sitting on our first evening in St Mark's Square, sipping a glass of white wine as the sun subsided on our left. Behind us in the café a string quartet played. In front was the backdrop Canaletto painted. But in this one all the tiny figures were moving about. We'd stepped into one of his paintings and, in that moment, I remember thinking this was the most beautiful city I'd ever seen. When you finally see most places you've heard about, they're not quite as you imagined them. The photographs in the brochure didn't show that gasworks over there. Fancy building a MacDonald's right opposite like that. But Venice is different. It exceeded my expectations by a very long way, and it always does.

Four years on, we've been back twice. We stay in a small hotel that overlooks the waterbus stop on the Lido. From our rooms you can look across the grey-green lagoon to St Mark's. And the four of us go over and lose ourselves in the tangled streets around the Grand Canal. We stop for lunch and watch people as they stroll, talk, eat or float by. It's a good place just to sit in and look around because everything there seems to be part of that same aqua-tinted painting I found myself sitting in on our first evening.

Proust had a point. Just as the pondy whiff of a drain can transport me to the Grand Canal and the smell of that college kitchen near Waterloo dragged me reluctantly back to school, so the smell of sun-cream takes me straight back to Ramla Bay on the north coast of the tiny island of Gozo.

Here on the amber sand surrounded even in summer by green fields – for Gozo is more fertile than its sister-island Malta – we look out at a blue sea or up at the cliffs where Calypso captivated Ulysses on his voyage home. We return every couple of years and stay in a hotel above the tiny port of Mgarr. Our rooms, next to each other with adjoining balconies like the stage set from Act One of *Private Lives*, look across to the island of Comino and the yellow rocks of Marfa Ridge on Malta. On Marfa, when they were much younger, Alex and Vicky found and dismantled the wire traps some hunters had left there. Even on the Maltese archipelago, where there are relatively few animals, they seize any opportunity to play with one, whether it's a chameleon which they've found and put on their shoulders, or a passing dog which, in the enforced absence of Harris in kennels, they've decided to adopt for the duration of the holiday.

Once or twice a year we return to Derbyshire, where we stay in a pub near Chatsworth and take the landlord's labradors with us on long walks. In the evenings the two daft dogs, one black and one chocolate, sprawl on the girls' bed, share biscuits and watch television together. And we still go to Dorset, where we often stay in Robin's house near Dorchester, and revisit familiar places from their childhood holidays.

It's always difficult knowing what to do with a holiday. Do you go back to somewhere you know you like or do you try new places and risk finding yourself somewhere you don't? We try to do both, but it's difficult because time is limited. Do we go to Venice this Easter, as we have the past couple of years, or back to Derbyshire? We can't do both. The girls chose Derbyshire. They always will: Venice has no labradors. Do we go back to Gozo this summer or walking in the Lake District? This is a more difficult one because there are no particular dogs to sway the decision. At Gozo we have warmth and friends and an excellent hotel, but limited things to do apart from swim and potter about. At Lyzzick Hall, below Skiddaw, we have magnificent country, friends and an excellent hotel, but unreliable weather. We chose Lyzzick and it's something all of us are looking forward to.

And in August Lois and I are staying in Ypres for a few days. We hope to find the field at Givenchy where Wally was killed, the crossroads near Bullecourt where Len died, and one or two places where Bill and Vernon fought. The last time I was there I knew nothing about what had happened to either of my uncles. It will be good to go and, knowing what happened, see these places and the two memorials with Len's and Wally's names among so many. But we're resolved that the First World War won't dominate the trip: our afternoons will be spent doing something entirely different, and evenings will find us in one of the open air restaurants in the Grote Markt, beside the rebuilt Cloth Hall.

We've always had good holidays but, now money's a bit less tight, we have a wider choice. We're making hay while the sun shines, not only financially but also as a family. Alex will be twenty-four in a couple of weeks. She won't be with us many more years. When she went away to Oxford, I thought she wouldn't come back for long. Then she took two years off, travelled with Alison round Europe and is back with us for the moment. Vicky's already had one holiday without us and has booked another this year. The days of family holidays are drawing to a close. We'll all miss them. We enjoy each others' company. We like doing the same sorts of things: pottering in attractive country, interfering with wildlife, and then having a relaxed lunch or dinner and a long chat about what we've seen. There'll be other things we'll do together. Lois and I, in any case, enjoy doing things as a couple. But for the moment we're making the most of the time we have together as a family. Like their childhood in Derbyshire and those distant holidays in the cottage in Dorset, this time won't come again.

If you're passing, why not pop in and meet us all? Alex is out with some friends but Lois and Vicky are there. If you're on the M3, we're within five minutes of Junction 5 at Hook. Come off here and head towards Farnham, through North Warnborough, past the Swan pub on your right and then over the bridge across the Basingstoke Canal. The canal was built in the closing years of the eighteenth century, but the railways followed too soon to allow it to make any money. Today, it provides us with a couple of very nice walks with kingfishers, herons and occasional deer.

The road from North Warnborough will take you into Odiham High Street. Long and broad, it was a coaching stop like the one in that carving in my grandparents' hall. Although the houses mostly look Georgian – about the same age as the canal – some are much older. Behind those facades several are fifteenth century. The George pub on the left there is one of the oldest. It has wattle-and-daub walls inside. Because this is quite a wealthy area, we suffer from far too many estate agents and antique or gift shops, and we lack useful shops like grocers and bakers. Most of us do our shopping at supermarkets now and our local shops have suffered, but we still have an old-fashioned butcher's shop, run by Winston in his white apron and cap. As his name suggests, Winston's in his mid-sixties. My cousin Robin has long argued that the human race falls into two distinct types: radiators, whom one always feels better for meeting, and drains, who have the opposite effect. Winston is one of life's radiators. Like many of the older people brought up here, he has a soft Hampshire accent – like my great-grandmother Alice had. The generations that followed have lost that: although we're forty miles from London, they favour a cockney twang instead. I'm not at all sure this is an advance.

Our close is just down here on the right. The houses are all much the same and not very attractive. They're four- or five-bedroomed modern ones with small front lawns and a garage beside them. Ours has a clematis climbing up the front to try to relieve the otherwise unbroken expanse of brick. Park in the drive. In the garage is my pride and joy: a green two-litre Fiat Coupé with tan leather seats and an electric sunroof. It's seven years old now and I bought it four years ago for half its original price. It had belonged to a merchant banker or a stock broker, or someone of that sort, who had driven three thousand miles in his three years. I suppose he was too busy working to enjoy it. Since then, I've more than made up for the time he lost. Designed by Pininfarina, who design Ferraris, it's strikingly, curvaceously beautiful as well as being enormous fun to drive. I call it my mid-life crisis car.

But here's Lois at the front door. In her arms she's holding Monty's successor, Harris, who's doing his usual stunt of barking to let all our neighbours know you've arrived.

Predominantly black and tan, he has a white chest, four white socks and, because we don't dock dogs' tails any more, a long tail like a cat's. Compared to his illustrious predecessor, he's thin, has longer legs and is less sure of himself. When he joined us as a pup, he spent his first night in Alex's bed, draped across her neck in case she got up and left him. He still hates being left on his own, and long and loud is the rejoicing when one of us returns to end his lonely vigil. Life without dogs would be unimaginably sad – as we discovered when Monty died in the days before little Harris came to fill the enormous void in our family.

While Monty was a keen petrologist who constructed a rockery in our garden with the stones he collected one-by-one on walks, Harris's abiding interest is in tennis balls. Although we've never given him a tennis ball, he has assembled a collection of at least two hundred. He's an advanced case of collector's mania. To him each tennis ball has its own unique magic and, having decided which one he wants to play with today, he won't rest until he finds it from among all the others. This remains his *bal du jour* until the next day, when another is carefully selected. He's an exceptional catch and would have made an excellent slip fielder. Here. Take a tennis ball and throw it for him. He'll stop barking then and decide he likes you.

Step through the narrow hall, past the small study on the left (where I'm writing this) and take that door on the right into our sitting room. Vicky is in here working. Her exams are in May.

A seventeen-year-old girl with long blonde hair and a look of concentration on her face perches cross-legged on the sofa, surrounded by piles of open and closed history books. She looks up, smiles and waves. She can't hear us because she's got her earphones on and is listening to music on her Ipod. On her right is Grandpa Fletcher's writing desk and the blue plate recording Elizabeth Fletcher's birth on 3rd December 1738. This makes Aunt Elizabeth exactly two hundred and fifty years and ten days older than my Vicky. Over the fireplace hangs the watercolour of Abbeville that Bill bought Alice.

Through some glass doors is the dining room with a large window into our small back garden, which has too many trees. One of them's a large eucalyptus, which lends an antipodean air to our small piece of Hampshire. But Alex and Vicky would much prefer to have the koala itself than just this small bit of its habitat. I won't show you upstairs, which – especially Vicky's room – is probably a bit of a mess. In any case, it's pretty standard stuff: three good-sized bedrooms, a tiny spare room, a shower room and a bathroom. You glance up the steep staircase and glimpse a photograph taken from a hill overlooking Froggatt Edge in Derbyshire. It was our favourite walk and, for our silver wedding, my friend Steve drove out there, walked it and took a picture for us to keep. He's a gifted photographer. On the hall wall here, next to that watercolour of Gozo, is one of an Orkney beach he took after he and Bev moved up there.

What we could do, if you've a couple of hours to spare, is take Harris up the canal. He needs a walk. Lois has just gone to get her boots so if we just wait in the front garden – I told you I spend a lot of my life waiting for them, didn't I? But even Lois shouldn't take too long just putting her boots on and grabbing a coat…

If we turn right at Colt Hill bridge, you can walk for miles along the canal. If you like, we can go up through the woods to where the litter of fox cubs were last spring. We saw them one afternoon by chance and, after that, spent a lot of time watching them playing, just across the canal, around some fallen logs among the bluebells. It was a good place for the vixen to raise her litter, miles from any roads. One evening we saw her come back from hunting and bring them a rabbit. Here's Lois. Shall we go?

We've never had much money but, since Alex was born, we've always managed to live in beautiful places. Ten years in the Peaks, which I've told you all about. Two living in Yorkshire beside the River Wharfe, where Monty and Sandy had most of their walks. Here Sandy finally died at the ripe old age of fifteen. I took a day's leave and we spent it at Whitby, remembering him, talking about him and breathing the salt air. And now we're just clocking up twelve years here in Hampshire. Like the tracer my Bomber Command friends told me about when I was writing about Jack, the years seem to approach lazily at first before suddenly accelerating past you. I'm still only middle-aged and I've a sneaking feeling they'll speed up a great deal more before we're done.

I suppose our greatest regret, Lois's and mine, is that we didn't have more children. We would have done but for a succession of slipped discs shortly after Alex's birth that, as well as causing Lois a great deal of pain, made another pregnancy risky. After seven years we took the risk and the result was Vicky, but by then it felt a bit late to have any more. My ideal would have been to have had four children, but we're very happy with the two God sent us. Despite keeping me waiting a lot, they have countless compensating advantages.

With love,

Christopher

39: Valletta revisited

Odiham

Sunday, 19th February 2006

Dear G,

Have you places you often go back to? They're not necessarily the most beautiful or luxurious places you've been, but they have something that makes you want to go back there. I have several. One's West Bay. Far from the most attractive of the south coast towns, it sits in the centre of Dorset's most stunning stretch of coastline and holds magical memories of my daughters' childhoods. Another is Malta, yellow, rocky, savagely hot and sometimes ugly. I first went there when I was thirteen, returned countless times during my teens, learned to drive on the runway of the disused airfield at Taqali and spent my honeymoon there. It feels like home and we've been back every few years since. More recently, as you know, we've stayed on its less developed neighbour, Gozo, instead, but I always visit Valletta, which is one of my favourite cities and holds so many memories of different stages of my life.

When Lois and I went back in the late 1990s, the hotel seemed unchanged from when my mother and I had found it one dazzling August morning in the early seventies. It stood in an impressive square at the top of Valletta, across the road from the Prime Minister's Office.

On its left, the tiny Upper Barracca Gardens, with their countless Victorian plaques, busts and naval monuments, offered a shady respite from the burning sun and a magnificent view across the blue expanse of Grand Harbour to yellow Fort St Angelo and the three cities on the other side. Cospicua, Senglea and Vittoriosa were all much older than sixteenth century Valletta.

While La Vallette built his new city, conceived after the first siege of 1565, on rococo lines and proportions, over the water the three cities grew up higgledy-piggledy over centuries. Cospicua, my father said, had been the most heavily bombed place on earth when the Italian and German bombers tried to bomb the island into starvation and surrender.

My father left us by the gardens, agreeing to meet us back there in a couple of hours, and headed off to the meeting with his printers. After a stroll round several blocks of Valletta's grid-patterned and almost vertical streets, my mother and I found ourselves back in that same square.

The Castile Hotel looked an attractive place to get a long midday drink on a blazing hot day. In its marble-floored lobby a discreet receptionist directed us, via a tiny lift, to an equally small bar almost up on the roof. Here we were greeted by John Pace (pronounced *Parchay*). Tubby, bald and hospitable and exuding kindly concern for my mother, who was feeling the heat a bit, he greeted us, settled her in a leather chair and retreated behind his bar to prepare our drinks. His bottles and his bar shone like the silver tray on which he served our drinks which was covered with starched, white linen that dazzled like his mess jacket. That drink and John's hospitality revived my mother. We heard how he had spent half a career in the Royal Navy as a steward, serving in the Atlantic and off Norway during the German invasion, and how he had ended up as the American ambassador's butler, and, in that half hour, we formed the basis of a lasting friendship.

John was a professional to his fingertips. And his sense of professionalism, supported by his Christian faith and his war experience, provided firm evidence, if he ever needed it, that he was just as good as anyone else. Thus, when the wife of a middle-aged English couple off one of the yachts in Sliema harbour came into John's bar and announced in gin-saturated tones: "Oh, look, Peter. It's that little barman we met last year", John was unmoved. He knew his own value and he also knew theirs – even though their son might have been at Winchester.

Later, we met my father in the Upper Barracca Gardens and returned for lunch in the Castile's restaurant overlooking Grand Harbour. The headwaiter in the restaurant wore a black tailcoat and striped trousers; all his waiters wore white mess jackets with silver buttons. The young waiter who looked after us looked anything but Maltese. He was blond, blue-eyed, strikingly handsome and aged about nineteen. He was too shy to get to know on this first lunch, but later it emerged that his name was Louis (which the Maltese pronounce Lewis) Old, and his father was English. Like me, Louis was a product of the war. His father had been born in Briantspuddle, near Dorchester. Nazi Germany's invasion of Poland uprooted him from his picturebook village, recruited him to the Dorset Regiment and sent him a thousand miles away to defend a yellow lump of sandstone in the central Mediterranean which was being bombed to oblivion by Mussolini's Regia Aeronautica and Hitler's Luftwaffe. At the end of the war he married Louis's mother and settled there.

From then on, all our future visits to Malta were spent at the Castile. During the mid-1970s, we returned often to Malta, where my father was having a series of books printed. On each trip we saw John Pace who, after he had retired, would walk up the steep, straight streets from his house down near Fort St Elmo to meet us for a drink and a chat. He still spent long hours in the Upper Barracca Gardens, watching the ships in the harbour, and was devastated when the tiff between our two governments resulted in the Royal Navy's withdrawal from Malta. He told us how he stood, part of a pressing crowd, by the rails of the Gardens, to watch our very last ship leave. Many wept. It was, as the press reminded us at the time, the end of an era but, while that trite phrase conveniently captured one eminently forgettable episode in the reporter's existence, the particular era whose end he was describing had constituted the greater part of John's life. He couldn't understand how two nations, bound by history and mutual regard, could allow their politicians to destroy a unique relationship that had been forged in defence of democracy in the flames of his blitzed island. Nor – even now – can I.

The last time I saw John was by accident on my honeymoon. Walking past the Cathedral in Valletta, Lois and I bumped into him going in for mass. He gave me his slightly shy, warm grin and extended an aging hand as I introduced him to my new wife. Our next Christmas card prompted a response from his son to say that John had died peacefully a while before.

And now, returning with Lois and the girls twenty-five years after that first visit with my mother, it was good to find so little changed. Externally and internally, the hotel was much as I remembered it. The receptionist looked familiar. The restaurant could accommodate us for lunch and the head waiter was – Louis! His hair was greying, his waist, like my own, a bit fuller, but it was him all right, and he remembered me. We shook hands for a long time and exchanged news. His father had died; so had my mother. He had married that elegant young woman who sometimes worked on reception. He had become a very devout Christian and was saving for a pilgrimage, with friends from his parish, to Israel. He and his wife had no children but a smile lit his face when I introduced my daughters.

After lunch Lois and the girls took the tiny lift while I walked down the stairs from the rooftop restaurant. On the floor below, the stained wooden door hung open, revealing what had been John's bar. The bar, like John himself, had gone, its immaculate rows of shining bottles and John's smiling hospitality survived now only in my memory. Here he'd taught me how to mix a brandy Alexander, but today his bar was a store-room with a few pieces of forgotten furniture piled untidily on its bare floor.

As I walked down the wooden staircase each floor was revealed to be much the same as the last: faded rugs on the marble floor, whitewashed walls contrasting with the dark wood of the furniture and bedroom doors around the landing. One door was open and, broom in hand, an elderly maid was just emerging. The half-familiar features of her face jogged a memory that was just out of reach. I smiled at her. She smiled back, looked away and then glanced at me again. Had my features sounded a similar echo in her memory?

Perhaps it was this wordless encounter with the maid that did it. As I turned back to the staircase, I felt a curious conviction that on the next landing I might well bump into my seventeen-year-old self coming up. Bump would be the word. He'd be racing up the stairs, white Gozitan pullover tied round his neck, on his way to his room to have a quick shower before meeting his parents in the bar. Some Maltese friends were coming to dinner that night and they might be here in half an hour.

His small, white-washed bedroom held only a dark wardrobe and chest of drawers. On the bedside table lay Jon Stallworthy's new biography of Wilfred Owen which he'd bought just before coming away. Studying Owen for 'A' Level, he could feel suitably virtuous while still reading something he'd have chosen to read anyway. The war poets somehow opened a path into poetry that was acceptable for a seventeen-year-old boy. At the same time, Elgar was opening new musical vistas; he was getting to know a new work almost weekly. The latest discovery was the substantial *Dream of Gerontius*, and a very poor but enthusiastic rendering of the priest's stirring *Profiscicere anima Christiana* probably accompanied a hasty shower. A rapid glance in the mirror, a quick comb through the hair and off, up the stairs to the bar.

It was as though that teenaged self with his energetic, unchannelled enthusiasms was materialising beside me on the stairs. What would he have made of his burlier, balder middle-aged self with his straw hat clutched in one hand?

He would, I think, have been agreeably surprised to hear that a wife and two blonde daughters were waiting for him even now in the hotel lobby. Given the urgency of his present enthusiasms, he would not have been surprised to find that his joy in Owen, Sassoon and Elgar survived, although Sassoon has supplanted Owen as favourite. He'd have marvelled at the tiny electronic MP3 player I use on the balcony in Gozo to listen to, not Elgar – this isn't his landscape – but Mozart, Schubert, Ravel and Delius, while watching the white ferries and tiny, painted fishing boats chugging in and out of the little port of Mgarr below. He'd have grinned at my thickening waist and receding hair, and laughed aloud at the notion that he should have become, of all things, a lecturer. But, hearing that this was my first return to Valletta since our mother's death from Alzheimer's, he would have looked thoughtful.

With love,

Christopher

40: The view from here

Odiham

Monday, 20th February 2006

Dear G,

Sitting down to write the last of these letters, I've just realised that I wrote the first on the 140th anniversary of Kit's birth on 12th January 1866. Reconstructing his story and Alice's in these letters revived them in my imagination: Kit's no longer just the owner of that lock of sandy hair in my drawer and the writer of that rather ponderous note on his grandfather's letter. But they remain distant acquaintances. Others, closer to me, seemed to materialise beside me as I tried to recreate their speech and appearance in print.

Uncle Jon stands in my parents' hall at the end of a companionable evening. He dons his tweed cap back to front, grins at me and says: "Bleriot." Auntie Gladys's hand pats my forearm as she sits on the arm of my chair and asks me what I've been doing since she last saw me. Jack, in tennis whites, a cricket pullover tied round his shoulders, stands at my elbow as I write about that evening at the Beeches Tennis Club. This is less of a surprise because I got used to his company seventeen years ago while I was writing *Portrait of a Bomber Pilot*, when I even found myself dreaming of bomber operations. And, perhaps the biggest surprise of all, Bill – Grandpa Faux – whose trench irony rings down the years as he enquires in that familiar voice of his: "Writing the story of your life, are you, Horace?"

I wasn't expecting him to return so vividly. I'm glad he did. I'm glad they all did. They're welcome ghosts.

And the experience has had another completely unexpected effect that just concerns me. Ever since my late teens I'd never been able to feel any connection with the young boy – me – I could see in old photographs. It was like looking at a picture of someone else: someone I didn't know. It was as though the present me had been so disfigured by unhappiness at school that I could see no similarities between that boy and my older self. Between his carefree life and mine was a jagged chasm which I'd crossed and he hadn't, across which we couldn't communicate. And then, as I wrote that very first letter to you, he quietly appeared beside me with a toy rifle and Nobby at his side. I could hear his voice, and he was saying things that reminded me of my mother and of Alex and Vicky, and of me. For the first time in thirty-five years I could see the link between us, recognise bits of myself in him and see how he became the me who's writing this. And one more thing: I found I rather liked him.

Alex found the riddle from which I chose the title for these letters – *the chance that made me* – in one of her books of Anglo-Saxon. It struck me at once as capturing a fundamental point about the whole story: that, if one day any one of these ancestors of ours had turned right instead of left and not met the person they married, not only would I not be writing this, but you wouldn't be reading it either. If Bill hadn't encouraged Peggy to move that wardrobe, if she hadn't miscarried my older brother, I wouldn't have been born. Look back a generation and, if a German paratrooper on a railway crossing near Cleves had been a better shot, or a Luftwaffe night-fighter pilot over Tellingstedt a worse one, I wouldn't be here. Back another generation: if Bill's experience on the Somme had mirrored Wally's at Givenchy or Len's at Bullecourt, I wouldn't be here. If Bill's father, Kit, hadn't fallen for the maid, Alice, at Fairmead…

You and I, like everyone else, are the product of an almost infinite number of events, a few of them dramatic, most utterly unremarkable, that might just as easily not have happened or have happened differently. One tiny difference in the seemingly endless chain of haphazard links and we'd not be here. A statistician reading this might calculate some telling probability figures. Arithmetically, it's impossible to contemplate, and our brains reject it. Self-importance rejects it too, while common sense and pragmatic self-preservation urge us to ignore the frightening possibility that we're simply the chaotic result of millions of random chances. Faith offers a simpler, better ordered, more explicable alternative. It's the one I choose – not only for this reason, but for others too. It seems to me that, despite all the suffering, ugliness and injustice, there is too much evidence of altruism, beauty and love for an atheist explanation of life to be plausible. But I realise that, so far, I've been very fortunate indeed: one of life's winners. Perhaps its losers feel differently.

Certainly, measured by Wally's, Len's or Jack's standards, I'm a very lucky man. I wrote Jack's biography when Vicky was born and I was in my early thirties. Conscious that he had had one daughter and died aged twenty-eight, I felt I'd just passed two milestones he'd not been allowed to reach. Seventeen years on, I remain conscious of that privilege and of another that lies ahead: that, all being well, I shall be allowed to watch my children grow to adulthood, to know my grandchildren – your parents – and to die in my bed. I've been conscious too that mine was the first generation since the nineteenth century to be free to choose a career straight from school and who weren't required to fight, kill and face death. No one asked me, as they asked Len and Wally, to live, sleep and die in a muddy trench or, as they demanded of Jack until the statistical odds against survival finally caught up with him, to drop tons of high explosive over a blazing German city spitting flak into a black sky. Measured against that, professional ambition or material wealth have long seemed trivial. I'm safe, comfortable, have enough to feed, house and clothe my family, and I face the prospect of living out my natural span.

I've tried to introduce you to some of the winners and losers in this, our story. Sometimes I've been uncertain who are which. Wally and Len, killed in their early twenties, from my perspective seem to have had a raw deal but, from where I stand now, I can't see much beyond the fact and manner of their deaths. There would have been so much more to tell you about them, had I known them, had they survived. Their sister, Winnie, I did know. She was allowed to reach her late eighties, but I think perhaps she had an even rawer deal than her brothers had. I sense that perhaps Bill also thought of himself as a loser, which makes me, his only grandson and someone who remembers him vividly, sad. Was Dora a winner? She seemed mostly to get her own way and died in her sleep aged eighty. Sid similarly seemed to get what he wanted by putting his own interests first. But neither seemed to me any happier as a consequence.

What about Jack? Although he had a few more years and a bit more of a life than Len and Wally, from where I stand he still seems to have missed out on a great deal. And yet, when I was writing *Portrait of a Bomber Pilot* and met his friends from forty and fifty years earlier, they spoke of him with considerable and immediate warmth and amusement. To them he was not simply a remembered face from the past. "If I can help, then Jack knows I'll do my best," said Ray, the Battle of Britain pilot. "We owe it to Shorty to get this right," said Ian, the elderly Air Vice-Marshal. "I'm glad you've written a book about my Jack," wrote Auntie Mamie, "I love him." Like Cordelia's in *Brideshead Revisited*, their love knew no past tense. I find it impossible to classify anyone remembered so vividly and affectionately so long after his death as one of life's losers.

After my mother's death, when my father couldn't face sorting through her things, we bundled them all up and brought them home. Among them we found an exercise book, beginning: "I have just returned from my son's wedding…" and describing her feelings. She wasn't happy. All three of her children had left home and her relationship with her daughters was not what it should have been. Her relationship with her parents had been wrong from the start. But she had been lucky in love. "I married the same type twice."

Right at the end, when Alzheimer's Disease finally exerted its full icy grip on her mind, and her soul no longer seemed to be in the deflated sprawl of wrinkled skin and protruding bones that lay in her nursing home bed, I was never quite sure if she had the remotest idea who I was. But she seemed to sense that I was someone she loved, and her love shone through the chill fog that surrounded her institutionalised existence. With my father, however, something approaching a miracle occurred. Shortly before she died, suddenly summoning long-lost lucidity from somewhere, she seized and kissed him and said – she hadn't spoken for weeks – "I do love you, you know." It was an appropriate end to their marriage and, having patiently nursed her through most of the Alzheimer's, he deserved no less.

I was holding my mother's hand when she died in the nursing home on 30th January 1995. She had made no sound and hadn't moved a muscle for hours. We sat for a long time until, quite suddenly, something changed. I don't know what it was. It was as if for a couple of hours I'd been watching a film of someone not moving and then, in an instant, sensed that it was no longer a film I was staring at, but a still photograph that would never move again. Physically, visually the change was imperceptible; spiritually, intuitively it was immense. The physicality of death was a tiny, unremarkable step; the departure of the soul was a transformation. I found the experience more reassuring than upsetting.

My father himself I find most difficult to assess in these terms. It's like trying to fix the bubble in a spirit level. His boyhood and schooldays seemed to label him, as that school photograph did, a loser, while his army life and marriage to my mother were the opposite. His life in publishing and most of his relationships with colleagues he found unfulfilling and ultimately a waste of his time and talents. His book links back to his army career and it's one to be proud of: thoughtful, sensitive and professional. He mishandled his relationship with his daughters and, ultimately, threw away his relationship with me and his grand-daughters.

It's like describing two quite different men. The one I thought I knew was a good husband and tried to be a good father and affectionate grandfather. The one now living in France deceived his family and no longer communicates with any of us. Those communications he does send – to a few people who know him less well – are propaganda, designed to persuade their recipients how superior France is in every respect to his own country. *Methinks he* – like a lot of ex-patriates – *doth protest too much...* Is he happy? Opinion on this point is divided. I can't see how the man I knew could be happy in the situation he has created. Alex, who spent hours at a time over several months trying unsuccessfully to persuade him to confront the reality of the choice he was making by rejecting his family, thinks the present him doesn't care enough about anyone else to have a moment's regret.

Perched on top of the contents of a box of unwanted family photographs he thrust at me when, two years ago, he was packing up his flat when he led me to believe that he was moving to Winchester, was a card to him.

Sydney darling,

Thank you for everything during our twenty-five years & to let you know I look forward to another twenty-five just as I did in 1947!

All my love, always,

Peg

Alex may be right.

Perhaps as we get old we simply run out of energy and turn inwards. Some of the people in these letters did, many did not. I hope I know which I'd choose, but I can see it only from my perspective. And that's all you'll get of the people in these pages. On those I knew you'll get my perspective: what I saw from my angle, how I interpreted it and how I remember it. On other occasions in other company people may have behaved differently. Perhaps some people remember Auntie Gladys and Uncle Jon unhappily. Perhaps some have fonder memories of Dora or Sid.

And of those more distant figures, whom I didn't know, the evidence is still more suspect. It's hearsay: what I heard from those who did know them, how they and I have interpreted it and how they and I remembered it. What I'm offering you here is a series of pictures seen through my lens. Like any photograph, each is taken from a particular spot at a particular time. Some – especially more distant views – are a bit blurred, others even distorted. Some show their subjects to real advantage, others make them look ugly or disagreeable. It's the best I can offer and I hope it will help you to create your own mental photograph album of people, vital to your existence, who otherwise might be just faceless names on a few, slowly fading bits of paper in a drawer in your desk.

We began with that letter from William Faux, annotated by his son, William, and grandson, Kit: "This letter from my dear father came into my possession Mch 11 1907 the 42nd anniversary of his wedding day". I told you that the Fauxes had a slightly self-important sense of posterity and, as I come near completing this exercise, I realise I must have inherited it. As far as I'm concerned, you are posterity. So, having told you a great deal about myself and the various relatives we share, it's about time I turned to you and thought a bit more about what you're like.

I am to you as Kit is to me. If we'd been able to ask him as he sat at his mahogany desk, bulky fountain pen in hand, writing that note in 1907, who he thought might be reading it a hundred years hence, what would he have replied? He was younger than me – forty-one – and his father had just died. Eighteen years married to Alice, who five days earlier had celebrated her thirty-eighth birthday, he was living in reasonable comfort in Southport with their three sons. Bill was seventeen and working as a clerk; ten-year-old Vernon and six-year-old Reg were at school. If Kit had stared hard out of his study window and into the future, what could he have seen?

He'd have seen a few motor cars, which were becoming a bit less noisy and a touch more reliable and were appearing in growing numbers, so he might conceivably have predicted their entirely replacing the horse. He might have predicted the gentle decline of the British Empire which had already begun but, however astute an observer of foreign policy he may have been, he could not have predicted either of the world wars that would devastate the next half century and dominate his sons' and grandchildren's lives.

What would he make of me and my family? We'd hold some surprises for him. We'd all be tall by his standards, but he'd recognise Alex's and Vicky's hair colouring. He'd think our style of dress rather casual and the women's clothes inadequate and very daring. He'd find our manners casual too, and our conversation informal, even familiar. He'd be astonished that, while maintaining a house and family, Lois works and yet still remains what he would call "a lady". He'd look at the variety of our meals with wonder and perhaps a touch of suspicion. The words "new-fangled" and "foreign" might figure more than once in his description of them as he reported back to his wife. But I doubt he'd spot any real difference between his relationship with Alice and mine with Lois, and I'm sure his feelings for his sons are pretty much the same as mine are for my daughters. I imagine he'd be pleased about that.

Kit's study seems a bit gloomy from where I sit, in mine. It has dark, solid furniture and heavy curtains. Mine seems smaller but lighter, less cluttered, in comparison. We have less space but use it better. Tastes have changed and the fabrics we wear and use to decorate our homes would seem to Kit's eyes colourful, even garish, and, because they are so easy to wash, unnaturally clean. Perhaps it's inevitable that my taste will seem as old-fashioned to you as Kit's does to me, but the armchair I sit in isn't fundamentally different from the one Kit pottered off and sat in once he'd blotted the ink dry on his note and got up from his writing desk.

So, if I sit here at my desk and stare hard out of the window, can I do any better than Kit would have done at imagining you and your family and the world that surrounds you? What do the physical things around you look like – your clothes, furniture and the equipment you take for granted at home or when you're working? If you have a car, does it still have a petrol or diesel engine? Or is it entirely electric or perhaps powered in some way which I can't imagine because it has yet to be invented? Do you still need a keyboard as I do to write this, or do you dictate to a machine that writes for you? Because of my much freer access to the written word, I'm probably more literate than Kit and Alice were. Will further advances have made you more or less literate than I am? It can work both ways, as we're finding with some younger ones now.

Does the now I inhabit seem to you either dangerously libertarian or heavily centralised and a bit authoritarian compared to your time? Is the government that serves you and your family democratic and accountable? Sometimes, perhaps because of our longstanding political stability, I worry that we take both too much for granted and are too ready to sacrifice them to the lesser gods of efficiency and expediency. Which way did we take in the longer term? Is our national obsession with social class, which for good and ill survived the twentieth century and remains in robust health in 2006, still going strong? Does the countryside that's so important in my family's life look much the same when you visit some of the places I've mentioned here? Have you found a cure for the Alzheimer's Disease that took my mother?

When I was a boy there were a great many popular books and magazines that predicted what the world's high-technology future would look like in the twenty-first century. Without exception, they seem to have got it wrong. Computers didn't get bigger and more complex; they got much, much smaller and simpler to use. We landed on the moon when I was twelve. 20th July 1969 found me on holiday from Hurstpierpoint on the island of Elba, where my parents and I watched the landing on grainy black and white television with Italian commentary. But we haven't colonised space as many predicted we would. Although technology has replaced almost all unskilled, manual jobs and improved our standard of living, it hasn't created a society with a great deal of leisure time. I'm pretty ruthless in guarding my free time but I still seem to have less of it than my father or father-in-law had in the 1950s and 1960s. Technology means that work intrudes on us more, not less. So forgive me if I avoid these sorts of physical predictions because I've no doubt at all I'd get them just as wildly, comically wrong as those books and magazines did.

Instead, I'll predict this and I hope I'm right. I imagine monogamy will remain for most people the ideal they try to maintain, that the social family unit of parents and children will survive, and that your feelings for your family will be no different from mine or Kit's. I imagine you'll glow with pride as I do when one of my children does something unselfish, clever, demanding or worthwhile. I imagine that, although the manifestation of social manners may change to become more or less formal, the spirit behind them – of putting others' interests, and especially those of the vulnerable, before one's own – will remain unchanged. I imagine that much of our countryside will remain unspoilt, and that sometimes it and the music you love will make you catch your breath as I have so often caught mine. I imagine you'll have family holidays in beautiful places and remember them as nostalgically as I do ours. I imagine you'll have animals around your home to enjoy their company and to teach your children how to love. I hope one of them's a dog. And my final prediction is this: that the differences between us, like those between Kit and me, will be as superficial as our clothes and furnishings.

Driving back from shooting yesterday morning past Upper Wield's prosperous looking houses and the open fields beside the tree-lined road to Bentworth, I remembered Alice's great-grandmother, Jemima Westbrook, whose precarious, octogenarian existence ended in a draughty wooden shack beside the chalk pit there. We – I and, I hope, you – are much luckier: our world is so much more comfortable and secure than Jemima's was. But humanity doesn't change much. We're each the sum of the genetics that created us and the experiences that shaped us: the chance that made me. At heart I doubt we're very different from Jemima.

And, like the human heart, the familiar view across those Hampshire fields is unchanged since the teenaged Alice glimpsed it for the last time on her way to catch the train to Fairmead, where her dark hair and lively manner captivated the young Kit and sent the fortunes of the Faux and Westbrook families in an entirely unexpected direction.

With love,

Christopher

Faux, Fletcher, Westbrook, Wetherly and Lightfoot relatives mentioned in the letters

- William Faux b 1784 — Andalusia Pannat b 1807
  - William Faux b 1833 — Mary Ellen Alabone b 1847
    - Francis Christopher "Kit" Faux b 1866 — Alice Westbrook b 1869
      - (parents of Alice: James Westbrook b 1839 — Charlotte Knight b 1842; 10 siblings including Robert and Arthur)
      - Francis Reginald Faux b 1901
      - Arthur Vernon Faux b 1897
      - William James Christopher "Bill" Faux b 1889 — Dora Elizabeth Fletcher b 1889
        - Marjorie Alwyn "Peggy" Faux b 1917 — Jack Harold Wetherly b 1914
          - Elizabeth Jary b 1948
          - Anne Wetherly b 1942
    - 7 siblings (including Uncle Jon's mother)

- John Fletcher b 1834 — Mary Ann Whiteside
  - Richard Ashton Fletcher b 1861 — Ada Eleanor Denham b 1864
    - Dora Elizabeth Fletcher b 1889
    - 7 siblings (including Lily, Gladys, Mamie and Alwyn)

- Harold Wetherly b 1890 — Gertrude Toms b 1885
  - Jack Harold Wetherly b 1914

- Sydney Walter Jary b 1924 — Marjorie Alwyn "Peggy" Faux b 1917
  - Christopher Jary b 1956 — Lois Lightfoot b 1949
    - Alexandra Jary b 1982
    - Victoria Jary b 1988
  - Elizabeth Jary b 1948

- David Evan Lightfoot b 1918 — Joyce Beatrice Eynon b 1913
  - Lois Lightfoot b 1949
  - Carol Lightfoot b 1942
  - Elaine Lightfoot b 1946

Jary, Rogers, Wetherly and Lightfoot relatives mentioned in the letters

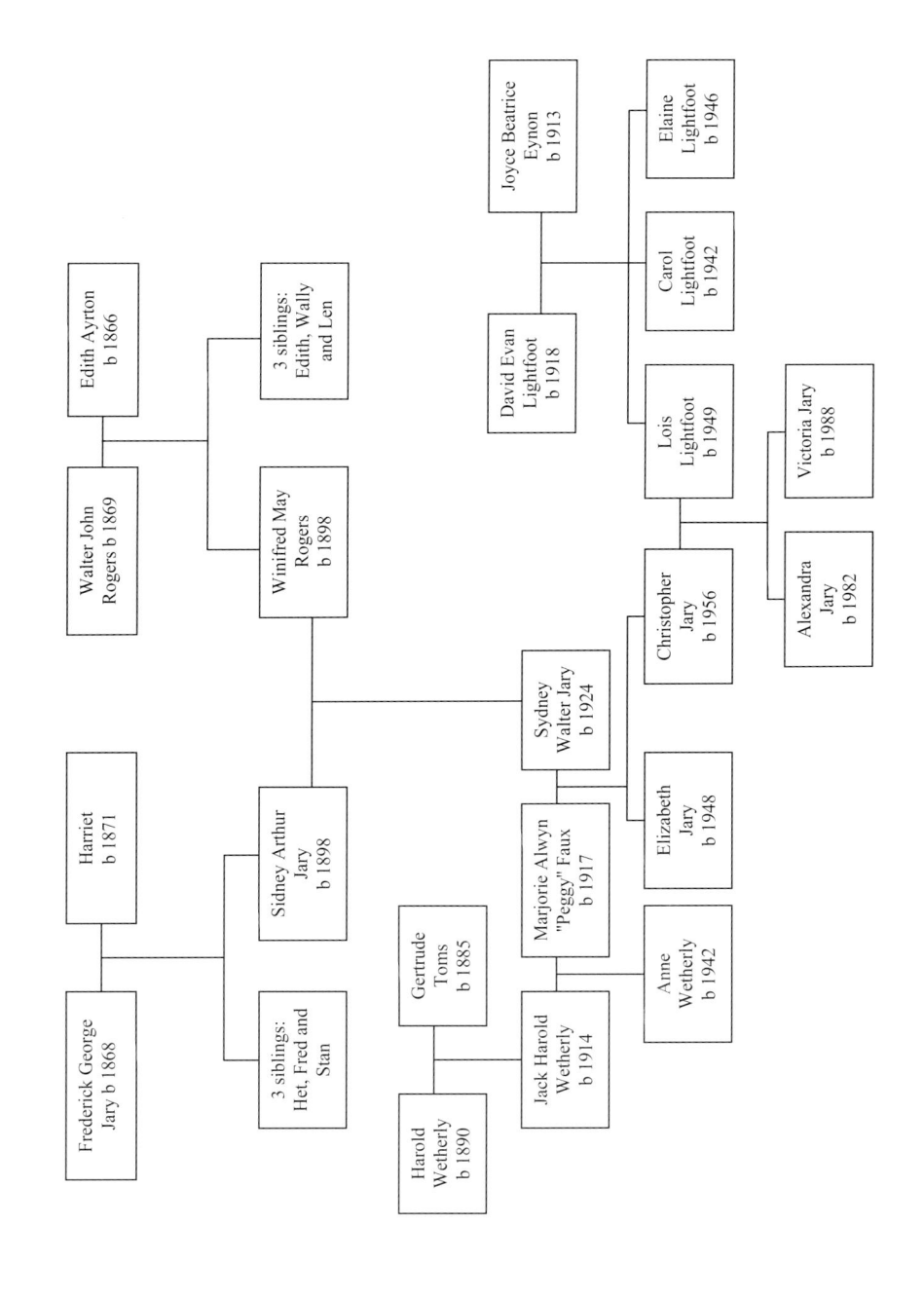

- Frederick George Jary b 1868 — Harriet b 1871
  - Sidney Arthur Jary b 1898
  - 3 siblings: Het, Fred and Stan

- Walter John Rogers b 1869 — Edith Ayrton b 1866
  - Winifred May Rogers b 1898
  - 3 siblings: Edith, Wally and Len

Sidney Arthur Jary b 1898 — Winifred May Rogers b 1898
  - Sydney Walter Jary b 1924

- Harold Wetherly b 1890 — Gertrude Toms b 1885
  - Jack Harold Wetherly b 1914

Jack Harold Wetherly b 1914 — Marjorie Alwyn "Peggy" Faux b 1917
  - Anne Wetherly b 1942

Sydney Walter Jary b 1924 — Anne Wetherly b 1942
  - Elizabeth Jary b 1948
  - Christopher Jary b 1956

- David Evan Lightfoot b 1918 — Joyce Beatrice Eynon b 1913
  - Carol Lightfoot b 1942
  - Elaine Lightfoot b 1946
  - Lois Lightfoot b 1949

Christopher Jary b 1956 — Lois Lightfoot b 1949
  - Alexandra Jary b 1982
  - Victoria Jary b 1988